TRUTH AND THE PERSON IN CHRISTIAN THEOLOGY

TRUTH
AND THE PERSON
IN CHRISTIAN THEOLOGY

A THEOLOGICAL ESSAY
IN TERMS OF THE SPIRITUAL PERSON

HUGH VERNON WHITE

New York OXFORD UNIVERSITY PRESS 1963

FOR

MALCOLM VERNON

BARBARA HELEN

NINA JEANNE

THEOLOGICAL construction and exposition always constitute in some degree a confession of faith, even if it is in biblical
or historical theology. Certainly the interpretation of the faith in
systematic form, if it is done seriously, is an expression of personal
conviction. However open-minded the theologian may be to op-
posing opinions, and however frankly he may confess the limitation and imperfection of his own thought, it is always his hope and
purpose to communicate truth. All forms of the Christian ministry
are affected by and involved in this truth-seeking and truth-
speaking.

The first part of my ministry was in the pastorate. Even in the
modern world, when the pastor has so many duties to perform,
the most important thing he does is the preaching of the gospel.
But no one can preach the gospel without constantly seeking a
better grasp of its meaning and ways to make that meaning more
evident to his congregation. This is primarily a theological undertaking. There is also in preaching a constant undercurrent of
apologetics, a defense of the faith against general skepticism which
exists even in the Church, and against the reasoned rejection of
the faith which today has many, sometimes sinister forms. My first
and most agonizing theological work was done in the preparation and preaching of sermons.

The second part of my ministry was in the world mission of the
Church. My specific assignment was to interpret and commend
to the Congregational Christian churches the work of missions in
carrying the gospel to the world. I quickly discovered that the

main problem was not a matter of method or organization, but the truth of the faith itself. I found myself often occupied with the strange endeavor to convince ministers of Christian churches that the gospel they were presumably preaching was true. And when it was not a matter of convincing, it still meant engaging with these pastors in the task of clarifying and strengthening the faith. This raised broad questions concerning Christianity and the non-Christian religions, the relation of religion to culture, and the maintenance of Christian faith in a world of social and political revolution. Deeper still were questions of the nature of religion, and of the relation of Christian faith to religion as such.

The American Board of Commissioners for Foreign Missions not only provided me with every kind of opportunity to get at the realities involved in these questions, but also gave me a free hand in dealing with them. Travel in the Orient, and many contacts with leaders of non-Christian faiths and with leaders of the Christian Church in several countries, provided clarification and concrete help. The crucial issue always was the truth of the Christian gospel and its saving relevance to the common spiritual condition of men.

It was my good fortune to be called upon to spend the last period of my ministry in the teaching of theology. My quest for truth had led me to that high undertaking. I had taught philosophy in college and philosophy of religion in seminary. Philosophy quite properly puts a limit on itself. It maintains, on principle, a sort of reserve toward religious faith through its commitment to rational abstractions. But theology works with and within a believing community; it is the intellectual or "belief" aspect of faith. The truth it seeks is frankly a truth of conviction and life commitment, a personal truth. It does not cautiously feel its way and protect itself by reservations and hypothetical procedures. Its ultimate object is not its own constructions, however important and "true" they may be, but God revealed in Christ and worshipped in the Christian Church. So theology is free to use all the powers of the human mind—faith, reason, imagination, memory, and moral will—to represent systematically the meaning of the faith. In terms of thought the truth it seeks is a truth of personal conviction.

I made this venture of faith, grateful for the discipline of philosophy and also for the experience of preaching and the dozen years spent in interpretation of the Christian world mission. This book represents my own faith and my own theology. I shall not even try to indicate sources and individual thinkers to which and to whom I am indebted. They are too many, and I should never be able to recall them. But perhaps it will be interesting to the reader to know that I grew up in an atmosphere of liberalism in which the historical study of the Bible, of Christianity, and of religion was dominant. The Social Gospel was at the height of its influence, and my first definite perspective theologically was Personal Idealism. All this I appropriated and preached with all my might. But with it all I never lost my hold on a strong biblical, evangelical faith in Jesus Christ as Lord and Savior.

I carried this faith into my interpretation of the Christian world mission. It has never ceased to bother me that, because I presented a "liberal" philosophy of missions, I was said to hold that the world mission is "man-centered," and that it is mainly a matter of "service" rather than the preaching of the gospel. What even in my most liberal period I contended for, and do still, is the preaching of the gospel supported and complemented by the manifestation of Christian love in service. I suppose the writers who have so misrepresented my position did it because they assumed that a liberal necessarily held such a position as they attributed to me, and many did. At any rate I am glad in this place to deny and repudiate this too common report of my theology of missions.

Like most liberals in the 'thirties, I fought—and misunderstood— the so-called neo-orthodox theology. This was due not alone to my own prepossessions, but also to the fact that my first contact with that theology was through Karl Barth's early and often extravagant writings. But when I read Emil Brunner's *Man in Revolt* it seemed to me that I was simply hearing, in a new form of utterance, the word of the gospel which I had always assumed to be the substance of the Christian faith. As I moved into the field of systematic theology proper I found much in this "new" theology that restored and expressed the substantial content of the historic Christian faith.

But we have passed the era of neo-orthodoxy. I am indebted to it, as I am to Personal Idealism. But this book must stand (or fall) on its own merit. No one can be held responsible for it but myself. It is not a finished product; in the effort to be concise and brief I have often only outlined a position. But the main ideas have all been taught and/or preached many times. Here I acknowledge my main indebtedness, which is to the students whom I have tried to teach and to the ministers with whom I have sought to make more explicit and meaningful the truth of our Christian faith.

Claremont, California
September 1962

HUGH VERNON WHITE

TABLE OF CONTENTS

TRUTH AND THE PERSON IN CHRISTIAN THEOLOGY

CHAPTER I

INTRODUCTION:

THE TWO PARTIES—GOD AND MAN

CHRISTIAN FAITH, when it takes the form of belief and so becomes theology, has two ultimate terms—God and man. It is thus religiously and historically oriented. These two terms represent the ultimate realities. The ideas and the systematic development of thought which constitute theology refer directly to God as the Party of the First Part, and man as the Party of the Second Part in an order of personal reality which is ultimate. God is the creator of the world and man. Man is a creature in the image of his creator, able to know and have communion with God. The world as a creation of God, and all its laws, processes, and potencies are subordinate to and dependent upon God. God is not laid under necessity by any general principle discovered in the world.

Man, a creature in the likeness of God, has the capacity to know the presence and the power of God and to respond to him in the basic act of faith. His knowledge, or his thought, of God is not derived from study and understanding of the ways of nature, or from examination of the forms of his own consciousness, but from the immediate presence and act of God which is apprehended by faith. Among men universally, God's manifestation of his presence and power, and man's response in faith, is the origin of religion. There is nothing in man's development of intelligent understanding of the world or of himself that can either prove or invalidate this primordial knowledge of God. The many aspects of thought, scientific, philosophical, and theological, with its principles, postulates, categories, and logic, are functions of the conscious creature—man. Reason, or rationality, is objectively valid only within a given finite system; it does not create or give existence to the system. The "world" is such a system; it can be indefinitely understood in terms of its internal logic or structure, but its origin cannot be known by reason. Reason, as the act of human consciousness, is an ordering function capable of almost infinitely varied structuring; but it is not an ultimate power competent to turn upon the man himself whose act it is and invalidate his basic consciousness of himself or God. Reason is reasoning, the ordered sequence of thought of the human person; it is not all of the human person, nor the highest power, but a marvelous instrument of both analytic and constructive thought. Reason does not do anything of itself but serves the interests and purposes of the total man whose vital impulse is translated from the biological level to the intellectual and eventually to the spiritual.

Theology is concerned with the world as the creation of God and as the sphere of his sustaining and providential action. Theology is also concerned with history as the scene of the man's relative freedom and his service of God. But it is concerned primarily with God in his direct relation to the human spirit, with his self-revelation in history, with his judgment and grace known in the personal life of faith. Man in his total and responsible action and in his relation to God is the human ultimate, not to be reduced to any of his own functions or relations to the created world. Therefore, the ultimate terms of reference of Christian theology are not postulates, principles, or categories, all of which are forms of human thought, but God, the transcendent and absolute origin of all existence, and man, the created spiritual person who exists in responsible relation to God.

The terms here used, especially "spiritual person," will be critically defined and their meaning elaborated in the course of the present work, which I would characterize as an essay in systematic theology. This will involve a rather extended outline and discussion of method and methods, but I think this is necessary because basic assumptions and method actually determine meaning. But first I should like to mention some common ultimates in theological construction which obscure, or even deny, the real personal ultimates of Christian theology, and replace its religious-historical orientation with one of subjective consciousness or abstract idea. These ultimates tend to come in pairs, which is probably due to the basic polarity of rational thought. They are ultimates for rational thought but not for the total life of the spiritual person. Certain theological systems are explicitly or implicitly constructed within the universe of these ultimate categories.

1. *Finite-infinite* is one of these pairs. Thought moves between the poles of the finite being and the infinite, which takes the place of or is identified with deity. These terms constitute limits of thought. The ultimate problem of human existence lies in the fact that man is a finite individual but somehow endowed or bedeviled with a deep hunger for the infinite. All theological meanings are organized within this tension. Salvation means the attainment in some manner of the infinite. In the rich and complex theology of Schleiermacher, all meanings are determined by the oneness of the individual with the whole, other terms for the union of the finite and the infinite.

2. *Nature-spirit* constitute the ultimate pair of categories for the theology that stems from Ritschl, who, in turn, took them from Kant. With Kant the fundamental dichotomy was that between the autonomous will and the system of "necessity" or complete causal determination in nature. Here the opposites are *freedom* and *necessity*. Ritschl transferred this philosophy into the realm of theology and made *spirit* and *nature* his ultimate terms. This is akin to, but not identical with, the "spiritual" man and the "natural" man of the New Testament. It represents an analysis of the human person into his two radically different elements: spirit which is free, moral, and good, and nature which is causally determined and hostile to the naturally divine character of spirit. The problem of religion becomes the triumph of man as spirit over man as nature. This conflict is within the man himself, and does not lie in a direct relation of man to God and his fellow man.

3. *Being* and *non-being* constitute another pair of ultimates, very ancient in speculative thought and made central in our time by Nicholas Berdyaev and Paul Tillich. These terms, like the others mentioned, embrace the total content of human discourse. Everything that exists is or has being. But once it was not, so it came out of non-being. The ideas of both being and non-being

are taken in complete generality, capitalized, and declared to represent the real ultimates. The nature of ultimate reality, in these terms, is set forth in *ontology*, which means the science of being. These terms are held to be more basic than person, or spirit. They are themselves verbal symbols, derived from the participial form of the word "to be" or "is," the *to on* in the Greek language. Put in crude English translation *ontology* might be called "isology," or the science of "is." They lend themselves, however, with the addition always of a concrete historical religious tradition, to unlimited abstract elaboration of thought in the realm of religion. The peculiar structure of the Greek language contributes to this doctrine since it has, like English, a copula. Formally, ontology arises from the hypostatizing of the copula.

4. Another important set of categories for speculative philosophy and even theology is that of *subject-object*. This is derived, of course, from the act of knowledge, the basic terms of which are knower and known. It is interesting to note that each one of the pairs of categories discussed, including this one, is derived from a certain aspect of experience, or universe of discourse. *Finite-infinite* is essentially a quantitative distinction, indicating the part which is limited, and the whole which has no limits. *Nature-spirit* is a category of action which distinguishes between action that is wholly determined and action which is free. *Being-non-being* is a distinction in the category of thought itself, a purely logical antithesis suggested by the fact that everything that exists once did not exist, but elevated to the pure realm of thought in which the non-being is as real as the being, indeed with Berdyaev it is the more important of the two.

The categories *subject-object* are derived from the act of knowledge and represent the distinction between the knower and that which is known. This is very important for philosophy which is always preoccupied, often supremely so, with epistemology, or the theory of knowledge. When religion is thought of as the knowledge of God, then God becomes the object as man is the subject of knowledge. Man is the knower and God is the known. But that seems to be an impossibility for man's knowledge cannot extend to and encompass God. The more insistently "knowledge"

is defined in terms of rational thought, the greater the impossibility of man knowing God. It was Hegel who defined religion
as thought and who claimed to have overcome the difficulty. He
did it by making God, or Spirit, both the subject and the object
of knowledge. Spirit-in-itself is Subject, and Spirit-for-itself is
Object. Spirit (God) therefore knows himself. But, it may be
asked, what has that to do with the religion of man, and his
knowledge of God? The answer is that Spirit (God) has this
knowledge in the mind of individual man, so that man's knowledge of God is really God's knowledge of himself. This, of
course, is not ordinary knowledge; it is not "ordinary thought," or
knowledge of the *Vorstellung* (the conception), but real thought,
knowledge of the *Begriff* (the Idea). This is comparable to Tillich's distinction between scientific knowledge as technical reason,
and knowledge of Being as ontological reason. However it is
done, it seems a kind of *tour de force* to claim knowledge of God
by identifying subject and object, and affirming that God knows
himself, or by positing an identity of structure between reason
(in man) and Being.

5. *Process-reality* constitute another set of ultimates. Indeed
they form the title of the book in which Alfred North Whitehead
sets forth his speculative philosophy.[1] These two terms are taken
from the confrontation of man by nature, a rationally baffling
combination of fixed form and change. Reason is completely at
home with the "eternal," or the perfect and changeless form, the
"idea" of Plato. But empirical fact is in constant change. This is a
radical problem for metaphysics. Which is real, or original, the
eternal form or the fact of change-process? The most thoroughgoing rationalist says that only the changeless, the eternal, is
real; the change is illusion or appearance (phenomenon). Parmenides, and Sankara, Greece and India, speak for this position. But
there is always a Heraclitus who insists that only change is real,
who says that process *is* the reality. Whitehead tries to comprehend these two polar opposites in one system of great ingenuity
which is inclusive of all elements of human experience and knowledge. All meanings—scientific fact, mathematical form, person-

[1] A. N. Whitehead, *Process and Reality*, New York, 1929.

ality, and God—are derived from or involved in this union of the two categories, *process* and *reality*. Historically this represents the rejection of Kant's "bifurcation of reality" into the autonomous will and the realm of necessity (nature). First the Romantic movement, and in our time *organicism*, continue the insistence that there is no real break or opposition between freedom and determinism, or between spirit and nature, between the divine and the human, and so forth. This was the position of Schleiermacher.

These categories that figure so largely in philosophical theology are ultimate generalizations of thought by which the mind seeks to understand rationally itself and the world in which it lives. They are necessary terms of philosophical understanding. But Christian faith is not primarily concerned with the world or the nature of rational knowledge. It is faith in God who is not the most general character of the world, nor the soul of the world, nor the real essence of the human consciousness. God is creator of the world, transcendent to and immanent in the world but not identical with it. Scientific knowledge of the world, and rational understanding of the world and of himself, so far as such understanding is possible, do not give man knowledge of God. God is the Other, both to the world and to man, and is known by his own act of self-revelation and man's responsive acknowledgment of faith.

Theology is the systematic interpretation and exposition of the meaning of the faith. It is thought, "rational" insofar as it is orderly and consistent and intelligible. The ultimate terms of theology are God and man. These are not rational concepts or categories; they are designative rather than definitive. Theology is not concerned primarily with deity and humanity, but with God and man. *Deity* and *humanity* are general ideas, or definitions of "natures." But theology has ultimate orientation not to these general ideas, but to the God who acts in the creation of the world, and who reveals himself in Jesus Christ. It is also oriented toward men, each and every individual man and all men as they actually exist in history. Theology, therefore, is a discipline of thought among Christian believers which is oriented to God's eternal act of creation and his acts in history toward men.

Its ideas are not formal *concepts*, but *conceptions*,[2] with the depth
dimensions given by the full scope of life in faith involving emotion, feeling and imagination, and will, as well as rational structure. The "logic" of theology is the logic of free personal or
spiritual action and relation. It is an order in which love, obedience, sin, repentance, grace, reconciliation are primary terms
because they designate the responsible acts of persons, and the
free acts of God. These terms and these conceptions do not need
to be demythologized; they are not symbolic, save as all human
words (and ideas) are symbolic of what they represent. These
terms refer directly to the acts and relations of spiritual persons,
God and man. This is the proper universe of discourse of Christian theology.

The theology of the present essay is cast in these primary
terms of Christian faith. The immediate knowledge of God is
faith itself; the next step is theology in the terms of God and man,
as here set forth. There is also a philosphy of religion and specifically the Christian religion which is the expression in general
or abstract terms of prevailing ideas and of the general principles
of religion, and specifically of the Christian religion. Such a philosophy properly deals in abstractions; it uses the categories of
the infinite and the finite, of being and non-being, of subject and
object, etc. This is comparable to a philosophy of civil law which
is useful for the lawyer's understanding, but which is no substitute for a specific knowledge of the actual laws of a state.

Theology is not interested primarily in religion, but in God.
Religion is a phenomenon in the historical existence of man,
identical with culture except as it is challenged by a transcendent
Reality and Authority. God is the transcendent Other who sustains and judges and redeems the man who creates culture in history. The man himself, including his reason and moral will, is
part and parcel of culture; culture is the man as he is in history,

[2] Susanne K. Langer makes the illuminating distinction between concept and
conception in *Philosophy in a New Key*, Cambridge (3rd ed.), 1957, pp. 49ff.
She says (p. 49 fn.): "Note that I have called the terms of our thinking conceptions, not concepts. Concepts are abstract forms embodied in conceptions.
Their bare presentation may be approximated by so-called 'abstract thought,'
but in ordinary mental life they no more figure as naked factors than skele-
tons are seen walking on the street."

and his religion is part of himself. But God stands above both history and human culture, including religion. Hs is the Creator, the judge of history and the redeemer of man. Accordingly a philosophy of religion may assume the intimate unity of culture and religion and find all its materials in the religion-culture complex. But theology is not an exposition of the nature of religion as the depth dimension of culture; it is the rational interpretation, according to its own logic of spiritual act and relation, of the self-revelation of God, and the response of man in faith. Christian theology shares this character with all theology; and it holds that the ultimate truth of God is disclosed in the word of the prophets, and in the incarnation of the Word. Its "truth" does not lie in the perfection of its statement, or in the formulation of its doctrine, but in the reality it designates; in the God who speaks in history, and who is known by faith in Christ. Human thought will never be able adequately to apprehend, and doctrines will never fully and infallibly set forth this truth of God in Christ. But it is under solemn obligation to persist in the attempt. The present work is an essay toward greater clarity and adequacy, and is especially concerned with the right basic orientation for Christian theology.

CHAPTER II

BASIC METHOD—HISTORICAL

CHRISTIAN FAITH is not primarily a form of doctrine; but man is a thinking mind, even though he is much more, and the implicit affirmation of any faith is that it is true. The teacher of the faith is a truth teller; he sets forth to both the believer and the unbeliever the truth of the Christian faith. The first form of this telling was the *kerygma*, the events of the life, death, and resurrection of Jesus Christ. But the "preaching" and the epistles, especially those of Paul and John, already involved interpretations of the meaning of the *kerygma* in the form of moral instruction and doctrinal affirmation. Formation of the early creeds came as a response to the demand of the believing world of the second and third centuries. In a time when both religious polytheism and philosophical monism flourished the Christian Church had to explain what it meant by saying that Jesus Christ is the Son of God. The formal answer was the doctrine of the Trinity—God is three Persons in one substance—and the christology of Chalcedon—Jesus Christ is the God-Man, two distinct natures in one Person.

Both the *kerygma* and the creeds were held to be "truth." The controversies and constructions of the first five centuries were a composite of religious and scriptural affirmation, and rational definition in terms of Greek philosophic thought, which itself was by no means fully unified in method or meaning. But out of this process which reached its most elaborate and influential expression in the mind of Augustine, the Christian Church of the West found itself endowed with an abundance of material for the theological industry of the Middle Ages. Christian faith came to be acceptance of the truth of the doctrine, and obedience to the Church that preserved and taught the doctrine.

The doctrine or theology of the Church, Roman Catholic and Protestant, is not only a system of beliefs, or truths; it is such a system developed according to the possibilities and limits of a method. The Church of today is heir to a long process of theological development in which the meaning of particular doctrines and ideas is limited and to some extent determined by the method used in their formation. Affirmations that are meaningful within the operation of one method may be quite invalid or changed in their meaning when another method is introduced. Some of the confusion of present-day theological thinking is due to the fact that different voices speak in the language of quite different basic methods. It is therefore not only important, it is indispensable to clarity and mutual understanding, that we trace out historically and distinguish critically the methods that have been and are being employed in the interpretation of the Christian faith.

1. THE SCHOLASTIC METHOD

Scholasticism is the method developed by medieval theologians when theology was the queen of the sciences. It represents the great synthesis between Greek, especially Aristotelian, thought and Christian faith which generated the philosophical problems of the medieval Church. Though very complex in detail it is simple in basic principle. There are two elements—*revelation* and *reason*. First principles or truths are supplied by revelation; the organization, demonstration, and expression of doctrine are developed upon the basis of these primary truths by reason. Aristotle is the authority in method, as revelation is the authority in substance.

Revelation is to be found primarily in scripture, but also in tradition, and takes the form of statements or propositions. These statements are found already written in scripture, or they are the formulated judgments of the living Church (tradition). There can be no conflict between these two sources because both are media of the revealing act of God. Doctrine grows and develops in answer to the needs and questions of the faithful, but new

statements of doctrine are really only further elaborated meanings of the changeless truth of the primary revelation. In this
elaboration of doctrine, reason as found in the Aristotelian tradition is the absolute guide. Aristotle often is not even referred to
by name, but simply as "the philosopher." Thus God and Aristotle collaborate in the scholastic method. This is a method of
exposition, proof, and instruction, not of the discovery of new
truth. There may be new truths in the sense of new expressions
and specific applications, but these are valid only as clearly de-
duced from the truths of original revelation. This makes reason,
if not the equal, at least a very substantial partner of revelation.

A similar method developed early in Protestantism. But Protestant theologians recognized scripture as the only source of
primary revelation, rejecting the authority of tradition which,
for the theologian, meant dogmatic formulas accepted on the
authority of the Church. They did, indeed, accept the pronounce-
ments of the ecumenical councils and were as orthodox in their
theology and christology as the Church of Rome. But the sole
ultimate test of all doctrine was the word of scripture. Protestantism never developed an official philosophy or logic as did the
Roman Church. But its theologians were equally committed to
reason as the method of theological construction upon the basis
of the propositions found in scripture. It was still God and reason,
or God and Aristotle, that furnished the matter and the method
of theology. The primary revelation is still in the form of propositions, which constitute the first principles of theology, and of
religious belief. And complete reliance is placed in the validity
of reason.[1]

For all scholasticism, Roman Catholic and Protestant, the form
and substance of theology are wholly determined by these two—
revelation and *reason*. Not only do they not conflict with one

[1] Cf. George Foot Moore, *History of Religion,* New York, 1919, vol. II,
p. 369. "When Protestant theologians of the second generation began to construct complete systems of doctrine, they not only reverted to the scholastic
type and built upon the great mediaeval synthesis of Aristotle and revelation
as on an impregnable rock, but drew directly and largely on the Neo-
Thomist theologians of the Spanish school for material and argument."
Cf. also Perry Miller, *The New England Mind,* New York, 1939, especially
pp. 99-107.

another; they have an inner and essential kinship. For revelation is in the form of the primary element of rational thought—a *proposition*. Revelation is thus assimilated to reason. This seemed to give definiteness, certainty, and power to the faith of the Church. Even a doctrine which could not have been arrived at by unaided reason, but which is given by revelation, as for example, the doctrine of the Trinity, is still a statement in the form of the proposition. Although it is beyond human comprehension it is still rational, indeed, a higher order of rational truth. To this, orthodox Roman Catholics and Protestant theologians of the scholastic period would agree. The higher reason is God's reason; it is essentially the same as the reason of man, but whereas man is imperfect and prone to error and is essentially limited in his power of rational thought, God is perfect, free from error, and all-encompassing. This proper humility as regards man's reason does not hide the fact that the essence of man, his soul or spirit, is found in his power of reason, and that in this also is found his, however imperfect, likeness to God. Even revelation is revelation of higher and purer affirmations of rational truth.

Despite the acknowledgment that it must be supplemented by revelation, a momentous concession was made to reason in the scholastic method. This led to developments, through definable stages, of (1) a strictly rational theology; then following skepticism, and the critique of reason by Kant, (2) subjective rationalism, the philosophy of religious experience. In our own day reason in theology appears in diverse and sometimes surprising forms. The modern period in philosophy shows a waning belief in God and reference to God. This is not surprising for reason alone, that is, reason freed from all propositions provided by revelation or dogma, cannot establish or ultimately recognize the existence of God. It is worth noting, in this connection, that reason alone is also unable to establish the existence of the world. Or, to put the matter quite simply, reason cannot establish existence. In this, Kant's *Critique of Pure Reason* stands as a permanent, if negative, accomplishment. The relevance for theology of this comment on modern philosophy lies in the fact that the developments noted above are reflected in corresponding changes of *method* in the field of theology. For theology does not provide its own method. It is an artifact, a work of man the thinker, and the processes of thought generally assumed to be valid are consciously or unconsciously employed in its construction. The basic requirement, therefore, for a good theology, is a method appropriate and adequate to the faith it would formulate. This calls for a critical review of the methods that have been followed, and their consequences for theology. Orthodox, dogmatic theology, both Protestant and Roman Catholic, remains outside this movement, not wholly untouched by it, but staunchly defending the reality of revelation as the communication of basic truths, and the use of reason in the construction of doctrine.

2. RATIONALISM: OBJECTIVE

The term "rationalism" needs to be defined. It does not mean merely the careful, responsible, and critical use of reason in thinking. The one who rejects rationalism is not an irrationalist. In this connection much adverse criticism of present-day theology is beside the point. The rationalism that many theologians, and others, reject is the assumption that reason can by examining and analyzing its own laws and structure arrive at the truth about Reality. What may be called the *rationalistic postulate* was formulated by Spinoza, although it had already been assumed by Descartes—"The order and connection of ideas is the same as the order and connection of things." [2]

This may be called *objective* rationalism. The form of truth is found in the reason itself; therefore truth is present and attainable. But this truth is truth about the world because it is assumed that the fundamental character of the world is rational, i.e. has the same structure as the mind. Mathematics seems to be the most perfect form of this rationality. The seventeenth-century rationalists, Descartes, Spinoza, and Leibniz, were all mathematicians. "Reality" was taken to be that which can be measured. Knowledge, said Descartes, is always knowledge of *superficies;* that is, it is geometrical. Spinoza even undertook to write an ethics in strictly geometric form. There is no "inner" meaning to anything; final causes or purposes are rejected.

[2] Spinoza, *Ethics,* Prop. VII.

Now this is pretty good physics; at least it is a pretty good start for physics. Despite the fact that these thinkers were keenly interested in experiments (Descartes discovered the circulation of the blood at about the same time as Harvey, and both he and Spinoza were greatly interested in experimental optics), their fundamental assumption was that a science of physics could be elaborated by the process of abstract rational construction. This is what the "objective" means when rationalism is qualified by the term.

But while these philosophers were primarily concerned with natural science and developments in mathematics, they were also men who believed in God. Descartes was a Roman Catholic whose closest advisors were Jesuit scholars. Spinoza was a Jew, not an orthodox Jew indeed, but still a "God intoxicated man." And Leibniz was a Protestant who was deeply interested in the re-union of Christendom and the missionary extension of the faith. They all had something to say about God. In fact the reality of the world, which rationalism cannot establish of itself, was accepted by Descartes on the basis of the veracity of God. The first principle of Spinoza's metaphysics was the one substance which has two attributes—thought and extension. *The substance is God.* This reveals a characteristic of all true rationalism, medieval or modern—the formulation of a highest category, an all-inclusive idea upon which all lesser ideas depend, or within which they are all included. When this idea is called God we have pantheism; when it is called the world we have naturalism. Spinoza called it both—*Deus sive natura.* But this really means that thought is God, for the *Deus sive natura* is another way of representing the provisional or relative dualism of *thought* and *extension* which Descartes called substances and Spinoza attributes. Actually, for Spinoza *natura* is extension and *Deus* is thought. The hallmark of rationalism, from Parmenides in Greece and Sankara in India to Paul Tillich, is the identification of thought and reality, or reason and God. The problems of change, of life, of freedom that arise in rationalism are dealt with variously. Orthodox theologians supplement reason with authority of church and/or scripture; philosophical theologians, with mysticism and "existence."

It was this philosophical movement that brought the age of

enlightenment. The theological outcome was the deism of the eighteenth century. Deism was a theology that depended more on reason than on revelation. Theology itself had invited this demotion of revelation. It is true that in scholasticism revelation comes first and then reason, but the revelation itself is in rational form, viz. the form of statements or propositions. Rationalists took the next logical step by assuming that if the ultimate truths are rational, a thoroughgoing reason could itself arrive at those truths. The astonishing success of reason in discovering the laws of the natural world led irresistibly to confidence that the existence and nature of God also could be rationally known. Descartes, despite his agreement to leave matters of religion to the Church in exchange for freedom to follow reason in matters of science, still was moved to construct an ontological argument of his own, an argument which was based on the medieval concepts of substance and cause.

In deism, theology surrendered to the rationalism of the philosophers and turned to nature as the key to or validation of the revealed religion historically received. This is accomplished by the use of analogy. The classic argument is contained in the essay by Bishop Butler published in 1736 and significantly entitled: "The Analogy of Religion, Natural and Revealed, to the Constitution and Cause of Nature." Faith is thoroughly rational. God is the First Cause, and the order of nature reveals his purpose and his rational government of the world. God, freedom, and immortality are rationally demonstrated, and the service of God and the destiny of man are described in terms of a rational morality. Faith is an act of reason, as we still hear in Addison's hymn, "...in reason's ear they all rejoice." Even God is subject to this rational order of natural and moral law.[3]

Thus the first result for theology of modern rationalism was to reverse the roles of revelation and reason. Whereas in scho-

---

[3] Joseph Butler, *Analogy of Religion*, London, 1841, p. 256: "...there is in the nature of things, an original standard of right and wrong in actions, independent upon all will, but which unalterably determines the will of God, to exercise that moral government over the world which religion teaches, i.e., finally and upon the whole to reward and punish men respectively as they act right or wrong; this assertion contains an abstract truth, as well as matter of fact."

lasticism the total faith and its meaning are given and validated by revelation, and reason functions only as a subsequent demonstration and elaboration of the truth (rationality) of the faith, which is received on the authority of the Church; in objective rationalism, the ultimate validation of the historic faith is reason which finds objective embodiment in nature. This puts upon reason the main burden for support of the faith. The enlightened theologians doubtless felt a great freedom and exhilaration in thus being able to maintain the faith without submission to the authority of a Church. It meant, however, that the fortunes of the faith were in a perilous manner bound up with the developments of philosophy and science. Above all faith was dependent on the ultimate success of Reason itself to provide not only a method for theology but also the first principles or truths upon which a theology is to be built. However, for the time the alliance between faith and reason seemed secure; the faith was proved to be rational and reason reigned as the ultimate arbiter of truth.

3. RATIONALISM: CRITICAL

Then came skepticism, followed by the "Copernican revolution" of Kant's critical philosophy which challenged and overthrew the rationalistic postulate. Here was reason holding itself up for a critical examination that left it devoid of authority, either analytically or analogically, to defend and support the claims of revealed religion. Revelation had passed out of the picture, and now reason takes over, but it is a chastened reason with no high claims to objective knowledge of God or even of the world. But the critique of reason was still a strictly rational matter; it was reason criticizing reason. Therefore, in place of *objective rationalism,* which assumed an order of nature identical in its structure with the order of the rational mind, and which claimed to demonstrate the existence of God by an ontological argument, we have a *critical rationalism* which is systematically agnostic. Pure reason knows only phenomena or appearances and orders them according to its own forms and categories in the scientific knowledge of nature. But this is all subjective; it has to do strictly with the contents and categories of the mind.[4] The thing-in-itself, that is the outside world or object, is not known. Neither is God known. The "things" of the world are assumed as the ultimate causes of the phenomena with which reason deals through a rather complicated process of imaginative construction. But God is only a necessary or regulative idea, a postulate of reason, required to complete the moral philosophy and to validate the final rationality of the world.

4. RATIONALISM: SUBJECTIVE

Immanuel Kant believed in God and considered himself a Christian. He rejected the common rational arguments for the existence of God, but he put a moral argument in their place. He wrote a "philosophy" of religion entitled, "Religion Within the Bounds of Reason Alone" *(Religion innerhalb der Grenzen der blossen Vernunft)*. But Kant was not a theologian. The philosophical theology of the post-Kantian period, however, developed directly out of his critical analysis of the human mind. He identified will and understanding as the rational mind, and set aside feeling as having no part in knowledge, or in rational, which meant true, religion. But these three basic elements of consciousness had been clearly distinguished, and consciousness itself had been made the immediate and direct subject matter of human knowledge. The total consciousness is immediately present and presumably the same in all men; it is a unity of thinking, willing, and feeling. This recalls the three ultimate values of platonic thought—truth, goodness, and beauty. The degree to which this orientation of religious faith permeated the thought of nineteenth- and early twentieth-century Christians can be seen in the common representation of the ultimate values of Christian life as truth, goodness, and beauty. These values are subjective qualities of the human consciousness; it became a primary concern of idealists to prove their objective reality.

There is another contribution to the ground plan of nineteenth-

[4] Cf. H. D. Aiken, *The Age of Ideology*, New York, 1956, p. 52. "Kant conceived the laws of rationality, not as a reflection of the structure of things in themselves, but as forms of the human understanding." See also on "subjectivism," pp. 15 and 16.

century philosophy of religion made by Kant, viz. the distinction between the order of freedom based on the autonomy of the moral will, and the order of necessity, or the world of nature which is the realm of the unbroken and unqualified reign of causality. This "bifurcation of reality" was accepted by some and rejected by others in post-Kantian thought; the philosophies of religion constructed by Schleiermacher, Hegel, and Ritschl represent attempts to give accounts of religion, and specifically the Christian religion, in terms either of the acceptance, or the rejection of this Kantian dualism. Schleiermacher and Hegel denied the dualism, but Ritschl turned the duality of freedom and necessity, or of the moral and the natural, into the more religious dualism of spirit and nature.

It is not my intention to give a full account or even a comprehensive outline of the systems of Schleiermacher, Hegel, and Ritschl, but only to exhibit them as impressive examples of the method of subjective rationalism. For they are strictly rationalistic in that they admit of no revelation. Ritschl, the most Kantian of the three, rejects explicitly both dogmatic Church doctrine based on revelation, and the objective rationalism of pre-Kantian days, as indeed did also Schleiermacher and Hegel. Put briefly, Schleiermacher made feeling the basis of religion, Hegel made thought its substance, and Ritschl gave the place of honor to morality. All the doctrines and meanings of the Christian faith are translated into terms of the God-consciousness (Schleiermacher), the Idea, or *Begriff* (Hegel), or moral purpose (Ritschl). There is no supernatural, no revelation. When the word "God" is used as it is constantly, of course, what is meant is not a transcendent Spirit or Person, but the universalized and absolutized element of the human consciousness immediately known as God-consciousness, or Idea (Thought), or moral purpose. Revelation is the personal realization of truth, of the consciousness of the divine or, and this was a common assumption fraught with unrealized difficulties, the emergence in history of Jesus Christ, and the extension through time of his authenttic influence, purpose, and power. Faith becomes identified with this subjective consciousness; it is rational, moral, psychological, but not a response to a God who speaks as the Other.

Many other movements of thought affected the Protestant theology of the nineteenth century, but the basic method is the subjective rationalism exhibited most fully and influentially in these three types of religious philosophy. Two influences which appeared but, as it were, lay dormant for nearly a century were the philosophy of Schelling and the religious writings of Kierkegaard. The existentialsm of Kierkegaard was a clear and devastating rejection of the subjective rationalism of Hegel. Interestingly enough it was done by one who asserted that "truth is subjectivity." Hegel had claimed objective validity for his "thought" by identifying subject and object, Spirit-in-Itself and Spirit-for-Itself. His system is called objective idealism; there is only one real Knower—God. But God is also the Known, the Object. "Object," for rational thought, means a concept grasped by the rational mind. Kierkegaard denounced the presumption of the "System" for making God an Object, and so subject to rational conception.

The revival of Schelling in brilliant form, modified by mysticism in the "depth of reason" and combined with the existentialism that stems from Kierkegaard, is found today in Paul Tillich. This is what might properly be called *ontological rationalism*. For the philosophical basis of the whole work is set forth with great clarity in volume I of his *Dogmatic Theology* in the affirmation that the structure of reason is identical with the structure of Being.[5] God is not *a* Being but Being, or Being Itself; and Being Itself embraces not only reason which, of course, simply *is*, that is, is static, but also the "depth of reason" which is the abyss of mystery, and is dynamic and creative, and the source of revelation through ecstasy. The *theology* consists in a "correlation" of basic Christian doctrines with the categories and concepts of this richly modified rationalism. It is Christian, because Tillich himself is a Christian, deeply rooted in the historic faith. One wonders whether, if he were a Hindu or a Buddhist, he could not work out with equal success a correlation between his philosophy and his religious faith. It is reasonable to assume that he could, for the nature of ontological reason is precisely to be the essence

[5] See, for example, *Systematic Theology*, vol. I, Chicago, 1951, pp. 20, 21, and 178, 179.

of all that is, physically, intellectually, psychologically, socio-
logically, politically, or, in a word, culturally. His philosphy is,
in fact, just the critical elaboration of the nature of reason, its
concepts, categories, processes (cf. pp. 18, 19 of *Systematic Theology*). This means that it is a method which man brings to all
his experiences and actions to give him understanding and to guide
him. Therefore, however widely and helpfully the instrument
is used, in the treatment of culture or of the Christian faith, we
must not lose sight of the fact that the method is strictly rationalistic. Even mystery, creativity, and revelation erupt from the
"depth of reason."

5. THE AGE OF IDEOLOGY

A recent book by Henry D. Aiken, entitled *The Age of
Ideology*, provides a critical and illuminating essay on the development of philosophy since Kant and furnishes the general background for the method of nineteenth-century theology as it has
been set forth in the preceding pages. "Ideology" is a correlate of
"subjectivism." Philosophy, as well as theology, has been working
with the content and process of the human mind. Strictly speaking, "truth" has not been the end sought, but "meaning." The
philosophy has been basically agnostic about God and the world,
and has turned to the elaboration and even exploitation of the
interests and possibilities of the human consciousness. Aiken
writes of a varied group of thinkers: Kant, Fichte, Hegel, Scho-
penhauer, Comte, Spencer, Mill, Marx, Nietzsche, Kierkegaard,
and Mach. The more recent outcome of this development includes pragmatism, phenomenology, semanticism, existentialism,
positivism, and ontological rationalism. It might be said that
philosophy has given up its ancient passion for truth and reality,
in short for metaphysical achievement, and has accepted the role
of a methodology, specific or general. This is the outcome of a
rationalism that first claimed to know God more truly than the
religious man as such could know him, and that also claimed to
know the world of nature in its essence as common experience
could never make it known.

6. RETURN TO REVELATION

Our time has witnessed a return to revelation. This is at least partly due to the exhaustion of the rational method in whatever form it might appear, objective, critical, or subjective. In the age of ideology, the rational process, honestly appraised, is an enterprise of the human mind and can be made subservient to the ends of men, scientific, social, political, or religious. No clear and sure objective reference, natural or divine, lays upon it the demands of truth, and holds it responsible for its operation and results. Little wonder that the world turned away from philosophy and religion to the economic and social struggle, and that ideologies— mechanism, fascism, communism—freely manipulated the mental process to provide a rational and even "scientific" justification for the massed passion and purpose of men. The old mythologies of religious faith were replaced by the new mythologies of secular faiths. Reason, once a master, laying its austere demand upon the mind of man, is now seen as the servant of man, his ambitions, his desires, his great passions.

What had happened in the general field of philosophy had its parallel in theology. The philosophical theology of the nineteenth century, as has been shown above, was in the form of a subjective rationalism. What is commonly called idealism, or post-Kantian idealism, is a form of this subjective rationalism. Its great figures were Schleiermacher, Hegel, and Ritschl. It is a shocking thing to observe how readily the idealism of Hegel was turned, *via* Feuerbach, into the materialism of Marx; and how easily the same idealism could support the national socialism of Hitler's Germany. Indeed, Hegel's *Philosophy of History* gives ample justification for amoral conduct on the part of the "world historical individual" and the "world historical nation." Even as gracious and socially idealistic a thinker as Josiah Royce could say in his *History of California*, "It is the State, the Social Order, that is divine. We are all but dust, save as this social order gives us life." [6]

A religious faith, therefore, resting not on revelation but on reason—subjective reason—found itself at a disadvantage when

[6] Josiah Royce, *California, From the Conquest in 1846 to the Second Vigilance Committee in San Francisco*, Boston, 1886, p. 501.

confronted by the violence of the world and the demonically
inverted idealism of the totalitarian movements of the present
day. It was the realization of this predicament, plus the revival of
Kierkegaard, that brought into being the biblical theology, or
theology of crisis, or neo-orthodoxy, of the past generation. A
central feature of this theology was its re-affirmation of revelation as the ground of Christian faith.

Despite many differences in the understanding of revelation
there are some things in which a large measure of agreement is to
be found in the theological developments of recent years. (1) The
first is that revelation is not the supernatural communication of
"truths" in the form of statements or doctrine. The intellectual-
ism of the scholastic method is quite generally rejected. (2)
Revelation is seen as God's act of self-disclosure, or of self-communication. If the question is asked, What does God reveal? The
answer is, God reveals himself. (3) The revelation is made to
man and man receives the revelation by faith. Faith is the human
correlate of revelation. The initiative is with God; he acts in
sovereign freedom. But man's act of faith is also free; in it he
knows the God who makes himself known. (4) The chief obstacle to the reception of God's self-revelation is not man's limited
intellectual powers, nor his finitude, but his sin. Pride, egotism,
self-will obstruct the revealing act of God; faith, obedience, love
open the way. But there are also intellectual limitations that interfere, and wrong and mistaken ideas of God and man and nature
create obstacles to faith. This points up the importance of theological understanding.

The foregoing agreements are in the realm of theological
thinking. A certain convergence of conception is to be found
more generally in the ecumenical movement. Here the existence
of the Church itself in history and the faith by which it has
lived provide a concrete meaning for revelation as God's act of
self-disclosure. Rationalism in any form is individualistic. Reason
aspires to universal categories, indeed, to a Universal; but reason
shows itself complete in the mind of an individual thinker. The
faith of the Church as a believing community, or a community of
faith, is personal, but it is the shared consciousness of a fellowship whose reality is an existence in love for one another and

common obedience toward God. The meaning of revelation is found in this social and historical character of the Christian faith.

1. It is an "historical" revelation; God reveals himself through his acts in history. This is quite a different thing from the historicism of the nineteenth century that found in the historic process itself the gradual disclosure of the truth and purpose of God. What it signifies is that God's dealings with the race and especially with the people of Israel, as understood by the prophetic mind, are his acts of judgment and grace. The "mighty acts of God" is a common term in the language of ecumenical discussion. There is no disregard of God's self-revelation in creation, but the greater relevance is found in history because here God is dealing directly in moral and spiritual terms with man himself. God reveals his own holiness, his own goodness, his own grace precisely in his acts toward and his demands upon man. But man lives in history, therefore this dealing is seen in events whose inner meaning is the act of God.

2. The supreme act of God is Jesus Christ. God reveals himself in his proper Person in the man Jesus. The historic, human reality of Jesus Christ is the basic and normative reality of revelation for Christian faith. This is, methodologically, the direct answer to and refutation of the idea that revelation is in terms of statements, propositions, or "truths." The "Word" of God is not a sentence or a doctrine; it is not an idea, but a Person. God was personally present in this human person, in whom he revealed himself. Jesus Christ is the revelation of the living God who is Love, who is Savior. The task of theology still remains to say "how" this incarnation is to be understood. But this should not obscure the fact of the general agreement that Jesus Christ is the revelation of God.

3. Ecumenical thinking is biblical. In this also there is agreement in current theological thought. The Bible is an historical literature in which are found the fact and the form of revelation in various ways. It records the "mighty acts of God" and the "word" spoken to the prophets. It is a literature of faith and contains a "history of salvation." Its theme is various but centers in the dealings of God with man. The modern churchman, like the modern theologian, knows of the historical and literary

criticism of the scriptures. He has no doctrine of verbal inspira-
tion or of infallibility. He does not find, as did the scholastic,
supernaturally revealed first principles of theological truth. But
he does see in the Bible the authentic witness to the presence
and action of God in history. Technical difficulties about the
authorship and the meaning of the text will never be fully resolved and, if they were, they would still not bring to theology
a propositional basis for systematic doctrine. In what sense and
to what extent the text must be "demythologized" or "re-
mythologized," to put its meaning fully into our contemporary
thought, is an open question. But all this being granted, it is still
true that the essential self-disclosure in scripture of the God who
creates and redeems is the beginning of all Christian theology.

4. Revelation, also, is seen as historical in that the living
Church through history has been and continues to be not only
the house of faith in which the faith is preserved, but the locus
of God's continuing self-revelation. God not only spoke through
the "mighty acts" of past time and the word of the prophet; not
only, even though supremely, in Jesus Christ. As Holy Spirit he
is present and speaks in the Church. The Church is the continuing
community of faith, hence the continuing receiver of revelation.
Revelation is not only historical, in the sense of coming through
past events which are the history of salvation; it is an ever present
historical reality in the living Church.

These main points present-day theology shares with the ecumenical consciousness of the Church. Theology is thus the systematic formulation and exposition of the faith of the Church.
In this it differs radically from the philosophical theology of the
past, and much of the theological philosophy of the present,
which is a product of individual experience and reflective thought
and which is communicated to others to persuade or instruct
them. Recent theology is not rationalistic, nor is it irrationalistic.
It holds that the subject matter with which it deals is not the
rational structure of the mind nor even the assumed rational
structure of the world, but the reality and act of the self-revealing
God.

CHAPTER III

THEOLOGICAL METHOD—CONSTRUCTIVE

AGAINST THE background briefly outlined in the preceding chapter, I shall set forth the method which seems to me valid for Christian theology. The method, so far as it is valid, will support and give a basis for the interpretations of Christian faith which follow. On the other hand the actual form of those interpretations will reflect back upon the method and, to some extent, justify it. I do not have a name for this method; the preceding characterizations of method as scholasticism and rationalism, objective, critical, and subjective, are based on an historic development which is the common knowledge and background of us all and so easily subject to classification and description. The return to revelation and biblical conceptions certainly does not invalidate all that has gone before; indeed, it makes possible creative use of elements in those methods. Perhaps the "new theology" is now sufficiently developed to disclose, both in its unity and in its diversity, both in its success and in its failure, the main elements of a method by which theological construction can proceed confidently today and tomorrow. At any rate, anyone seriously attempting to write theology should be clear and candid in regard to his method. This will enable those who feel that the method is wrong or inadequate to save themselves the trouble of reading any further; it will put on notice to those who proceed what meanings can properly be attached to the doctrine as it is set forth.

REASON, IMAGINATION, AND FAITH

The fundamental elements of theological thinking are reason, imagination, and faith. All these are primary forms of the act of

the mind; they are involved in all knowing. The complete and
actual thought of man always involves all three. Usually we are
more conscious of one element than of the others. Sometimes we
are wholly unaware of one or the other. As a matter of fact in
most of our thinking we are not aware of any one of them as such.
Thinking is the characteristic form of human activity and of
conscious interaction with the world, with other persons and with
God. In no aspect of his mental activity is man infallible; no
aspect of his thought is absolute. The mind of man, in its most
comprehensive activity, or in its most disciplined, specialized, and
tested functioning, prescribes no laws to reality. But the concep-
tualizing act of the reason, the creative construction of the imagination, and the assurance of faith are all indispensable for the
living of a full human life and the apprehension of truth. In
science the reason is dominant; in the arts and industry, imagination; and in religion, faith. Yet all are involved in each and every
form of human activity and all are needed if the full meaning of
truth is to be found. They merge into one another. "Pure" science is almost exclusively rational, that is, a matter of the logic
and *ratio* of concepts, yet it merges into technology which is the
concrete construction, by the imagination, of mechanisms, methods, and processes by which the theory may be put to work in
the actual world. Religion is faith in the transcendent and in the
absolute grounding of the human spirit in meaning and reality.
But it always appears in the forms of imagination which legend,
myth, and sacrament give it, and is constantly distilled into a
theology. The fine arts approach the form of "pure" imagination;
still the artist always needs a medium—words, pigments, sounds—
and is at once involved in the technical matters of language, can-
vas, brushes, musical instruments, or stone and chisel. And there
is a philosophy of art. The *faith* of the scientist may be almost
wholly implicit, and the worshipper may seem to lose the *rational*
structure of thought in his act of faith but the faith is there in
the one case, nevertheless, and in the other, the reason. What we
have to do with always is the *man*, the thinker, who in his wholeness acts in his apprehension of and relation to all that is in and
over against him.

REASON IN THEOLOGY

For theology "reason" does not connote a fixed structure, either objective or subjective. Theology today, like the other serious disciplines of human thought, is aware of the fact that both objective and subjective rationalism, as described above, have proven inadequate. But while rationalism has had its day, *reasoning* remains as the process of clear and criticized thinking by which such truth as man is capable of is achieved in any field. But there is nothing mysterious or absolute about reasoning. It is simply ordered and coherent thought. It does not prescribe laws to reality although it may formulate "laws" for human understanding; it is not infallible in any field; and it is always relative to the particular subject matter with which it deals. It might be said that reasoning is logical thinking, but "logic" itself is a relative thing. Logic means, fundamentally, "order." Logical thinking is orderly thinking. But the order is always an order of "something" if it is to lead to "truth." There are as many logics as there are forms of reality. The logic of family life is different from the logic of business procedure. The logic of education is different from that of manufacture. Thought and language, which are inseparable, seek for a universal logic.[1] The Aristotelian logic and Euclidian geometry were for a long time assumed to be universal forms of thought identical with "reality." But Aristotle and Euclid respectively have had to give way to empirical thinking on the one hand, and on the other to the non-Euclidian elaboration of geometry and the general developments of mathematics. In both cases logic and language are seen to be a responsible human, or mental, interaction with and communication about reality. Language may be quite simple, as simple as the naming of an object in the world of common experience. Both logic and language may become so complex and specialized, so far removed from any direct perception, that only the specialist can understand them and, indeed, only remotely do they relate to the immediately experienced world. The development of symbolic

[1] Cf. Descartes's quest for a universal language. This, in its proper functioning, is what mathematics constitutes.

logic and mathematics today, and the pre-occupation of philosophy with language attest this fact.

Reason, for theology, is reasoning. As such it has a logic, and constitutes careful, ordered, and critical thinking. But its logic and its language are the language and logic of the spiritual life. It is a logic of God, and man, his creature. It is a logic of spiritual, that is, personal, reality and relations. It speaks of a Creator and creation; of judgment and grace; of obedience and sin; and of repentance and forgiveness. It cannot express its meanings in terms of physics, or biology, or even in terms of ethics alone. Ethics speaks of the good, of the good will, of the free moral act. But theology takes the whole man in his wholeness and in his relation to other men and to God, and speaks of love, and obedience, and disobedience, of reconciliation, of repentance, and of forgiveness. This is not the logic of a rational ethics, but of actual personal relations between man and man, and between man and God. This language and logic is based on the fact that the primary or ultimate terms of theology are the concrete, or existent actual persons—individuals not generalities; persons not ideas are the ultimate units or referents of thought in theology. Insofar as theology has become philosophical, what it has gained in cogency and clarity it has gained at the sacrifice of the fundamental stuff of real theology, which is the personal spirit and its acts and relations.

Faith

Theology is based on and determined by faith. It is actually the rational or systematic interpretation and expression of *a* faith. A faith, or religion, is a serious, developed, and widely held form of man's life in relation to ultimate reality and the ultimate meaning of his own life. There is a sense in which faith exists without a clearly defined relation to any religious tradition, in the more or less conscious personal construction of a religious outlook. This actually occurs only among the relatively small percentage of mankind who have the interest and the intellectual ambition to attain such a faith. Even in such persons, the "faith" is likely to have the form and color of a dominant religious tradition. For, as Schleiermacher insists, there is no such thing as "religion in general," and the real faith of men is an historic and more or less organized system of life and meaning. This is certainly true of Christian faith, and Christian theology is the systematic setting forth and communication of the faith.

Psychologically, faith is the hopeful and positive attitude. All faith has this aspect, whether it is well conceived or based upon a tragic illusion. "Have faith; be hopeful," we may be told. But the question is, Have faith in what? Be hopeful of what and upon what basis? A psychological description of faith, taken as the substance of it, leads to pure sentimentalism. Or it may lead to superstition because it is at random attached to the most convenient or superficially attractive object. Still it is true that faith is basically a hopeful and confident attitude, and we need faith for confidence and for accomplishment in humaan life. Faith is both belief and trust.

But faith is also an act of knowledge, or a factor in all knowledge. Put simply, faith is the apprehension of reality. Reason analyzes and interprets, but does not provide the substantial and objective material of knowledge. The "pure" reason has only its own form for object. Even perceptions are modifications of the mind though referred to objective fact. But the reality of a world, of a thing in the world, of other persons, of God is apprehended directly in the total act of the personal spirit and the best word for this is faith. One might call it intuition; it is certainly intuitive in the sense of being an immediate apprehension. Faith is the essentially objective outreach of the consciousness. Science "accepts the world"; it knows the process but not the reality of the world except by this unargued act of faith. It is only common sense to accept the world as real. But common sense includes the element or act of faith. One may say that faith is the reality sense. Theoretically we can say, as did Descartes, that the world *may* be illusion. But practically we don't believe it. We do believe that the world is real, and the belief, though implicit, is the root of our knowledge. Faith, therefore, is a matter of response and responsibility: response to the world that is there, that is real, and that makes life meaningful; responsibility, in that we take the world for what it is, deal with it realistically both in conforming to it and in transforming it to suit our own ends.

So faith "accepts God." It does not "know" him as the scientist knows the process of the world. But it knows his presence, his reality, and the demand he makes upon man, and the promise of his help. Faith is a response to God in his reality and it makes man responsible to him, as he is. Theology is the elaboration of a rational structure of meanings derived from the primary act of faith. This is "belief," the form of all knowledge; it is, in this sense, knowledge. It is not infallible; no human knowledge is infallible. It is not free from the danger of illusion; no human knowledge is free from such danger. It is incomplete; all human knowledge is incomplete. It is not a knowledge that can be forced upon anyone by logical proof, or by outward demonstration— which means miracle, and miracle cannot demonstrate truth. But in the realm of personal, or spiritual, relations and reality, it is the direct and only ultimate form of knowledge. A man can know his neighbor *as man* only by faith. So man can know God, *as God*, only by faith. Any object or being of which anyone claims rational knowledge apart from faith, is not God but an idea, i.e. a form of his own mind.

IMAGINATION

The primary act of the thinking mind is imagination; in it are both reason and faith, i.e. order and a sense of reality. Imagination is not the irresponsible play of fancy, as in a waking dream. It is rather the serious and responsible form in which thought deals with reality not immediately presented in perception. It sets the presented world in the context of a larger world both imagined and conceived. The greater part of the world of thought is not present in time or in space. From the vantage point of here and now the mind moves into a temporal and an extended world both imaginatively and conceptually. Its task is to construct a complete world. This is accomplished first mythologically, that is, in pictorial form. Then, with the emergence of abstract reason, a conceptionally complete world is constructed. Neither the world as construed by myth, nor that constructed by abstract reason, is ever actually complete or adequate. Neither imagination nor reason can encompass reality. Neither the myth nor the metaphysics is literally true, nor completely false. As a matter of fact, there are many mythological representations of the world, and there are conflicting systems of metaphysics. Theology has always worked closely with both religious mythology and philosophical metaphysics, although it is identical with neither, and it has, on its own grounds, revised and rejected much of both. For example, Christian theology early rejected the hierarchies of Neo-Platonic spirits and demons. But it also rejected the rational monism of Greek thought. Thomas Aquinas accepted the main structure of Aristotelian metaphysics, but as a Christian he added the ideas of creation and the Trinity.

Both myth and metaphysics are symbolic representations of reality. Neither is or can be literally true. Even the language of Tillich's "ontological reason" is symbolic. "Literal truth" is only the truth of the letter, or of the written word on the page. It is an assertion about a finite meaning within a limited and clearly defined agreement on names and meanings. No assertion about the whole can be "literal." However, this need not dismay the serious thinker, theologian, philosopher, or scientist. For thinking is precisely the representation in thought, by symbols, of reality on any level. The issue is the appropriateness and adequacy of the symbolism.

Not even the approximately precise and experimentally proven propositions of natural science are literally true; the most generally valid formula or equation is a symbol of what cannot be literally known or sensibly presented. Energy is not seen, heard, or felt, therefore not literally and simply known in the formula $E = mc^2$. Nature is not literally like anyone's conception of nature. Nature cannot be directly and in its own full and proper reality "presented" either to the senses or the rational mind of man any more than God can. Yet nature is a "whole," a complete reality about which universally valid formulas can be made. The scientist would be in as much of a predicament if the layman should demand, "Show us nature," as Jesus was when one of his disciples said, "Show us the Father." The conception of God and the concept of nature are practically, vitally, and morally meaningful and both have a certain kind of truth. They constitute knowledge of God and nature. Neither theology nor science claims a "knowledge" such as that of classical metaphysics in which an identity of reason and reality was assumed.

Thinking is largely, and probably primarily, a projection in consciousness of action into the future, a plotting of the course of life in advance of actually living it. The mind scouts the course the man must take, it enacts in imagination the conduct of tomorrow in the actual setting and conditions of that action. It views the scene as it is remembered or imagined, considers the possibilities and calculates the difficulties to be encountered. It estimates the resources of skill and strength of the man against the conditions, and in thought goes through the whole action to see if it can succeed.

The original form of this preview of action is doubtless concretely imaginative, a three-D representation of the future with sound, and also smell and touch added, a little like the cinema in Huxley's *Brave New World*. And the future is the next hour, or day, or brief period in which a course of action can be fully foreseen. So there is a maximum of reality in thinking at this stage. The man thinks with his body, with the sense of action and strain, of pain or pleasure and of accomplished act.

The conceptual form of thought is likewise basically a preview of action, but *in abstracto*. It is true that there is the aspect of pure contemplation in abstract thought, just as there is the moment of immediate enjoyment in the simpler form of imagination. This is a sort of provisionally passive form of consciousness in knowledge. But thought is mainly active and action looks toward the future. The form that conceptual thought takes is that of a general, but precisely calculated and defined pattern of future action. It is a form lacking in the full-scale concreteness that characterizes imagination, but by the same token it is more precise in indicating possibilities and difficulties. Still its character is essentially the same as that of imagination, in that it is a preview of action in a real world. Only the action is viewed conceptually rather than imaginatively. Yet the possibility of action is still the primary key to the knowledge value. Thus highly complex mathematical processes are required to give a conceptual knowledge of the maximum speed at which a car can take a curve of a certain degree, on a surface of a specific kind, with a certain kind of tire, etc. But motorists are daily making swift, and usually successful calculations in imagination, judging speed, distance, traction, and so on. The purest form of conceptual thinking is mathematics which formulates the general rules for movements in space.

Both these ways of thinking are symbolical; one forming *conceptions* of the imagination, the other forming *concepts* of reason. The symbolism of imagination is in terms of concrete life experience, and is therefore nearer to reality as man can know it. It is a mental representation of the full reality of experience. However, the reality of the form is gained at the cost of a degree of inaccuracy and even the possibility of illusion. In pathological cases a wholly unreal world can be imagined. But this is man's first and most basic way of thinking and of his conscious dealing with the real world. Perhaps it always will be. Accordingly, men generally have a sense of strangeness and unreality in the modern world of mathematical and unimaginable entities. The artists are trying to represent and make real this world by "abstract" forms or symbolism. Perhaps they would do better to deal meaningfully with the basic forms of human experience in symbols that are the common language of mankind and so assert the primary value of such experience.

The symbolism of conceptual thought constitutes a sort of shorthand, a system of terms and signs representing no particular existing reality, but the form, proportions, and relations of reality in general. These are the special intellectual tools of the scientist, and he uses them as such. They are technical and operational; they *work*. They attain a high degree of theoretical accuracy which, taken with the actual accuracy of measurement of the physical world that is now possible, means that action in and on the natural world can be calculated with a high degree of certainty.

Different as these two ways of thinking are as regards the medium—picture or concept—they are both acts or products of living minds. They are both practical or instrumental in character. They serve a purpose. They are mental means by which a living man plots his course in both the short-term actions and in the long-term undertakings to which he gives himself, including the all-inclusive action of life as a whole. The mind thus forms and follows *intentions* and tests out ways to fulfill them in both modes of pre-vision. But there is a certain important difference between these two functions of the mind. Conceptual thought, ultimately, is concerned with possibilities and techniques; imagination is concerned also and even more with the worth of the intended act and the reality of the world in which it takes place. Both of these concerns, of course, are important, and human thinking and living must take account of both. Both are rational but in different senses. A process of thought is rational if it is coherent and if it arrives at conclusions logically derived from its primary axioms. This is rationality within the thought process itself. But we have asserted that thought is instrumental to action. Indeed its truth is largely attested by the success of the action for which it is carried on. But there is another important meaning of "rational." One asks if an action itself is rational. By this he means, Does it contribute to a certain end? If, for example, one is planning an auto trip and he spends his time drawing maps of the playground on which he played as a child, we would say that his action is irrational. It has no relevance to his auto trip; it does not contribute to the success or enjoyment of the trip. But if he spent his time studying maps of the states through which he was to travel, if he collected information about motels and places of interest, if he provided himself with sun glasses and a portable ice box, in all these things we would say he was acting quite rationally. So, in court, if a defense attorney can prove that the accused would have had no reason for doing things he was said to have done a presumption is created in his favor. Reason in that sense comprehends both motive and purpose.

Now, for most persons, the reason *for which* they live is more important than the techniques *by which* they live. Even if one's main interest is some form of technical action, that action functioning as an end is the reason for his living. Yet even here it may be said that it is the satisfaction that the man has in the technical accomplishment, rather than the process itself, that is the reason for his life.[2]

Theology, and historically philosophy also, has been primarily concerned with the true end of existence and the nature of the divine or eternal order in which that end is realized. This is a concern for the rationality of life as a whole. But the two disciplines tend to use different methods. Philosophy has put its trust in the concept from the time of Socrates. Theology, while it has often become absorbed in concepts as such, has never completely given up the imagination. It finds conceptions in imaginal form more adequate and true to its meaning. This is certainly the case with Christian theology in which the basic symbols are taken from history and from the person of Christ.

TRUTH AND ORIGINS

If thinking is primarily a mental preview of the future in the interest of action or living, human thinking is also, and from earliest times has been engaged with the past. The earliest thought about the past, like the first way of looking into the future, is imaginative, that is, it is a full-scale realistic and dramatic portrayal. Primitive man has his cosmogonic myth which he relates in story and enacts in ritual. He has his mythological and legendary accounts of the origin and life of his tribe which he endlessly repeats in his epics and in the folk lore which precedes history. His gods are primary figures in this moving drama of the past; they are not separate from the world or man, and are different from himself mainly in power. Knowing is imaginal, its expression dramatic, either in words or dance ritual.

Why this interest of man in his past? It is not mere curiosity, nor an attempt to explain things as they are. It is a practical

[2] As, for example, in mathematics: "The beauty of a mathematical result is the fundamental motive for its pursuit. Every creative mathematician is essentially a creative artist. The most important and fertile discoveries in the whole field of mathematics have been made by men who were guided by aesthetic motives—men whose insight into unsuspected relations between apparently diverse phenomena led them to replace an ugly and unsatisfactory chaos by a beautiful and illuminating order." From an article by Professor Edward V. Huntington in *The Scientific Monthly*, April 1931, p. 48 fn.

interest, as practical as man's anxious pre-viewing of the future. His own security is bound up in both directions of his thinking. If he looks forward to test the action of tomorrow in imagination because his survival depends on a true picture of its conditions, he looks backward to discover or see what he himself is, and to reassure himself of the alliance of his limited and dubious power with the greater, more steadfast, and dependable powers or power in which he originated and which are in a larger sense what he is. He quite reasonably feels that his security is much more dependent upon this origin and his identity with the greater powers, than it is upon the success of his plans and calculations about the future. More generally we may say that man finds the meaning of his own life and being in this originative past and in spiritual oneness with the greater powers recognized, honored, and appealed to in his religion. Things have come to be what they now are through the intentional action of higher powers, but those powers are akin to man and despite their fearful aspect they are on his side, and can be so approached and addressed as to be helpful to him.

When man has become consciously and reflectively rational he is at first more preoccupied with the past than with the future. He first tries to find out what is the true nature of the power or powers that are obviously prior to and greater than himself. His understanding of the world is the first element in his understanding of himself, as well as the key to his security. *Understanding*, therefore, is the nature of this kind of thinking; but it is still practical in character, because it is the (usually) unspoken conviction of the philosopher that to know or understand is itself the basis of man's true being and security. Man comes to know what he himself is by knowing what the original nature of the world is. But though rational thought may tell us what the original nature of the world is, it cannot properly tell us anything about real origination. It can tell us the constitution of the world but not how it came to be. If it does the latter it forges a philosophical myth, such as Plato's creation myth in the *Timaeus*. Rational metaphysics in its fully mature form, as in Aristotle, has no account of origin, only a description of the changeless structure of an eternally existing universe. This is the classical "metaphysics" which means, as we must continually remind ourselves, not a science of something beyond nature (*phusis*) but only the first principles of nature, or of reason. God is defined by Aristotle as the first principles of reason. But God does not create the world; he simply is, as unmoved Being, wholly rational in his nature.

A more limited (self-limited) rational account of the world appears with modern science, which abandons completely any attempt to account for the world's coming into being. It seeks to know how things are. Its interest in the past is strictly an interest in the essentially uniform process of an existing world. The "past" means the preceding states or changes of the world, just as the future means the possibilities of states or changes that will take place of themselves or can be determined by the actions of man. As science, it can press back indefinitely into a "past" the inquiry as to what preceded any given state of the world, but cannot ask about the origin of the process itself. There is no "beginning," only a continuing. "Creation" is not a scientific term or idea. Science, therefore, does not try to "understand" the world in the mythological or philosophical sense. It seeks to *know* the world in terms of a present which is extended without basic change in nature both into the past and into the future. No light is thrown on any alleged creation, or purpose of the world. Knowledge of the world does not give man any knowledge of the meaning of his life. If we ask what is the ultimate purpose of human existence, science has no answer. This is not its responsibility, and its method excludes the question.

But if philosophy has, by its own rational method, abandoned the quest for man's origin or the origin of the world, and if science has never acknowledged the quest as legitimate or meaningful, theology is primarily concerned with this issue. The main concern of theology is the truth about man's origin and destiny. Fundamentally, theology is the "theory" or "knowledge" of God. Its object is God. But this is because God is the source of man's existence and because the meaning of man's life is found in him. When we think of God, we think of him as Creator; when we think of the world, we think of it not primarily as "nature" but as "creation." In knowing the world as the creation of God we know it not in terms of its natural process, and the regularity and consistency of that process; we know it is an order of things originating in the act of God, and under his creative control. Man thus finds meaning in his own existence. He knows what and who he himself is; in his own being he sees a likeness to God; in God he sees the Lord of his being, and the Father of his spirit. In this religious conception of the world and its Creator, theology starts with the self-revelation of God and the faith of man which is the response to that revelation.

THEOLOGY AND HISTORY

Religious faith is rooted in the past of man in terms of history. And the past goes back to the beginnings of man as man. If primitive man knew himself akin to the world in which he lived (in this he was as "naturalistic" as modern science), he also knew that world not as an inanimate or sub-human physical process but as living and possessed of such powers of sensitivity, intention, and free action as he knew in himself. In this he held the same position as the most enlightened Christian of today. It is the conviction that man is thus "in the image" of God that has given real meaning to his existence, even when he is most threatened with complete submergence under the powers of a natural world that does not know him and is not concerned with him or his destiny.

The history of man's dealings with God or of God's dealings with man goes through the forms of pure mythology, of mythology supplemented by legend, of history as the prophetic mind apprehends it and, in the Christian faith, as centered in the person of Christ in whom the Creator God reveals himself also as the Redeemer. I say "history as the prophetic mind apprehends it," because in the prophets of the Old Testament we have real history, namely an account of at least one people in terms of God's demand upon them, and his judgment and mercy in dealing with them. Here is a conscious response of the human spirit to God and it is in terms of his dealings, first with one nation, and then with the race. The appearance of Jesus Christ, and the faith of the Christian community, most explicitly as formulated by

Paul, furnish a total meaning for the life of man as man in terms of the revelation of God as Father of all men, and Christ as Savior. Christian theology starts and finishes with God. It finds the historic self-revelation of God in the prophetic word of the Old Testament and in Jesus Christ. He is Creator; he is righteous; he is Love. This revelation is in history; it emerges in the drama of real historic existence. History takes the place of myth in the original sense. Legend gives way to history. It is history as known in its depth dimension by faith and as recorded in the life of a community of faith and in a scripture which knows the act of God in the event. It is like myth in that it has the depth of meaning. It is like legend in that it preserves the sense of the greater power. But it is true history in that the prophets lived and spoke and staked their lives in a concrete historic situation, and that the Christ was a real man, living in a moment and in a place in history, giving his life in witness to the Father who sent him, and dying as a final act of faithfulness to God and love to man. This is all history in the fullest sense of the word. It is history not just as record but as past event with present meaning and promise for any future that man can have.

Christian faith is an historic faith, therefore, not only in the sense that its origin is in the career of Jesus Christ, so that a calendar, for example, can begin with the assumed date of his birth, with a B.C. and an A.D. for every known event in the life of the race. It is historic in the much more important sense that the revelation of God to which this faith is response comes in that historic Christ, and in the specific self-communication of God through the Old Testament prophets. But this specific line of revelation is within the total context of man's age-long dealings with God back to the crudest beginnings. What might be called the basic sense of God, the awareness of the all-encompassing mystery of deity, which is a basic form of the human consciousness and which conditions and accompanies man in history, this is the context of Christian faith as it is of all religious faith. It is the sense of *presence*, more fundamental than Otto's sense of the *holy*, without which true human consciousness could never have appeared.

Religious faith is faith in God; the development of religion and the religions represents the relative success or failure of men in apprehending the *truth* implied in the faith. In its claim to truth the Christian faith shares with all religions the conviction of the essential authenticity of the sense of the presence and the power of God. In this the Christian and the primitive man agree. Early man was not all wrong; he was fundamentally right when he knew himself in the presence of higher being or beings akin to him and concerned with him. It is doubtful if the human mind could have faced the conditions of actual existence and had courage to make what progress it has, had it not found some essential support and kinship for its humanity in the world about and within.

With profound regard for all the great traditions of religious faith, and the essential authenticity of their basic sense of the presence and power of God, the Christian holds that the historic development through the prophets of Israel which came to its fulfillment and judgment in Christ is the unique history of God's self-revelation in his essential character and in his redemptive purpose for man. To believe that this is true does not condemn nor discredit the faith of other religious communities, nor assert that God's self-revelation failed completely in them. But historic developments in Israel, the gradual formulation of ideas of both man and God, the emergence of communities and personalities, and the free response of the prophetic spirit to God, are all needed to make the event of Christ possible and to give it re-demptive power.

Christian theology has to do with history not only in the sense that it acknowledges a self-revelation of God in history, but also in its dependence upon a transmission of the truth of that revela-tion through history. God spoke through the prophets; he was incarnate in Christ. To those who heard the prophets speak and to those who knew Christ, who could say, "that...which we have heard, which we have seen with our eyes, which we have looked upon and touched with our hands, concerning the word of life..." (I John 1:1),[3] the revelation was a contemporary event to be directly known by faith. But following that moment in history the revelation must be received indirectly through a

[3] All biblical references are to the Revised Standard Version.

"testimony" first made by word of mouth and then committed to writing, and thus become "scripture." Christian faith and the truth sought by Christian theology here encounter the relativity of historical knowledge.

This relativity is neither all loss nor all gain. It certainly represents a loss; what one may call the "factuality" of history is called in question. One may go to the extreme of denying that any such person as Jesus ever lived. Thus the basis of factuality is completely removed and one can either reject the faith completely or, as many have, "spiritualize" it by making the person and the teaching of Christ symbolic of a religious reality wholly identified with present experience. The opposite extreme is that taken by those who affirm, in the face of all difficulties, a supernaturally preserved accuracy in the writing, editing, transmission, and translation of the scripture.

The nineteenth-century theologies assumed an authentic transmission through the centuries of what they took to be the essential element in the event of Christ. With Schleiermacher it was the "impulse that came from Jesus," that is, the full realization of the God consciousness, which proved itself at any time in the actual God consciousness of the believer. With Ritschl it was the moral reality of God revealed in Christ as his "self-end" or purpose, which each believer accepted as his own and so came into immediate realization of the saving power of Christ and the consciousness of the forgiveness of sins. This was an essentially subjective matter, a form of experience, first attributed to Christ and then enjoyed by the Christian. The real point of beginning for the Christian was not historic event but present consciousness. This kind of faith tended to make of Christianity a really non-historical religion. It did not assert any direct or even historical relation between the individual believer and God or Christ.

Let us say, at the outset, that Christian faith cannot be "proved" by historic fact. No detail of the life of Jesus even if completely established as factual, no amount of detailed knowledge about him in the ordinary sense of historical knowledge, can establish that "God was in Christ reconciling the world unto Himself." What Jesus said and did; where he was at any particular time; what social facts and natural phenomena constituted the locus of

his career, even if fully known, would not constitute authenticity
for his claim upon men or validate the faith of his disciples. Those
who knew him best, as friends or enemies, or just as spectators,
in the main saw in him no full and decisive revelation of God.
That was only seen by faith, even by those most intimate with
him. "Flesh and blood" did not reveal God, rather God himself,
and he revealed his presence to men of faith. Even this was a
revelation that grew upon the disciples. Both the reality and the
meaning of the revelation came over a period of time, and the
one to whom it came with greatest clarity and power—Paul—did
not actually see or know Jesus in the flesh. He knew him by
"testimony" and by a "vision." It was the affirmation of another
of the best "receivers," attributed to Jesus, that the Spirit which
was to come after his departure would lead the disciples into "all
truth" (John 16:13).

The gospels, however factual and even, at many points, "matter
of fact" in character, are more like the work of an artist than an
historian. They are moving portraits of Jesus rather than photo-
graphs, or even motion pictures. For the artist gets the "real"
person by selection and discernment. Formal accuracy may be
absent, much may be omitted, but the real "person" is there. So
with the portrait of Jesus. He is not an imaginary person; he is
historically real. But he is what the heart of the believer grasps
and communicates. The act of faith is an art of the spirit, and the
artists were unsophisticated men whose faith and love and self-
involvement made them authentic witnesses to the God they
knew in Christ.

But the transmission of the Christian revelation in history is
possible because that revelation is constantly renewed in the life
of the believing community. It is not as though God spoke once
or to one generation and then left with men the responsibility to
preserve a "deposit of faith" and transmit through memory and
writing what he had "revealed." It is precisely the truth of
Christian faith that God is fully present in humanity through
Christ and through faith in Christ. The incarnation establishes the
presence, and the Church constitutes a community in which that
presence is known by faith. Theologically this is the meaning of
the Holy Spirit. The Holy Spirit is God immediately present in

the Church and to the individual Christian. The revelation is never the communication of truths or doctrines; it is always God making himself known. The same God who spoke through the prophets and who was incarnate in Christ is present now and through all time, as Holy Spirit.

Both the continuity of the community of faith and the constant presence of God make "history" a living thing and make the historic act of God in Christ a present possession and power in the Church. The living "memory" or continuing experience of Christ is the correlate of the immediate presence of God as Holy Spirit. A "revelation," any revelation of God to man, is in history and comes to a particular individual or community. It creates and nourishes the faith of the community. But this is possible only because the community lives in the presence of the same God who, as Holy Spirit, renews and extends the revelation he first made in essential fullness in Christ.

All historic knowledge assumes the essential and continuing uniformity of human nature, just as all scientific knowledge assumes the uniformity of nature. The story of man can be told. Earliest artifacts reveal the mind of ancient man only because it is assumed that the mind of man is essentially the same. The earliest written records of men can be read and understood with an approximate degree of understanding by modern man only because man is man despite the cultural and intellectual changes made through the passage of time. If in science the reason is the central power of knowing, in history imagination is even more important. The power to reconstruct and clothe with living, concrete meaning the records of the past is the essence of historic knowledge. Science, in dealing with the biological or geological past, reconstructs full-scale models of vanished species by creative use of imagination. The historian can do this to a much fuller degree because he can assume a man inwardly like himself. So he can construct a history of human emotions, ambitions, purposes, and faith. He can write the story of political movements and social developments.

Religious faith uses imagination in a similar way, but to an even greater degree. For here the historian sharing the faith of past generations can enter into their deeper experiences and even their knowledge of God through his self-revelation. Faith itself, as an element of knowledge, is here the central thing, more important even than imagination, from which it cannot be separated. For faith is the apprehension of God and imagination gives the qualitative character to man's immediate experience of God. This points to the meaning of "myth" in revelation and faith. God appears in human actions, in historic events, in the life of Christ. The concrete form of his self-revelation is the living wholeness of human life. It is thus the imaginative rather than the conceptual representation and reproduction of the event that conveys its true and full meaning as revelation. The imaginative knowledge of event merges into the proper function of myth as the form in which faith knows the presence and act of God. Some of the events of great importance to the first Christian believers are related in semi-mythological form because only in this way can their reality and meaning to those who experienced them be communicated. Most important of these is the appearance of the risen Lord, first to the disciples who had just seen him die, and later to Paul. "Secular" history has no place for these appearances, except to report that there is a literary account showing that early Christians believed in the risen Christ. No "secular" reporter or photographer present at the times and the places with the disciples would have seen or recorded the presence of a risen Christ. But to these men of faith he was there; it was not an illusion, but a presence of the same one they had known "in the flesh." The special vision of Paul had immediate physical effects, his temporary blindness, and permanent spiritual effects.

This is a knowledge which formed one whole with the knowledge of Christ as he walked and talked with his disciples. For even then, at one point at least, they saw in him "the Christ, the Son of the living God." That which they saw and heard at Caesarea Philippi was that which they now saw after the crucifixion. No one *saw* the resurrection, although there were visions of an empty tomb and angels saying "He is risen." What the disciples saw at various times and in various guises was the risen Lord, who so impressed them with his reality and with his identity that the resurrection was for them established as a fact. The early Christian community was one in which there was not merely belief that Christ had risen from the dead, but that he was actually present with them in their common life and worship, and that he was the center of their lives both socially and individually. So Paul writes of the Church as the body of Christ, of Christ as the head of the Church, and of Christ being formed in the Christian. He even says, "It is no longer I that live but Christ that liveth in me." The dying and rising of Christ is assimilated to the change in the one who enters the fellowship by baptism; "We were buried therefore with him by baptism into death, so that as Christ rose from the dead by the glory of the Father, we too might walk in newness of life" (Rom. 6:4). This is not just a subjective experience; it is patterned on and determined by the objective event of Christ. It is not just a theoretical representation of the spiritual deliverance of man from sin to righteousness, but the fact of that deliverance itself.

It may be said that the appearance of the risen Christ to the disciples and his presence in the community of faith is historic event; the ultimate nature of this event and its reality are to be found in the faith of the believers. No explanation or even account of this kind of factuality can be given by a secular history. But the full account of human existence is never merely secular. There is always a depth meaning, or a transcendent element, in human life. This is "known" and represented in the form of imaginative accounts, historical and mythological. It is known to "faith." There is great peril here to "truth." Irresponsible exercise of the imagination has produced endless angelologies and demonologies, apocalyptic drama, and cosmic speculations. We may be grateful that so much sanity was exercised by those who fixed the canon of scripture. The Christian faith is vulnerable here to the skeptic. A literalistic defense of the faith is futile and even fatal. But also a complete "spiritualizing" or demythologizing of the faith eventually eliminates it. A recognition of the real validity of imagination and faith as forms of religious knowledge, continuous with and to a degree responsible to conceptual formulation and rational criticism, and inseparable from competent historic inquiry, must be the basis of Christian theology.

THE TRUTH OF HISTORIC FAITH

The total reality of man in history is involved in the quest for truth. It is the whole man who seeks truth, and truth involves an appropriation and involvement by man in his wholeness. Truth is as much a matter of the will as it is of the intellect; it is a practical as well as a theoretical attainment. Truth for the real man is that to which he can commit himself with confidence; his theoretical judgment, his emotions, and his actions. The rather vague but ultimate term "reality" comes near to being a synonym of truth. If reason furnishes a critical test for reality, it is also true that imagination gives more fully the qualitative character of reality, and faith is the conviction of reality itself.

While truth is this impact of reality upon man in his wholeness, and his living involvement in it, knowledge of truth is attained by man or mediated to man by particular facts and events. Scientific truth is mediated by natural facts, and historic truth is mediated by events and is a truth of events, that is, of what actually happened. But the form in which man holds either kind of truth is a construction of his own mind. Historic truth takes the form of an imaginative reproduction with full dimensional meaning of the past story of man. It is an interpretation in terms of man's motives, emotions, purposes, and satisfactions. The truth of this interpretation rests technically upon the methods of historical science, but it also rests upon the imaginative power of the historian to enter into the constant elements of human nature and really discern the full meaning of the event. A similar imaginative participation is required even by the natural scientist who can test his theoretical knowledge by specific experiment and establish a wholly impersonal formula which invariably works when the prescribed conditions are present. The "testing" of historical knowledge is not so simple or impersonal. It is the testing of life itself. False conceptions of past events are eventually refuted by the experience of the race, and true interpretations find confirmation in continuing experience.

There is also a sort of testing in the history of revelation, or rather a testing of the truth of revelation, as mediated by event. The past event cannot be repeated or re-enacted as can experiments in science. But in every historic event, in every happening in the life of man in time, in which God is known, there is a super-temporal element, namely, the act of God. The event recedes in time but God is constant in his presence and action. All "knowledge" of God is a knowledge of present event and the action of the eternal God.[4] The knowledge of faith is a knowledge always that occurs in present event, so is "historic." It is also the product of the co-presence of the transcendent and eternal God. Every "truth" first known through event or historic fact can be renewed because of the steadfastness of God and the fact that man is always essentially the same.

But truth *must* constantly be renewed, or be gained anew. Truth is the ultimate but fleeing goal of both faith and reason. It is this truth that theology seeks. *Pure* reason does not give that truth as the rationalists believed. *Pure* experience does not give the truth as the idealists thought. *Pure* history does not give that truth as the historical school affirmed. There is, in fact, no "pure" reason, no "pure" experience, no "pure" history. There is always the whole man with all his defects and limitations in history, knowing God by an active and living faith, as he reveals himself in events and in the heart of the believer. God makes his power and wisdom known in creating the world. He makes his personal being and action known in Jesus Christ. He makes himself known immediately in the community of faith as Holy Spirit. Revelation comes in the creation; it is in the Event of Christ; it is in the life of the believing and worshipping Church. It is this cosmic, historic, and ever present reality of God with which theology has to do; and all its affirmations and formulations are to be held responsible to his self-revelation.

Christian theology is biblical in the sense that the primary apprehension of God's revelation is recorded in scripture and that the common form of the faith is found there. In the use of this record the theology that calls itself "biblical" is highly selective. But any theology that claims to be Christian must be biblical, and must also accept the responsibility and the hazard of this selectivity. Selectivity is unavoidable if a systematic, that is rational,

---

[4] There is this element of truth in Karl Barth's radical doctrine of revelation.

interpretation of the self-revelation of God in event is to be made. The task of critical study of scripture cannot be renounced. But beyond that, the essential Word of God to be found in scripture must be sought in terms of its living and present truth. This may involve a certain amount of demythologizing, or better, re-mythologizing. But more important is the present guidance of the Holy Spirit. The discovery of the living truth is not only an enterprise for literary and historical criticism, but it is also, and at the same time, a task for the present faith of the Christian community.

This task of interpretation is always incomplete. All forms of theology are imperfect. Neither infallibility nor finality is to be found in human thought, and theology is an exercise of human thinking. But a growing fullness of truth is possible to critical and reverent faith. Real discoveries are made which powerfully affect the life of the whole Christian community. Such was Luther's discovery of the truth that salvation is by faith and grace. Such a discovery was that of the unique meaning of *agape* in our own time. These discoveries are also "recoveries," in that the truth they bring to light is already to be found in the New Testament. But they, like all effective truth, must be discovered by each generation, and indeed, by each individual. *Revelation* is the act of God received by faith. But the *truth* of and in the revelation is discovered, and rediscovered, by men. The work of the theologian, therefore, is this continuing discovery, which is recovery, of the meaning of God's self-revelation, and its valid and meaningful presentation in terms of the language and conceptions of the time. While all theology is dated, as, indeed, is all human knowledge, it is judged by the eternal and undated reality of God.

The form of Christian theology, as has already been set forth, is determined generally by the full exercise of all our human power of knowing through reason, imagination, and faith. It is a knowledge of God as he has made himself known in history, and as he constantly makes himself known to faith. The eternal God reveals himself in time, in all times and places. In the knowledge created by the human response to God there is an objective and a subjective pole. This is true of all knowledge. The most objective rational demonstration of truth, or scientific proof of an hypothesis, becomes knowledge for any mind only when the mind for itself "sees" or "feels" its truth. This is the emotional element, the subjective pole in knowing. No man can know for another; I must make the judgment my own, and take responsibility for it. This is the personal and emotional involvement in true knowledge. The final act of knowledge is not understanding but "will." In so far, Descartes was right. But this is only a technical way of saying that it is knowledge for me, my knowledge. I am the subject of the knowing. If the evidence seems overwhelming and if all competent authorities agree, I am unconscious of any tension and of any emotion in the judgment. But if no one present supports me, and if public authority, for example, a medieval Church condemns me, my affirmation becomes a passionate personal act. And when I affirm what is to me the most evident truth in the face of opposition, I personally am involved; the subjective pole is dominant. "Objectivity" really means that there is so much agreement that the affirmation of truth is matter of fact. But it is still a subjective affirmation unless I am just accepting and repeating what someone else has said.

The subjective character of truth is more dominant and more evident in religious faith than in ordinary knowing. The technical scientist has protected himself by an elaborate system of tests so that he withholds acceptance of *any* hypothesis until general agreement has been reached. The "truth" he formulates, in any case, is not something that directly affects his personal being. But the truth of religious faith which theology seeks to define and formulate is essentially and intensely personal. It has to do with personal commitment in believing and in doing. It involves the basic meaning of life. The "person" himself is involved and committed. Past and future as well as present are implicated. In this "faith knowledge" man looks back to a "beginning" which is really the creative act of God. He looks forward to a destiny which is really the kingdom of God. In such knowledge, subjective assurance takes the place of rational certainty. The "evidences" are in the historic revelation and in the present knowledge of God as Holy Spirit.

But the "subjectivity" does not mean a mere personal preference.

It is not a matter of one believing what he wants to believe. All real believing has in it a sort of compulsion: I cannot but believe what convinces me, what seems true to me. Beyond that, the "subjectivity" of religious knowledge means just personal commitment and acting upon it. This is what Kierkegaard meant when he said "truth is subjectivity." It is true *for me*. And I live and act upon my real vision of truth. It is not theoretical, impersonal, but practical, personal. Over against this is the alleged "objectivity" of the knowledge of God in the Hegelian "system." To be an object for rational thought means to be grasped, handled, and used by the reason. Because of this the knowledge of God can never be objective as is the knowledge of the world or any part of the world. God is not known as an object, not even as *the* Object. He is known as the Subject who reveals himself, and his self-revelation is not rational knowledge about himself but the demand of his righteous will upon man and the assurance of his saving grace.

CHAPTER IV

MAN—SPIRITUAL PERSON

THE CHRISTIAN HERITAGE

There is a long, slow development in Western thought of the idea of man as personal. The Greeks were interested primarily in the soul. But "soul" is an ambiguous term. It can mean simply the principle of self-movement, or life. It has "parts" or, to put the matter in another way, there are several souls, the nutritive, the sensitive, the desiring, and the rational. Or, as Plato suggests, there are three souls; the lowest located below the diaphragm, the "spirited soul" in the chest, and the rational soul in the head. In any case it is the rational soul that is distinctive. For Greek thought, reason *(nous)* is the highest element in man. If man is akin to the lower creation in that he has a nutritive soul, he is also akin to God in that he possesses reason, for God is "the first principles of reason." Through all this diversity of thought about the soul there emerges a general conception of man as body *(soma)*, soul *(psyche)*, and spirit *(pneuma)*. Psyche is essentially life and sensitivity; spirit is *nous* or intellect.

Christian thinking about man begins with the Jewish heritage. Man is a creature of soul and body. At death the soul leaves the body (this is a view shared with primitive man). But in the resurrection body and soul are reunited to receive the judgment of God. Instead of self-analysis, the creative, sustaining, and judging power of God dominates the early Christian's thought of himself. What is important is not a rational understanding of his own constitution but faith in and obedience to God and the receiving from him of the new life which is his gift. It is not what man *is* that is important, but what God *does* for him. "It is he that hath made us and not we ourselves." "I am fearfully and wonderfully made, and that my soul knoweth right well." The mystery of our existence is beyond our understanding, but God "knows our frame," and it is by his will and power that we shall find life. For the Christian the meaning of life has been revealed in Jesus Christ. "We shall be like him for we shall see him as he is."

This basically religious idea of man, of course, encountered the reflective thought of Greek and Roman philosophy. Most important for the development of a doctrine of man is a new term introduced into Christian theology in the course of the third century, the Latin word *persona*. In the doctrine of the Trinity it is used to translate the Greek word *hypostasis;* Father, Son, and Holy Spirit are the three *persons* of the God who is one substance. Christ is one *person* in whom the two perfect and complete *natures* (divine and human) are united without separation or confusion.

The term was taken over into philosophy and the classic definition of *person* as applied to man was given by Boethius (d. 525): "A person is an individual substance of a rational nature." Here the essence of man is *rationality*. This follows the Greek idea that it is *nous*, or the intellectual part of the soul, or the rational soul, that is constitutive of man. This definition and conception prevailed throughout the Middle Ages. It constituted the point of departure for "modern" philosophy. Descartes, the so-called father of modern philosophy, began with the famous affirmation,

"I think, therefore I am," a statement that Augustine had made more than a thousand years earlier. But Descartes quickly limited "thinking." At first he said, quite reasonably: "But what then am I? A thing which thinks. What is a thing which thinks? It is a thing which doubts, understands (conceives), affirms, denies, wills, refuses, which also imagines and feels." [1]

But when he came to state critically what "thinking" is he reduced it to two factors, *understanding* and *will*. The other aspects of thinking—perception, feeling, etc.—were set aside because they represent confused and unclear forms of consciousness. Thinking,

[1] Haldane and Ross, ed., *The Philosophical Works of Descartes*, Cambridge, 1911, vol. I, p. 153.

in its pure form, deals with clear and distinct ideas and observes
their purely logical relations. This is the ideal of "reason." This
purified thinking is what Descartes designates as *understanding*,
the perception of clear and distinct ideas and the logical relation
of such ideas. What, then, of the *will?* The will is not a moral act
or decision; it is simply the soul's affirmation of the truth of the
relation that the understanding sees.

This is as far as Descartes goes in defining the soul; the whole
conception is taken up with the act of knowing, with its method
and validity. Even the will is wholly absorbed into this knowledge
process. Man is, of course, a body but the body is, apart from the
knowing mind, a pure mechanism. The real man is the soul;
Descartes uses the term soul (*l'âme*) constantly in his discussion
of the mind or consciousness of man.

It is, perhaps, unfortunate that philosophy is the work of philosophers, that is, of men whose chief goal is knowledge, or understanding. This quite proper preoccupation gives to all their
thinking a bias toward thought itself, or knowing. Much philosophy is epistemology or theory of knowledge. We have noted in
the first chapter the prevalence of rationalism in theology
throughout its history. Theologians, too, are thinkers; they easily
come under the spell of philosophy (many of them are also
philosophers) and tend toward a rationalistic, or intellectualistic
conception of man, God, and religion. This tendency is dominant
in Roman Catholic theology today. The instrument of thought is
reason; reason in its strict form is pure logic. Logic deals in concepts and their strictly formal relations. Thus theology tends to
follow philosophy into an increasingly formal and abstract order
of thought.

A major attempt to transcend this bias, although only partially
carried out, was that of Kant in his conception of the autonomous will. For Kant, the will is not simply the final act of the
knowing mind which affirms the truth of ideas observed by the
understanding. It is the *moral* will, the free and responsible determination of conduct by man. The essence of the act of will
is that it is free; this is in sharp contrast to the unbroken causal
determination of the events of "nature." The will is the realm of
freedom, nature is the realm of "necessity," or causal determina-

tion. Thus is continued Descartes's dualism of mind and matter, of soul and body. Only, with Kant, the freedom is freedom of the moral will.

But Kant was still the rationalist even in his drastic critique of Reason. The will is free, indeed, but it is a "rational" moral will which legislates freely the universal moral *law*. This sounds suspiciously like Descartes, who claimed that the will is free but also that when the will is confronted with a clear and distinct idea it automatically asserts the truth of the idea.[2] Curiously enough the only way the will can escape from this bondage to the understanding (reason) is to make an error, and this happens only when it makes its judgment prematurely, that is, before the understanding has become clear. Kant had to resort to "maxims" for the application of his universal moral law to actual cases of moral conduct, and the choice of the maxim and its application was left to the "heart." This is a strange but necessary abandonment of "reason" just at the crucial point of moral action.

Still, Kant made an important contribution to the doctrine of man in the autonomous will, even though he hedged that will about by reason, and in the end resorted to the "heart."[3] The modern conception of personality was two-thirds formed by this contribution. The person is not only rationality, it is also free will. However, feeling is still excluded. This radical deficiency was made good by Schleiermacher, who affirmed that the fundamental factor in man is feeling. Will and thought, he says, arise out of feeling, and are acts, as contrasted with the passivity of feeling. These three—feeling, will, and thought—constitute the total person. There is no "fourth." The subject of all three—feeling, thought, and will—is precisely the unity of the three and not an additional factor.[4]

Thus we have the outlines of the "person" or "personality" of modern idealistic philosophy, and specifically of Personal Idealism. But it is still a philosophical doctrine with a bias toward the

[2] Ibid. p. 175.
[3] T. K. Abbott, *Kant's Critique of Practical Reason, and Other Works on the Theory of Ethics*, London (6th ed.), 1909, p. 359. "...the bottom of his heart (the subjective first principle of his maxims) is inscrutable to himself."
[4] F. Schleiermacher, *The Christian Faith*, Edinburgh, 1928, p. 8.

knowledge function, and a certain aloofness from the bodily and emotional nature of man. Modern empirical psychology adds this final element to our conception of man. Personal Idealism, indeed idealistic philosophy generally, is analytic in method; that is, it accepts the consciousness of man as presented and, by analyzing it into its aspects and functions, arrives at a philosophical "psychology." Empirical psychology is inductive; it studies man as he is observed in his total existence. It observes neurological, behavioral, social facts as well as the facts of the waking consciousness. It posits an unconscious, takes account of the emotions and their physiological connections. The "personality" is now a much more complex thing, and organically one with the body. Incidentally this is a return to, or an arrival at, the biblical conception of man as one creature, formed of the dust, but with the breath of God breathed into him. D. R. G. Owen [5] points out that this is more akin to the modern scientific view of man than to the "religious" idea of man as a duality of body and soul.

However, psychology in the modern sense still encounters a certain frustration in dealing with personality. Psychology is a science. Science generally and the sciences in particular deal with nature. Psychology, therefore, views human personality as a natural phenomenon and seeks knowledge of it according to the methods, canons, and limitations of scientific method. But as a scientist the psychologist must himself resort to analysis; to know man he must first of all distinguish common traits or general factors to be found in all men. The scientific knowledge thus obtained, therefore, is not knowledge of a particular man in his wholeness but knowledge of general traits and factors in all men. The real, individual whole personality of John Smith is not known and cannot be known scientifically.[6] Such knowledge of personality in general as psychology attains must be "applied" to the particular man in the practice of psychosomatic medicine. But this application is an art, not a science. It involves scientific knowledge, of course, but the actual man being dealt with is not

[5] D. R. G. Owen, *Body and Soul, a Study in the Christian View of Man,* Philadelphia, 1956.
[6] This idea is developed in Gordon Allport, *Becoming,* New Haven, 1955; and Paul Tournier, *The Meaning of Persons,* New York, 1957.

scientifically known; or, to put it another way, he is not a scientific object.

The real man is not, then, a natural phenomenon. This sounds absurd. Every man is certainly a part of nature. But he is also spirit, and this is the key to what we mean when we say that man is *person*, or a person. In saying that man is spirit or person we do not say that he is not a part of nature, or that there cannot be a scientific physiology, or psychology, but only that all such knowledge falls short of a true knowledge of the man in his wholeness as a person. We cannot arrive at knowledge of man as person scientifically precisely because knowledge of the person is not just knowledge of the general traits or elements or processes that are common to all men. It is knowledge of this one, total, particular man in his character, in his exercise of a certain original and relatively free disposition of all his powers, and in his responsible relation to other persons.

Does this mean, then, that man is a mystery, unknowable? Certainly man is a mystery and in his wholeness can not be known either philosophically or scientifically. But he can be known; the knowledge of man is a religious, or theological, form of knowledge. He is known in relation to other men and to God. He is known as master of nature, as well as part of nature. He is known in terms of his freedom and responsibility within a society which is not wholly a natural fact, but also a moral universe. He is known in terms of his dependence upon and likeness to God. The proper source for this knowledge is *faith;* its development is a part of *theology.*

PERSON IS SPIRIT

It is necessary to discuss somewhat technically the precise meaning of the term "person." I have traced the outlines of the meaning of "person" from the purely metaphysical conception of the Middle Ages expressed in Boethius' definition, through the development of an idea of personality as the unity of consciousness; I have shown also how gradually the whole rational character was modified, first by Descartes's introduction of the *will* (even though will was simply a part of the completed act of knowledge), then by Kant for whom the will was a *moral* will and free (although its freedom was rendered problematical both by the rational law that it expressed and the need of *maxims* which not the will but the "heart" supplied). And, finally, I have mentioned the work of Schleiermacher who boldly introduced *feeling* as not merely a respectable part of consciousness but, indeed, the basic form of it. Out of this idea developed the various forms of Personal Idealism, which is the doctrine that *personality* is a unity of consciousness, the essential functions of which are thought, feeling, and will. The doctrine of man as *spiritual person* which is to be set forth in this chapter has emerged from a critical study and reconstruction of the idea of personality as conceived in Personal Idealism.

In setting forth this doctrine we must first distinguish between *personality* and *person*. The distinction is not original; indeed, it has a long history, although often the two terms are used interchangeably. The distinction lies in the use of *person* to indicate the total subject or agent in relation to other persons and to nature, while *personality* refers to the experienced and observed complex functioning of consciousness. Accordingly, the *personalism* of Bowne and others is a doctrine that finds the meaning of personality by analyzing and describing its essential parts or functions. It is, of course, taken for granted that personalities know each other and communicate with each other. But the full nature of personality is found by looking deeply and critically into the "inner world" of *one* person and understanding clearly what we find there. The personality, being just the unity of consciousness of the one who knows it, is fully accessible to observation and analysis. There is no metaphysical "substance" lying back of it. The total personality is "apparent." Fundamentally there is no mystery in it. Thus the personality (1) is the unity of consciousness, and (2) it is known in its completeness in the single instance.

Now, whatever may have been the meanings, theological or philosophical, in times past of the shorter word *person*, I am using it in a sense which I shall attempt to state briefly and critically, and then to develop in some detail. But here I shall point out that the *person* is not just the unity of consciousness; it is rather the

subject of that unity. This *subject* is not a *substance*, a "thing"
that thinks, but it is the *spiritual* agent and reality which fills the
void made by the abandonment of substance. Likewise, it should
be said that the *person* does not exist, and cannot be known or
described, as a single individual. It is essentially relational or social
in character. Its most important meanings can be stated only in
its relation to other persons and to nature as "other." The position
of Leibniz is an extreme but valid statement of personalism generally, namely that each soul is a windowless monad; or in the
terms of recent personalism each personality is completely external to every other (even if it has windows!). But in fact the
person exists in relations, and by nature seeks to and does enter
into other persons. To these statements might be added the further affirmation that the *person* is not observable and analyzable,
that in essence it is mystery and known not by reason but by
faith. It is the *simple* agent, man in the simplicity of his *act*, and
the wholeness of his relationship, as distinguished from the *complexity* and *diversity* of personality. This does not mean that there
is a "person" distinguishable even in thought from the empirical
personality; this is what the "substance" of a substantial soul
means. Man viewed in his totality and in his relation to the other
is a *simple subject;* man observed and described in all the infinite
complexity of his intellectual, psychological, and bodily composi-
tion and functioning is a complex but approximately knowable
organism. The *simple subject* known in act and relation is known
not analytically but directly, immediately by faith. This statement
expresses the meanings both of person and of faith. The person
is known by faith; faith is the immediate recognition, acknowledgment, and regard for the person.

Our account of man must go beyond the body and soul creature
of early Christian thought as determined by the Jewish tradition.
It must also both develop and transcend the Greek idea of body,
soul, and spirit *(soma, psyche,* and *pneuma).* This is due to the
fact that in both traditions the term "soul" is ambiguous, and also
to the fact that in Greek thought "spirit" is identified too simply
with reason *(nous).* There is both more unity and more diversity
in the human person than these ancient anthropologies recognize.

We may proceed by making four statements about man, as follows:

Man is body (*soma*).

Man is soul (*psyche*).

Man is mind (*nous*).

Man is spirit (*pneuma*).

This is a cumulative series of meanings or powers. Each one of these statements designates a form or quality and power of existence, of action and relation. They are all true of the same individual—man. There is indeed a kind of hierarchy observable; for example, "mind" is a higher order of reality than "body." But if this is taken to mean that there are four distinguishable and even relatively independent realities, the truth of man is lost. It is also true that in the natural origin of man the "lower" order appeared first, namely, the body, and that "mind" in the proper sense came later. But this does not mean that a human mind apart from a human body is either possible or thinkable; this is perhaps the main defect of idealism. On the other hand it is impossible to conceive of a *human* body apart from a human mind. Such a body would be an abortion, a monstrosity, an *inhuman* thing.

I have used these two terms, "body" and "mind," but the same assertions could be made with regard to any other pair that might be selected from the four. Man is *one* being or creature; whatever else may be truly said of him, at least these four statements are true about that one individual. The oneness is an inner, ineradicable unity; the unity of a true individual; the human *person* is body, soul, mind, spirit. There is a higher and a lower order of power and value to be recognized; but there is continuity throughout, as well as unity. Language, entirely apart from technical philosophical and scientific terminology, implicitly recognizes these four "powers." The commonest distinction is that between soul and body; from primitive man on it is assumed that for the soul to leave the body means death. That is, a body without life, thought, or spirit is a dead body. It *was* once human, it is so no longer; it is only the "remains." But "soul" itself is an ambiguous word. In popular as well as in technical language soul has meant life, sensitivity, the power of thought, and what is properly spirit. I have used the term here in a limited and more precise way. Soul, the *psyche* of Greek anthropology, is taken to mean the vital, emotional power of man.

But the human person also thinks. This is not his whole nature, but it is certainly a form of activity that is his peculiar distinction among living and sentient things. Man is *nous*, or intellect, and this distinguishes him from less-than-human animals. He is, as Aristotle said, an animal but he is also a *thinking* animal. However, we must not think of the "mind" as some existent thing that has been brought from some intellectual heaven and added to the living, emotional creature already existing. It is the living, feeling body that thinks. Or, to put it more accurately, mind or thinking, as well as emotions and bodily structure and function, *is* the man. But none the less is the man also living body, or soul and body. Thus the creature that we can call man is one that thinks; not a *thing* that thinks, as Descartes said, but this psychosomatic *mind* that thinks. But the mind, the thinking, is as much the man, is as essential a power of the man as the psychological and physiological processes. Still rational thought is not merely a psychological activity; mind is not merely soul or psyche. The man who thinks is a soul that has reached a power of rational activity that lesser souls do not have. No matter how badly a man uses this rational power, he is still a mind. But if he really does not have it, through disease or accident, then he is a truncated human organism; he is no longer really human.

While the four terms used of man are true and represent an ascending scale of powers, they still lose their meaning unless attributed to the *one* person who is as much the one as he is any other of the four. We err, strictly speaking, when we say that we *have* body, soul, mind, or spirit. Rather we *are* each and all of them. Yet we are one creature, one person.

The total person is spirit. As spirit the person is known in its unique power, act, and relation. The person as body, soul, and mind is a highly complex natural organism. Even the rational mind is a mental reflection of nature, its structure and functioning largely determined by natural origin and environment. The peculiar power of spirit is freedom which is a simple act of creativity. The total complex—body, soul, and mind—serves as instrument for the free act of spirit which is a simple whole, not process but *act*. The free act is both moral and creative. The full form of moral freedom is love; creativity in its simplest expression is the originality without which one is hardly human at all. While love and creativity are the essence of spirit, man actually is "spiritual" only in limited degree. Both love and creativity are costly and involve the discipline and use of "nature" which is another word for determinate structure and process. On the other hand the freedom that comes to full expression in spirit extends downward, giving biological evolution its variety and quite possibly extending in minimal degree to elementary movements of matter.

"Spirit" and "person" come very close to meaning the same thing. But there is a real and important distinction; "spirit" represents a certain power, while "person" designates the subject or agent of all the powers. The dual term "spiritual person" seems best to represent the complete human reality. *Person* is the substantive, *spirit* the highest power or activity of the person. It can truly be said that man is a bodily person, that he is a psychological person, that he is a rational person. It must also be said that man is a spiritual person. But it is because he *is* spirit, that he is truly a person at all.

"Spirit" is more than mind or reason. It is more than *psyche* or soul. Obviously it is more than body. Yet the human spirit is not something apart from body, soul, and mind; it is precisely the power exercised by the total person in what might be called in brief "self-transcendence," or just "transcendence." We have designated this power as "freedom." The freedom is moral; it is also intellectual. It is the power of love (*agape*); it is also the power to create. Unless rational thought is a purely mechanical operation (as some would insist it is), the thinker has a certain power to deal freely with "free" ideas and to construct combinations of them significant and useful for his purposes. This is a transcending of the world as it is and is known by some new construction of it. The "new" is first in imagination and then, if a really successful construction, it can be realized in the world of things. Love is the power of the spirit to transcend self-interest and even go against its demands in order to do something for the good of another. Creativity is the power of spirit to re-order thought and circum-

stance so that something new appears in the world.[7] Not only is
all great art the creative act of man but much of the lesser doings
of man reveal a modicum of creativity. Unless there is some
originality in a man he could hardly be called a man. Nor is all
this creativity a production of the good or the true or the beautiful; much of it is a debased and even diabolical exercise of freedom. So the root evil as well as the root good of man is spiritual;
that is, it is the outcome of his freedom.

Spirit means transcendence also in the sense of going beyond
one's self and living with, in, and for others. This is the power of
the person to be "distinct but not separate" from other persons.
Here we must reject the individualism of Personal Idealism and all
other positions that posit a complete mind or person external to
all others and capable of knowing them only as an outsider. This
externality is certainly true of the "personality" conceived as the
unity of consciousness. As such a unity I have a truly private life.
But the unity of consciousness is only an abstraction from the
total person. At this point the distinction between "personality"
and "person" is useful. "Personality" represents the unity of consciousness and the relative privacy of the individual; what Dean
Inge means by "distinction." It means that however intimately
and even inwardly one person may be involved in the life of
another they remain two distinct individuals. Neither one can be
the *subject* of the consciousness of the other.

But two individuals need not and should not be "separate." As
spiritual persons they not only communicate with each other but
communicate themselves to each other. It is this mutual self-communication that was lacking in Personal Idealism, and indeed in
the whole philosophical tradition which limited its conception
of man to *mind*. If man is just a mind, each one is wholly external
to the other; one cannot invade the privacy of the other's
thoughts and feelings. He can only infer from some outward act
or state of the visible body, or learn from language which sym-

[7] We speak of creative imagination. But creativity is an act of the human
spirit which involves both ideas and images; it operates in mathematics as
well as in music. The distinction between creative and merely logical thought
is therefore not between concepts and images but between rationally determined and free exercise of the powers of mind.

bolically expresses it what the mind of the other is thinking, feeling, or willing.

One can go further and say that one man can only know that the other *is* a mind like himself by this external and inferential process of communication. There is no direct and certain knowledge of the other. The ultimate situation is that of two self-contained and eternally separate "minds" signalling to each other across an infinite space of separateness. This is the outcome of the subjective rationalism of modern philosophy; the tragedy is that so much of modern theology has accepted this conception of man as mind, and so surrendered the deepest insights of the theological heritage of Christianity, and ruled out some of its fundamental religious affirmations.

For the spiritual being called man in the Christian faith is not just a personality conceived as a unity of consciousness. He is a spiritual person with the power of self-transcendence. And self-transcendence means the power to enter into the lives of others and to open his own life to them. I have quoted Dean Inge whose precise words are, "Distinction, not separation, is the mark of personality; but it is separation, not distinction, that forbids union." [8] Dean Inge uses "personality" here with the meaning that I am giving to "person." However he makes clear the distinction that I am insisting upon between the two terms.

So far is it from being true that the self of our immediate consciousness is our true personality, that we can only attain personality, as spiritual and rational beings, by passing beyond the limits that mark us off as separate individuals. Separate individuality, we may say, is the bar which prevents us from realizing our true privileges as persons.[9]

The primary language of Christian faith, of course, is not that of theology, but of religion. It is in the New Testament that we find the direct assertion of a spiritual inwardness in personal relations. In the Fourth Gospel the relation of Jesus with the Father and with his own disciples is so expressed. "He who abides in me, and I in him, he it is that bears much fruit, for apart from me you

8 W. R. Inge, *Christian Mysticism,* London (6th ed.), 1925, p. 30.
9 Ibid. p. 31.

can do nothing" (John 15:5). "... that they all may be one; even as thou, Father, art in me, and I in thee, that they also may be one in us ..." (John 17:21). Paul uses similar language, as the following passages from II Cor. 5 show: "... if anyone is in Christ, he is a new creation" (v. 17); "... God was in Christ reconciling the world to himself, ..." (v. 19). "... one God and Father of us all, who is above all and through all and in all" (Eph. 4:6).

This is pre-theological, religious language. It is a statement of the nature of spiritual relations as not external but inward. It represents a reality with which a strictly rational philosophy cannot cope; for reason seeks clear distinctions between ideas so that they may be related to each other logically but wholly externally. Any inner identification or overlapping of one idea with another is only confusion. But the relation of person with person is not a logical relation; it is a spiritual or inward one. If this is not true, then the whole case for religious faith is lost, and the spiritual reality of man is denied. It is undoubtedly true that this is the outcome for many thoughtful people. But for the man of faith, the Christian who believes in the God who was in Christ, and who as Holy Spirit is in the Christian, the language of mutual indwelling is basic to the reality of life. The philosopher who holds to the ultimacy of reason will say that these terms are religious and only symbolic of a truth which, when clearly stated in rational terms, has to do with the external relations of ideas and minds.

But philosophy has followed this course through both a rejection of the theological method and ignorance of the depth as well as the surface meaning of theology. That much theology needed to be rejected is doubtless true; as a matter of fact the thing that rendered dogmatic theology really objectionable was precisely that it had surrendered to the rationalism of philosophy, as I have pointed out in the first chapter. But the deeper currents of theological thought have preserved the depth dimension of meanings that are first expressed in the religious language of the New Testament and of Christian experience. At one point in particular, the one which here concerns us directly, the spiritual relations of persons is set forth in the doctrine of "coinherence." The idea first developed in exposition of the relation of Father, Son, and Holy Spirit in the Trinity. The three "persons" are represented by this doctrine as mutually each within the other. John 17:21 is quoted to support the idea. The theological achievement opens the way to a doctrine of man as spirit, although I do not know of any systematic development of it. At any rate we are now engaged in a modest attempt in that direction. However, religious thought and to some extent theological formulation have kept as a background this possibility and reality of the spiritual person.

Let us say, then, that the basic nature of the spiritual person is to transcend the limits of its individuality, and to enter into the life of other persons and take them into itself. And that this statement is no more symbolic than any other language; rather that, when we are speaking directly of the life of man the spiritual person, it is as literal as words can be in conveying meaning and truth.

One difficulty we encounter both in comprehending and in communicating the meaning of "spirit" lies in the use of "inward" or "inner." Despite the assurance often given that these terms are not employed in a spatial sense, it is assumed that they do have that meaning, that spirit is literally "in" man. The same difficulty arises when we speak of "mind" or "soul." We can see the body, but we cannot see the soul, the mind, or even less the spirit. The classic expression of this spatial idea of soul is that of Descartes. Descartes indeed made body or matter identical with extension (space), and he also said that none of the concepts applicable to extension are applicable to mind or soul. This is metaphysical dualism. But he had to find some point of relation between these two distinct substances in the actual man, so he located the place of meeting at the pineal gland in the brain. The soul, he said, is present at this point to receive from the brain sensations and movements of the body, and to communicate to the body its direction of those movements. Apart from this control exercised over it by the soul the body is, like the bodies of animals, a complete mechanism.

It is easy to see the crudity of this conception. Yet in one way its essential error is almost universally present in our thinking about mind and spirit. We think of them as in some spatial sense "inside" the body. We have the feeling that if we could go beyond neural processes and the chemical and electronic activities of the brain cells, we could see the "thinking" or the "feeling," or, perhaps, the "mind" or the "soul" in its own proper character.

Now, it may be said, quite simply, that the soul, the mind, the spirit are no more inside than they are outside the bodily organism. They are powers or activities of a subject who is more than a body, but still a body. They are the mental activities and spiritual powers of the whole man. The "soul" or vitality and emotional consciousness of man comes into being precisely because of the organic totality of an animal body developed in certain fashion and degree. Further development of the living soul issues in the power of rational thought. The emergence of "spirit" is the final creative act of God who addresses the conscious person and evokes a response. In this response the *humanum* is created. The human spirit is, first, a response to the creative Spirit of God. The whole process through which the body, soul, and mind that are man, are brought into being in the world of nature is the creative action of God. The emergence of man as man comes when God awakens in the creature a sense of his own presence and therewith opens the way into the world of personal existence. This final act of the creation of man is in the realm of conscious and rational being; yet it is an act that completes what might be called the natural process of development.

But this "natural" process is itself the form of God's creative action. Man represents the completion of the creative process in which the creature's own consciousness and freedom of response become one with the act of God. The man is the image of God, but a pretty dim and troubled image. There is the beginning and the possibility of full humanity. Man is created in relation and response; in his essential humanity the presence of God is involved. Man exists from the beginning in relation. He is not man apart from God; he is man through this final, even if fitful, response to and engagement with God. The "image" is not an impression upon the creature as though the divine form were a seal and man the plastic material; this is a wholly external idea of likeness. The original response is the indwelling of God, the creator, and the entrance into God of man the creature. Here is the primary involvement or engagement of man with his creator and of the creator with man. Here is the basis for the meaning of spirit, the person who is himself and distinct from God; but whose personal being is constituted by his inner relation to God, a relation in which some degree of consciousness, responsibility, and communion are involved.

The actual history of man, religious and moral, is the story of the uneasy and sometimes terrible sense of the divine presence, of its uncompromising demands upon man, of the unimaginable possibilities to which he is called. The fear of God, and no less the finding of security in God, are the basic form of man's consciousness and represent a certain spiritual polarity out of which come the whole accomplishment and meaning of human existence. It ought to be pointed out that this is not the story of men as separate individuals. The religious aspect of man's primary relation to God has its complement in the social relation of men with one another. The creative environment in which humanity appeared was a social as well as a divine order. That is, man comes to his full humanity, he is awakened to consciousness of and response to God in the profound social unity of family and clan. It is in community with his fellows that the creature meets God and hears his voice. The community is the organ of consciousness of God and response to God. Man is one with his fellows as well as one with God; in tension as well as in comfort. The first reality of the true person is more union than separateness, more a sharing of a common life than the maintaining of a distinct existence. The real problem for human consciousness is to realize the possibility of individual existence rather than to know the reality of other persons. Individualism is an accomplishment and to a certain degree a restriction of our humanity. It is only the rational and external way of viewing ourselves that marks the sophisticated mind which creates a problem of "knowing" the other as a mind or person. Deeper in our consciousness than the sense of distinct individuality is the consciousness of our oneness with others, and thus, necessarily, their reality and presence.

"Inwardness" means that the reality of man is not merely superficial, that is, a perceptible object. Descartes said that all scientific knowledge is of *superficies*, or surfaces. Essentially it is geometrical which means that it has spatial form and can be measured. There is no "inside" that cannot be made an "outside" by divi-

sion. Therefore he banished "final" causes, or purposes, from the
realm of rational knowledge. For a purpose is mental; it is not a
fact or a movement in space. Natural science methodologically,
and to its advantage, follows this principle. To know any segment
of nature is to observe what the sequence of events actually and
invariably is, not why it is that way. The good scientist may become a bad philosopher by denying that there is any such thing
as purpose in the universe and by asserting that the world is a
great mechanism. But even if such an assertion is made the scientist certainly has his own purposes in his research and experimen-
tation. He is consciously and purposefully trying to find out
what the answer is to questions he and other men have asked; and
he is trying to devise methods by which he can control the invariable processes of nature to his own ends, and the ends of the
society of which he is part. But these purposes of the scientist and
society are not objects in space to be observed as things among
other things with their specific functions in a natural process. The
purpose of any mechanism is not some vital part of the machine;
it is not even the energy that moves its parts; it is a meaning
disclosed in the use of the machine. A missionary told of a native
chief in Madagascar who had been given a piano by Queen Vic-
toria. The piano was taken out of its case, but it was set upside
down. The chief and his court could not imagine what it was for
or how to operate it. The missionary had the piano set right side
up and his wife played it. The chief was charmed and offered to
trade six handsome young women for the musician so that he
could enjoy the operation of this wonderful instrument. No
mechanism is "understood" until it is operated. Its purpose is not
in some central and hidden part, nor in a label pasted on the outside. The purpose is known in the *use* of the mechanism.

Of course, the world is not a mechanism, although there are
discoverable almost infinite mechanistic connections and possibilities. But the point here is that any purpose, or final cause,
either in creation or in the work of man, is not an object among
objects, an event among events, in the observable world. And our
brief discussion of purpose is only illustrative of the fact that the
"inner" character of spirit does not mean that deep, deep inside
the human psychosomatic organism there is a spatial center, even

a point without mass, which is this spirit. "Spirit" means the wholeness of man, in his power of free action and self-transcendence. There is a certain polarity of meaning in the term. It represents that which man most essentially, most basically is, but also that which he is in his most complete being, relation and action, that which he is most comprehensively. So we say, he is deficient in this and wrong in that, but the spirit of the man is right. That is, taken in his wholeness the *man* is right.

It might truly be said that man as spirit is most open to our knowledge, most obvious though not superficial. He is the man we know in relation, in action, in intention and in the most evident quality of his life. It is true that we can be deceived, and can deceive others. But deception cannot be entirely successful, nor for very long. A child, or a man of complete sincerity and simplicity, can usually detect the truth of another. The reason that lying and deceit are an offense against our fellows is that they conceal or distort our reality as spiritual persons. When we "see" or "know" others as spirit it is not by penetrating deep into their thoughts and motives through analysis but simply recognizing and accepting them as what they obviously are, free and responsible persons.

Immediate knowledge of another in a bodily sense is primarily a matter of physical contact; symbolically we clasp the hand, or rub noses, or embrace one another. Immediate knowledge of another as mind comes directly when we speak a common language (even though no one of us uses it perfectly). When one expresses his thought in any language he opens his mind so that the hearer "looks into" that mind. So he makes himself known in the only sense in which man as mind can be known. In similar and even more universal manner we know another as a living soul, or emotional being, when he expresses his emotion. Perhaps the oldest language is that of the emotions. So men have practiced the art of concealment of emotion, acting brave when they are afraid, appearing cheerful when they are sad. Thus men set up artificial and deceptive barriers between themselves and other men. All culture is a complex involving a certain degree of such deception. Rudyard Kipling once told the boys of a school that the invention of language had greatly increased man's capacity to lie. But suppression or perversion of the normal expression of emotions is an older and more prevalent form of deception.

But deception is possible and needed because the natural and spontaneous expression of emotion is a disclosure of the "soul." The soul of a child is, at least to begin with, quite open to view. The soul of a truly great man is likewise open, revealed in his life. For the great man is essentially simple and "open." Most of us, doubtless, fail to "know" him in his greatness, but that is our defect and not due to the fact that the greatness is hidden deep under layers of complex mental operations and subtle and sophisticated symbolic utterance. The greatness of the great man is in the simplicity and unity of the great emotions of his life, which are known in sincerity of word and deed. So we are known to each other in our greatness and in our meanness, despite the conventional disguises we wear and the specific acts of deception we practice.

Thus man is known to his fellows as a body, by direct physical contact, the simplest form of "presence." He is known as a mind through the "opening" of his mind by language so that others can see into it. He is known as a sensitive and emotional "soul" by expressions of feelings and emotions that "reveal" his soul. These mental and emotional realities that are not bodies or parts of bodies to be observed in and as themselves, which are the "inner" reality of man, are to the perceptive companion as evident as is the body which is the organ of their expression.

So, also, is the spiritual person who is the total man, known in his essential reality and in his relation to other persons. This knowledge is what I call faith, the immediate acknowledgment of the other as a free, responsible, creative person; one who can love and be loved; one with whom we can have a common life without either losing his distinct and inalienable identity; one who in his wholeness is thus immediately present and known; one essentially capable of self-transcendence; one created in the image of God; one who makes a silent but inescapable demand upon me for respect and love; one who can and should not only reveal himself to me as mind and soul but should also give himself to me, as I should give myself to him. This is the knowledge of spirit, the presence to each other of spiritual persons, the unity and polarity of individual integrity and social community. It is because man is spirit or spiritual person that he can know in the deepest and most immediate way his neighbor and share with him the life in God which is fully human existence.

CHAPTER V

HISTORY, SCIENCE, AND THEOLOGY

THERE ARE three kinds of truth: historical, scientific, and theological. Each represents a reality with which man has to do, and there is a most appropriate method or form of mental activity by which each kind of truth is more or less successfully attained. Theological truth is truth about God; scientific truth is truth about nature; and historic truth is truth about man's own life and works in time. The disciplines that deal with these three forms of truth are respectively theology, science, and history.

It might be asked whether there is not a fourth, namely philosophy. Philosophy, however, is not a quest for truth in some definable area of reality with which man has to do, but rather an endeavor to understand what truth means in any and every realm. "Understanding" is the clarification of meaning. Philosophy is therefore primarily a methodology for the critical study of all forms of knowledge, in all the areas of man's experience. Theology has its language which refers directly to God; science has its language which refers directly to nature; history has its language which refers directly to human culture. Philosophy is a sort of language about language, and is engaged in examination of the reflective thought of the human mind. It seeks to discover the principles of all rational thought and the limits and validity of all human judgments. If philosophy has an "object" comparable to God, the object of theology, and nature, the object of science, that object is the "Life of Reason," as Santayana has characterized it, that is, the realm of human thought. In times when the main preoccupation of educated men is religion, philosophy will actually concern itself a great deal with God; in times of predominant concern for history, philosophy will be preoccupied with the stuff of human culture; in a time like our own in which science looms so large upon the horizon, philosophy will be largely devoted to the meaning, method, and validity of scientific knowledge. In our own time the great prominence of phenomenology, symbolic logic, semanticism, and positivism of various kinds reveals philosophy's primary concern with methodology, that is, with the mind critically examining its own nature and operation, studying the grammar, syntax, and rhetoric of the language about language.

But the meaning of "truth" in human thinking is that there is an objective reality that thinking is *about*. The primary object of thinking is not thinking itself. A purely subjective rationalism makes such an assumption and so reduces truth to an analysis of the rational consciousness. But if thought is taken to be the limited but approximately successful effort of human reason to know reality as it is, and if men believe in God, and in the physical world, and in man himself as real, then the quest for truth becomes an endeavor to know these aspects of reality. Truth is a guide for action. The knowledge of God is a true understanding of what God requires of us and what God does for us. The knowledge of nature is that conformity of thought to the actual order of events that will enable us to acquire the goods and escape the dangers of nature, and so to exercise control over nature by our technics that it will increasingly serve our needs and purposes. The knowledge of history and culture can enlighten us so that we may avoid more successfully the dangers and acquire and enjoy the better values of human existence.

Different methods are required for the attainment of truth in whatever degree it can be found. These methods are not entirely exclusive, but each must be appropriate to the subject matter. However, it is one and the same man, one and the same mind, that is engaged in the quest whatever may be the "field of specialization." It is the same man who is theologian, scientist, and historian. True, any particular man may be predominantly the historian, or the theologian, or the scientist. One may deny that there is any real truth save that of theology, or of science, or of history. But some dimension of truth is always lost unless the full range of reality is taken seriously even though each man gives his main attention to some special area. The possibility of truth in each and all of these fields is due to the nature of man himself. In our analysis of man into the four major powers of body, soul, mind, and spirit, we have glimpsed the great diversity and complexity of the human person. This was an exercise in the critical understanding of man himself, despite the fact that it ended up in an affirmation that the human person is essentially simple in act, relational in character, and lives by a certain self-transcendence. Now we turn to the three great fundamental relations of man—to God, to nature, and to culture—to see what capacities are called into play as he participates in these relations, and in the typically human activities that make up the reality of his life.

Man *lives* in these three relations: to an Other (God), to the other (nature), and to others (men). His *knowing* involves both the particular or concrete (fact), and the universal or general (idea). The *form* of his existence is time and eternity. The possibility of participation in the three relations arises from his possession of the *powers* of spirit, mind, and soul which have been discussed above.

History

Culture is the total reality in time of what man makes of himself. Man has a history because corporately he *does* something and so makes a human modification of nature as it is in him and about him. Culture is both man's partial mastery of nature and a characteristic formation and expression of himself. The most immediate relationship within which man lives is this world of culture, which for each individual or generation is both objective fact and subjective realization.

Our special interest here is the "power" of man by which he both creates culture and lives in relation to it. The whole man is active in this as in each and every relation, but the special capacity by which he can produce culture and participate in it as his chief medium of existence is the power of soul or *psyche*. In the soul the physical energies of the body are united with the rational intelligence of the mind in living and productive activity. Through this activity something of the freedom and creativity of spirit finds expression in the cultural process.

Mind or *nous* as pure knowing produces nothing. Ideas do not act. There is, of course, no actual mind concerned only with ideas, at least no such human mind. What we see in human history producing the distinctive and varied cultural forms of different peoples is the *soul*, the living, imaginative, passionate consciousness of races and nations. Peoples form their life according to their own endowment and desire, as well as in conformity to their environment. Here our knowledge is especially concerned with concrete particularity. One may develop a general philosophy or theory of culture, but the knowledge of any culture is a knowledge of its particularity. This "particular" is not found alone in artifacts or pictorial representations of the products of a culture; it also involves an imaginative construction of the thoughts and feelings, the desires and values, and the self-understanding of the living men whose culture we are studying. The pole of knowing in this understanding of a culture is not the universal but the particular.

The particularity in this realm of knowledge is further seen if we distinguish between *mind* and *mentalities*. A scientific psychology deals with *the* mind or consciousness of man, whether the focus of interest is on its rational structure as with the philosophical psychology of an earlier day, or on the emotional and affective processes as with present-day psychology. This is a concern for the universal or general character of mind; there is only *one* scientific psychology no matter how diverse its forms of action, just as there is one physiology despite racial variations. But this universal mind actually appears in the distinctive and concrete mentalities of particular peoples. Essentially the mind either as intelligence or as psychic organism is the same in all countries, but there is a distinct French mentality, a Japanese mentality, and an American mentality. That is, the actual man in any culture is psychologically a product of that specific culture; this is the particularity that must be known if we are to have a real knowledge of any culture. The knowledge of history is especially concerned with this particularity, and can never be wholly reduced to a scientific formula.

Culture is pre-eminently the domain of time. It is the stuff of history. Time finds its true meaning in the doing of conscious agents,[1] and culture is what man does, not in the act of a moment, but in the prolonged effort of the ages. There is a past by which men live in the present, and a future toward which they move. The concern of man for his own past as suggested above lies in the fact that one generation knows itself in terms of its progenitors and their achievements; it is one with them. The primitive expectation of life after death represents the continuance of the tribe; essentially it was reunion with the ancestors. Certainly it was not eternal life, but a continuance of life in time with a diminishing intensity. The limitations of the meaning of life to a passage of time is disclosed when rational philosophy develops the idea of an eternity cyclic in character, which was done in Greece, India, and China. This is a projection of the particular, concrete, temporal character of culture, the essence of which is time, into the rational terms of universality and timelessness. The cycle itself is fixed and unchanging; the passage of time continues endlessly not in a straight line, but in a cycle, turning back upon itself so that in the new cycle the precise particular persons and events of preceding cycles are repeated. This is the illicit manner in which pure reason deals with the unique and unrepeatable realities of action which make up the stuff of human history. As over against this colossal error of rationalism, the reality of human culture and the true object of history lie precisely in the truth of the action which has a present, a past which is unrepeatable, and a future which is in some degree an open possibility. The time of reason is fictitious. Culture must be known in its true temporal character which is part and parcel of its concrete particularity. It is not eternal; it is not universal. It is essentially finite, changing, passing away; in short, it is temporal.

Man is this being in time who produces the works of culture, which represent not only his productive and creative power, the power of man as *soul*, but also reveal the temporal form of his existence. If this is all that man is, then he is essentially a creature

[1] Cf. John Macmurray, *The Self as Agent*, New York, 1957, especially pp. 132ff.

of time and nothing more. His imagination may hold out before him a reunion with the ancestors in an underworld, or in a celestial country, or in a western paradise, but that is itself a diminishing and devitalized existence that eventually fades out. Or his reason may construct a cyclic order in which the same weary round must be repeated in which time gets reality and permanence at the cost of endless and intolerable repetition. This is the result, in simple or in sophisticated form, of the attempt to absolutize culture, or to raise it to the dignity of an ultimate end for man, and to express the destiny of man in purely rational terms. This is the peril of identifying religion with culture. Culture is a work of man in time; if man has a real eternal destiny, it is not found in the absolutizing or idealizing of culture, but in the transcending of culture, which is the work of man, by religious faith in the true eternity of God.

SCIENCE

Science at least in current usage is the knowledge of nature. It is because man is mind (*nous*) or intellect that he can know nature. This statement might be turned around and the assertion made that nature is that form of the actual world that can be known under the categories of human reason. The world as we see it and know it in immediate experience is a moving, qualitative, and often confusing complex of sensations. The form of our scientific knowledge is a complex of purely abstract formulas and equations, a conceptual pattern. But it begins with the *observation* of fact. So here are both the particular (fact) and the universal (hypothesis). Here is also time, but time in a restricted and particular sense. The complete form of scientific knowledge is not only a universal judgment but one that is timeless, in the sense of being always valid under given conditions. A scientific "truth," if one can use the word, is a timeless truth. It does not depend upon the intention or passion of any human society, nor any human effort or originality. It is not "dated." There never was a moment when this truth was not true, nor will it ever fail to be true because of the degeneration of human effort. Despite the progress and development of scientific knowledge, insofar as any hypothesis is true it is, as it were, lifted out of time and is in no sense dependent upon human, or even divine, action. In the midst of all the change in nature, this truth remains unchanged; it has no before or after, not even a now. It knows no passage of time, for time is the form of action and is meaningful only if there are agents. The dimension of eternity, therefore, in our knowledge of nature is simply timelessness. This kind of truth man can have because he is intellect or *nous*. As scientist he can isolate this "power" or function of his total person and exercise it in a provisional disregard for all the rest of his powers. It is true, most obviously, in our time, that such dispassionate and purely rational knowledge contributes to the passionate activity of man as a member of history. It is also true that in the acquisition of such universal and timeless formulas of knowledge, the scientist is moved by his own emotions or interests, and further that not pure intellect but creative imagination is of prime importance. One might think that the scientist who by the free exercise of an educated and disciplined imagination is producing a new world every day, would be the one most able to conceive of an ultimate and infinite Creator who brings into being the whole vast system of the worlds, and endows man with something of his own power of creativity. In the words of Genesis this might be seen as God breathing into man the breath of life so that man becomes a living soul. However, in itself, the act of scientific knowledge is an act of pure intellect; its object or content is a timeless form, and eternity is simply the changelessness and time-lessness of the conceptual pattern.

THEOLOGY

The truth of theology is truth about God. We have discussed above the meaning of faith as the "reality sense," or the "sense of presence," or the immediate recognition of the other, whether God or man, as free and responsible person (or Person). It is because man is spirit *(pneuma)* that this kind of knowledge is possible. Always the form of knowledge is determined by the object of knowledge. So religious knowledge is first not knowledge "about" but the knowledge "of" God. For God is objective in the sense of being real, and not a product of the mind as idea or image. God is not an object in the sense of being a "somewhat" that is "there" for our disinterested or impersonal observation, judgment, and use. God is not object in the ordinary sense, but the Other. God is Spirit and spirit, in man or God, is not an object of observation, but is known by faith. This is the radical difference between science and religion. Science can deal only with that which can be observed, i.e. phenomena, which simply means that which appears to the senses. The beginning of scientific knowledge is in this observation of fact. Religion begins in faith in that which is not seen, that which does not appear. This is what is meant by mystery; not that which is not known, but that which is not seen or sensibly perceived. But mystery means more than that; it means that the One known as mystery cannot be controlled. Knowledge of nature gives man control over nature. Knowledge of God gives no such control, nor does it mean that we have the key to a divine mechanics by which we can manipulate God to serve our own ends.

Knowledge of God is essentially personal knowledge. We know him as the supreme and original Person who freely creates the world in which we discover order and the regularities that our reason can comprehend and that we can use. As Person he commands pre-eminently respect and love as do all persons. As the divine Person he also requires from us reverence, worship, and obedience. Our knowledge of God is a confession, an acknowledgment of One who has the absolute right to our obedience, and upon whom we absolutely depend. He is God because in him are the origin and meaning of our lives. We know him only as he makes himself known; we wait upon him and when he reveals his will we seek, with his help, to do it. Religion is the service of God; only those can know God who are willing to know him as Lord, and to render to him willing service.

The knowledge of God does not begin in observation of fact nor issue in hypothesis which is always tentative; it begins in God's act of self-revelation and issues in faith which is decisive. Such, indeed, is the nature of all personal knowledge—of man as well as of God. It is because man is spirit that he can have this knowledge; it is because God is Spirit that he can and does make himself known. Spirit, as Paul Tillich observes,[2] is the whole. Spirit is not known sensibly nor rationally but by faith, and by a response of the human spirit which in its perfection is love. Man in his personal wholeness is spirit; God as the complete and perfect One is Spirit because he is pure Person, the One who has power to create, to act in love, to give himself in grace. The complete and perfect power of spirit is in God alone; the created person of man has the power of spirit because he is created in response to the self-communicating act of God. This does not mean that man, being spirit, is naturally obedient to God. As a matter of fact, despite the fact that his very humanity is a relation to God, man is both disobedient and indifferent to God. That is why the universal obstacle between man and God is sin. The first choice of man is to do his own will and serve his own interest and so to put himself in conflict with God. Actually he must discover and accept his sonship to God by repentance and faith, and receive as a gift of God's grace the destiny which is implied in his creation.

The knowledge of faith is not theology. Theology is the systematic interpretation of the faith. Christian theology is the interpretation and communication of the knowledge of God that the Church has in and through Jesus Christ. The truth of Christian faith is God revealed in Christ; the truth of Christian theology, so far as it is attained, is the rational interpretation of Christian faith. The one is unchanging—Christ is the same yesterday, and today, and forever; the other is a changing, sometimes advancing, sometimes degenerating systematization of belief or doctrine.

The God known by faith is eternal, but not in the sense of mere timelessness. Culture was seen to be the activity of man in time; science was seen as a knowledge in terms of timeless laws or formulas. Faith has its own sense and meaning for time. Insofar as time is the form of action and God and man are agents, conscious, free, and creative, the life of God and men involves time. One might say that it produces time, or times. Certainly this is not restricted to the time of a spatial or physical order such as "this world." Eternal life is *life* and life is not timeless, static. The eternal life of man with God is therefore not a timeless state. The

[2] Paul Tillich, *Systematic Theology*, Chicago, 1951, vol. I, p. 251.

language of personal relations, of love and communion, of freedom and creativity, is more adequate to the reality of eternal life
than the language of timeless truth as it is used in rational discourse, either scientific or philosophical. The "time" of eternal
life is the time of God's creative power in which man as spirit
participates.

Now the whole man in his powers of soul, mind, and spirit is
the subject of the whole range of human experience and action.
As spirit he is in free and responsible relation to other men and
to God even when his whole conscious attention is given to scientific research. As mind he "knows" the natural world of which
he is a part even when most completely absorbed in the worship
of God. When engaged in creative activity in any aspect of the
social process (culture) man exhibits most perfectly, perhaps,
the living unity of the freedom of the spirit and his dependence
on and use of the regularities of nature. The man is always the
person, simple in act and relation, infinitely complex in the
structure and process of his empirical personality.

We may now return to the four basic statements with which
our discussion of the human person began and observe the
organic oneness in the person of the four "powers" represented
by these statements. There are two poles to this doctrine of man:
(1) the functional distinction, reflected in the common terminology of various languages, between body, soul, mind, and spirit;
(2) the intimate interdependence and interrelations of these
meanings. Thus body and soul share the common element of
life, but somehow life acquires a new dimension in soul, because
soul is conscious life. Soul also shares with mind the illumination
of consciousness, although in mind consciousness now has the
distinctive function of rational thought. And mind is not sheer
intellect or rationality; it also is one with spirit in the super-
rational power of freedom and creativity.

This complex and yet essentially unified and simple individual
has a polar relation to both nature and God. The dualism of body
and soul in which men have seen themselves as, in body, one
with nature and, in soul, one with God is so much of an over-
simplification that it obscures the inner diversity of man and also
denies his essential unity. However, it is true that in his bodily

constitution man is only one step from simple nature; so when death comes and life departs, "chemistry takes over." There is nothing human any more. At the other pole of his being, man is only one step from God. His "likeness" to God is a practical matter; when in the freedom of spirit he knows and serves God, God takes over, not for death but for life, for this is the realization of the ultimate meaning of human existence, to be one with God in freedom and in eternal life. This is a more elaborate and technical way of saying what the New Testament means by the terms "the natural man" and "the spiritual man."

Man is a creature. To think of the world as "creation" is to see the whole existence and process of the world as the act of God. As creation the world has, of course, a certain independent reality. This is the difference between creation, and the idea of the world as an organism of which God is the soul. But the world as creation, despite the increasing degrees of constitutional freedom that it enjoys and struggles with, still exists and is what it is by the creative act of God. So man is a creature. He does not exist by his own act; he does not know and understand himself save in a limited way and through intellectual effort. He does not have power of himself to be what he is, to exercise the lower or the higher powers of his own being. The endowment of life and mind has come through an age-long process of which he can trace out only the sketchiest outline. His freedom is most incomprehensible of all. "Our wills are ours, we know not how." He can never rationally know this freedom any more than he can know the power that originates and sustains the vast process of nature. Both must simply be known by faith. Nature *is*, man is *free*; neither statement can either be explained or proved.

Man, this spiritual person, is a creature. God creates him; he exists by the power of God rather than by the power of some natural process, or by virtue of some metaphysical substance that he is, or power of being that is inalienably his. He is the most complex and precariously sustained individual in creation. Viewed thus from the standpoint of nature he is ephemeral indeed; his dreams and visions of eternity are a delusion. But viewed as the creature of God, as one created to be a son of God and to participate in eternal life, the destiny of man is no delusion. His value and his security are not found in the "natural man," in any power of soul or of mind; but in the relation to God which makes him spirit, and in the power of God to bestow life. So Jesus answered the Sadducees who did not believe in the resurrection, "God is the God of the living not of the dead." The Christian who believes in the risen Christ says "because he lives we too shall live." This is not a natural outcome of our life, nor a rationally demonstrable destiny; it is wholly dependent on the creative power and will of God. Thus the destiny as well as the original existence of man is understood by Christian faith as the act of the Creator. The fragile and fleeting complex we know as man has no natural power to endure; but as the creature of God and the object of his love, man is heir to eternity.

As stated already, the world as created has a certain degree of independence. This means, first, that the world is not God, not even the body of God; and that God is not just the soul, or the inner meaning of the world. But it also means that the world, even though sustained in its existence by the creative act of God, is what it is, has a real autonomy, a minimum kind of freedom. Creation not only has an absolute beginning in the act of God but it also has a history of change, conflict, diversification, evolution, and development. The deist view that God made the world a perfect machine and then left it to run according to its fixed and changeless laws, is clearly false. The more modern idea that the world is in an evolutionary process without either an intelligence of its own or any control and direction by a present Deity, puts a fantastic burden upon the element of chance. But we do not have to choose between the simple mechanism of deism and the pure chance of a self-sufficient evolution. God is in the world, as well as before and above the world; this is the immanence and transcendence of God. And the effect of the immanent presence of God is the bestowal on the world in increasing degree of the power of freedom, that is the power to be itself at every moment and in every place. This freedom seems to show itself as sheer indeterminacy in the most elementary particles. It soon exhibits a "habit" in atoms, and a spontaneity in living things. With more complex structures higher forms of life appear, with more obvious freedom of movement and even some kind of conscious intelligence. Thus with vast patience God prepares the psychosomatic organism in which consciousness becomes self-consciousness, in which the creature hears the voice of the Creator, in which appears the dim and flickering light of a freedom like that of God. This is the freedom of spirit by which man becomes a maker of history, an artist and artisan, a reflective thinker turning his inquiring mind upon himself, to understand, to evaluate, and to remake himself. It is this creature, blessed and burdened with the responsibility not only of making a living, but also of realizing his own destiny, who lives the life of man in the three great relations—to nature, to culture, and to God.

Freedom takes on a different specific meaning in each one of these relations. In relation to nature it has to deal with what Kant called "necessity," that is, the impersonal laws of nature. Kant saw these "laws" as the expression of causality and nature as a system of such causes; this was the "necessity." Present-day scientists do not talk about causes in this sense, but the element of mechanism is still recognized in the invariable order of events in nature. Kant was primarily concerned to establish the freedom of the moral will in contrast to this realm of necessity. But it is not only moral will that is free. There is also the creativity of imagination by which man as mind "sits loose" to the fixity of nature, and both in thought and in act takes it apart and puts it together again to produce (create?) new substances. He also "sits loose" to the principle of mechanism so far as to form innumerable new machines himself, using freely the power of necessity to serve more and more perfectly his own needs and desires. This "sitting loose" is the form of his freedom in regard to the order of nature of which he is himself a part. This is really not a new idea at all; it is as old as the book of Genesis in which God is reported to have said to the newly created man, "Be fruitful and multiply, and fill the earth and subdue it; and have dominion over the fish of the sea and over the birds of the air and over every living thing that moves upon the earth." Man is made "of the dust of the earth." God never forgets this: "He remembereth that we are dust," and he never lets man forget it, for death continually reminds man of it: "You are dust, and to dust you shall return." Man is a part of creation; but God also put upon man the responsibility of being master of nature. The history of civilization is the long-drawn-out story, greatly accelerated in our day, of his fulfillment of this commission. But, always man must exercise his freedom and his control of nature in conformity to the "laws" or "necessity" of nature. Thus freedom is not the power to do anything one wants to do. It is conditioned by the fixed order of an already existing nature. There is not any conflict between freedom and necessity, but co-operation. Without the free intelligence of man he would not know the regularity of natural law; and without the fixedness and dependability of that law he could never exercise his freedom. Freedom and law are complementary; the freedom of man depends for its exercise upon the necessity of nature. Both are real; neither by itself has any power or meaning. It is in this environment of nature that man becomes free and it is by the laws of nature that he is both limited and released to live the life of man.

In relation to culture, or history, man also seems to be confined to a fixed order, and to be largely determined by his heritage and environment. If culture is, as we have said, the work of man and an expression of his freedom and creativity, it is so only by slow and almost imperceptible change. The mores of primitive man are almost as fixed an order as is natural law. The individual, in whom the ultimate act of free imagination arises, is seemingly bound not only by his physical heredity but also by the law of the clan. However, there is change in human society due in the first instance to the unpredictable doings of nature in variations of climate as well as specific occurrences of storm, flood, drouth, etc. Mores are altered both by geographical changes and by conflict and co-operation of clan with clan. Despite the submergence of the individual in the clan there are individual men of superior strength, courage and ability, and imagination. Thus change occurs and becomes the limited occasion for the vision of the seer and the creation of the artist, as well as the daring of the leader. This freedom must always work within the determination of time and place, and the constitution of the individual man. Freedom of thought, freedom of enterprise, political freedom are not absolute freedoms; they must take account of fixed

orders or they cannot endure. The visionary is one who sees his
vision but not the human and historical conditions in which it
must be realized. The utopian is the one who will be free without
recognizing the practical steps that must be taken in every "now"
as we move from the present to a desired future. Political freedom
is a mirage, as many newly liberated people are now discovering,
unless it is sought by means that deal successfully with the actual
state of the world and society. So in his relation to history and
culture man can be free only by accepting his fate, that is, by
recognizing and dealing with things as they are, and by finding
or making a way to something better. Even then the disaster of
war or the slow degeneration of culture can undo much real
progress. Such is the precariousness of human existence and such
are the conditions within which man can be free in history.

It is only the spiritual person, or the person as spirit, that can
act in full freedom. This act of freedom cannot be rationally
understood or explained, precisely because rational knowledge
is the knowledge of how things logically, that is, necessarily, are.
Rational thought is as "necessary" as is the causal connection of
events in nature; it is, taken strictly, the mechanism of mind.
Therefore freedom in thought or act is non-rational; it is not
sub- but super-rational. The control, therefore, over man as free
spirit is not to be found in a rational order, or law, nor in some
hypostatized Reason, but in God the original and true Spiritual
Person. Just as the freedom of man in relation to nature is conditioned by the fixed order of nature, and as his freedom in
history is conditioned by the relatively fixed order of society as
well as his own constitution, so human freedom in relation to
God is both made possible by God and subject to him. Freedom
in the world of nature is technically conditioned. But in relation
to God, the purely personal relation of man, his freedom is
spiritually conditioned. The creation of man as spiritual person
is the endowment of man with freedom. But the exercise of this
freedom at once becomes a moral problem. How to be free is
the supreme issue of human existence. Here the question is not
how to adjust oneself to fate or necessity, but how to determine
oneself, or *what* to be. The answer to this fundamental question
is not to be found in a natural law or rational principle. It is not

to be found even in a moral law. It is to be found simply and only in the God who has created man in his own image, the God who *is* the true Person. It is by knowledge of God, by obedience to God, by love of God that man exercises his freedom. It is by free acknowledgment of the Other as Lord, that man the creature finds and realizes the true meaning of himself. The word and the idea of obedience express the nature of this relation. It is not a rational, not even a moral term. One does not "obey" the laws of nature; he conforms to them by necessity. One does not "obey" the demands of the laws or mores of human society; he submits to them because he has to, or suffers the penalty if he does not. But one "obeys" another person, human or divine. Obedience is a personal response given in recognition of the rightful authority of another. There is no sacrifice of one's rights, dignity, or even freedom in such obedience. A child obeys his father because the child needs control and the father has the right and the responsibility of exercising that control. The soldier obeys his captain's order in which the command is rightly given. Our life has many orders in which we properly and without any loss of dignity or freedom obey the command of another. Democracy, perhaps more than any other system, depends upon the relation of command and obedience. It is always a person who commands, and a person who obeys. Obedience is essentially a personal relation. It is not a rational, or natural, or even, in the strictest sense a moral relation. The moral relation is, of course, the relation of persons, but it is a relation in which the personal has been resolved into laws, mores, or principles. Morality, therefore, is the conformity of personal conduct to relatively impersonal standards.

All the instances of obedience discussed above represent the authority of one man over another. But this is always a constitutional authority; it is never absolute. The one who commands does so by virtue of a generally recognized and accepted system within which and in conformity to which he gives his command. Because this is so the personal character of the relation of commanding and obeying is profoundly qualified. No human person, simply as person, has the right to command another. This is justification for Kant's assertion of the autonomy of the will. But there is a Person, God, who has the absolute right to command and whose authority all men rightly recognize. Nor is there any loss of man's personal dignity or freedom in this obedience, precisely because God is, above and beyond all the orders and constitutions of nature and history, the One who rightly commands. Religious faith is the recognition of this ultimate and absolute right. Therefore, for religious faith obedience is not mere compulsory conformity nor submission to a qualified personal authority. It is the free recognition of the divine personal Reality who is the source of one's own freedom and the realization of its meaning. "His service is perfect freedom." He can never be obeyed except unconditionally and freely. No doing of his will for any ulterior reason *is* obedience. Thus the full meaning of freedom is found only in this relation to God which is the supreme and essential personal relation. This is the point at which the meaning of freedom in the other relations of man's life is to be seen, although in those relations the freedom is conditioned as has been pointed out above. It is the spiritual person, and only the person as spirit, who knows the full meaning of freedom and who lives not in isolation but in free obedience to God.

CHAPTER . VI

GOD THE SPIRITUAL PERSON

THE TRUTH of God is more nearly akin to the truth of man than to the loftiest abstractions of rational thought, such as the Absolute or Being. It is found more in the wholeness of man as spiritual person than in the "world" or cosmos. The "nature" of God is more adequately expressed in such terms as Subject (the One who says "I"), Creator, Living, than in the categories of Idea, Substance, Being, all of which mean very much the same and all of which are fundamentally physical-rational in origin, that is, they allege to denote objectively the existing Cosmos, and subjectively the purely rational mind that knows it. These terms imply that man and God are ultimately *nous* or Pure Reason. If the word "Spirit" is used in connection with them, its strict connotation is still *nous*.

When the Christian says, "God is Spirit," he gives expression to a conception of God derived not from speculation on the nature of the cosmic order, but from the primary sense of a divine presence, developed and illuminated by prophets and pious men, and given full and concrete reality in Jesus Christ. God as Spirit is Subject, that is the Knower rather than the idea. God is Creator not the cosmos. God is the living God not one who simply *is*. This is what is meant by saying that God is Spiritual Person.

We have made the affirmation that the Christian faith finds its meaning in the two "parties," God the Party of the First Part, and man the Party of the Second Part. We have at some length sought to set forth the nature of man, as a true "party," in terms

of a complex creature whose simple wholeness is designated as
"spiritual person." Now we must reverently turn to the conception of God as Spiritual Person. The meanings given to "spiritual"
and to "person" in our anthropology carry over here but with
profound modification to our theology.

Despite the modification involved when we apply these terms
to our thought of God, there is a continuity of meaning which
should be stated here, both to reflect back upon what has been
said about man and to throw light upon what is to be said about
God. I have used the phrase "spiritual person" instead of the
more common one, "personal spirit." [1] I have said that man is a
spiritual person, and that God is the Spiritual Person. The reason
for this is that the term "person" is used to designate the subject;
it is a substantive, it indicates the one who is and does something.
On the other hand, "spirit" indicates the nature and function of
the person, namely, his wholeness, his freedom, his action and
responsibility. I hope this will help to deliver both words from
vagueness, and distinguish our use of them from a wide range
of meanings with which they have actually been used, both
popular and technical. To say, then, that God is Spirit means that
he is the Person whose completeness and unity are actual, whose
freedom is original or underived, and the perfect expression of
his own nature. God is not the "personality" of idealism; he is
the Creator, the Lord, the Heavenly Father of Christian faith,
whose powers, acts, and relations are spiritual rather than rational
or natural. A spiritual order is an order of free persons, just as a
rational order is an order of ideas, and a natural order is an order
of physical events. Through his rational thought man participates
in the rational order, and because he is a body he participates in
the physical order. It is because he is created a person that he
shares in a spiritual order; this, indeed, is the substance of his life
and being. The source and center of the spiritual order is God
the supreme and original Person. His fundamental relation to
man is spiritual, that is personal. This is more fundamental even
than the moral relation by which men are bound to one another.

[1] Cf. William N. Clark, *An Outline of Christian Theology*, New York, 1898,
p. 66. "God is the Personal Spirit, perfectly good, who in holy love creates,
sustains and orders all."

The spiritual order is one of creativity, love, and grace. Its substance is communion in freedom. In the Christian faith all this is involved in the Kingdom of God.

God is one; one supreme, uncreated, complete Spiritual Person who is Creator and Ruler of the world. God is self-revealing; in his works, in his Word, and in his Son. To make this self-revealing action more explicit, let us say that God reveals himself in nature, in history, and in Jesus Christ. The revelation is always to faith, just as light is manifest to vision, and sound to hearing, and rational structure to the mind. The same nature, the same history, the same Jesus Christ is there for all; but only to faith do they reveal God. "The heavens declare the glory of God" only to the man of faith. The word of the Lord was spoken by Amos and Hosea, but few heard it. "God was in Christ reconciling the world to himself," but only a handful of believers saw it. God cannot be found by searching; no method or apparatus of observation exists or can be devised that will penetrate the mystery of God and bring him out as an object for human knowledge, but he reveals himself to the humble and the pure in heart. Revelation is the free act of the divine Person; the faith by which it is received is the free response of the human person.

What, then, does God reveal? He reveals himself. He does not produce miraculously a book containing the truth he wants men to believe, and commanding the things he wants men to do. Still less does he reveal to speculative thought the mystery of his own being. He reveals himself. The truths and the moral demands of God upon men are apprehended by the man of faith in the forms of human thought and in terms of the actual conditions of history. The Bible is the product both of the revealing acts of God and the faith of men. Its form, rather its varied forms, are those of the historic situation and the human response and apprehension of God's self-revelation. They have the incompleteness and fallibility of human understanding as well as the reality and authority of the act of God. Only men of faith can receive the revelation, but faith in man is the response to the presence of God, the account of whose self-revelation is found in the Bible. Revelation is always in the present. It was in the present for Second Isaiah; it was in the present for St. Paul. For those who read

the words of these, and others, in the Bible the God who spoke
then is present speaking now. He acts and speaks in history but
he, himself, is the eternally present One.

But there is a form of truth in terms of human understanding
that emerges in the historic self-communication of God to men.
The nature of God and his righteousness emerge more clearly as
generation after generation of men hear and seek to do what
God makes known to them. This is real "progressive" revelation.
The goodness and mercy of the God of Israel become more apparent. It becomes more and more clear that God is one and
holy, that he is a God of love and grace. All this is no key to the
metaphysical structure of Deity, if there is any meaning in those
words. But it is a knowledge of God that can be entertained by
the mind of man and that is of the most surpassing importance to
man. Nowhere in the biblical writings, Old Testament or New
Testament, is God called Person. But the character and act of
God, his dealings with the world and with man, as we find them in
the Bible, are all such that this term serves most adequately in our
reflective thought about him. God acts; a person acts. God is
good; goodness is the attribute of a person. Above all, God loves;
and love is the act of a person in dealing with other persons. The
creativity and love of God are expressions of that freedom
which is the power of Spirit. This is what it means to say that
God is Person, that he is Spirit; the two words must be used
together to give the full and complete meaning of either. It is
this "truth" that is formed in the minds of men through the historical self-revelation of God. It constitutes a "conception" of
God; not a definition or concept, for concept implies completeness of comprehension and there is no such comprehension of
God. But it gives a real "knowledge" of God in terms both appropriate to God's own being, and supremely significant to man.

The ultimate act of God is his incarnation in Jesus Christ. In
incarnation both the presence of God and his self-revelation become historically actual. To say that God is incarnate in Christ
does not imply that he is not present at other moments in history,
or that he does not act in and through other men. Man is not
man apart from God. All response of man to God represents
his prior action in human life. Even the most rebellious soul is

engaged with God, only now as antagonist. But to say that God was incarnate in Christ means that in this man's life at this time and place in history, God did his full work of love and grace, and not only spoke his word clearly but fully performed his act of redemption. The word spoken by the great prophets, and received by men of faith, now was not a word only but a life. So for the Christian, Christ *is* the Word. He does, indeed, speak the word; so far as words can convey meaning, his words give us the truth of God and man. But still words are symbols; the reality is life, and the life of Christ is the full and complete embodiment of the truth. In the most literal sense the truth, or Word, of God is inseparable from God; it is God himself.

The life of Christ, therefore, is the truth and the act of God; it is the life of God in man. There are theoretical problems involved and we shall deal with them in a later section on the doctrine of the person of Christ; but this religious affirmation, that God was in Christ, was the faith of the first Christians long before the christological problem as such arose. The words here used are primary for Christian faith. Christology comes later as an attempt to elucidate and systematize their meaning. But such doctrinal statements can never take the place of the primary, factual reality of the faith itself. They can help as all theological construction can help to make the faith meaningful and to communicate it to others. And I shall try to formulate a christology in terms of the method outlined and the conception of spiritual personality elaborated above. The point being made here is that God, the one God, is a self-revealing God, and that the culmination of that self-revelation is Jesus Christ. If God is conceived as the Absolute, self-revelation becomes inconceivable, for it means that God comes into relation to the world and to men; and the Absolute by definition has no relations to any kind of other. But if God is Person, as we are affirming, self-revelation is not only not a problem; it is an act that expresses the very nature of God.

God is Creator. He creates the world—all things visible and invisible. "Creation" is not a scientific term. The act of creation cannot be rationally known, for to know rationally is to place an act or an idea in a logically defined relation to other acts or ideas. But the act of creation is prior to all forms of intelligible reality and cannot be so defined. Rational knowledge is possible only within a system, a "universe of discourse." But the meaning of creation is that the total system of reality is brought into being. The form of "knowing" that is rational does not reach to this prior act. Rational knowledge is knowledge of that which *is* (being) and possibility; it cannot comprehend origination.

When scientists write for popular reading about the creation of the universe, they do not mean real creation. They refer to the process by which some already existing mass was formed into the galactic and planetary systems that we know as the "universe." There was always something there and inherent in that "something" were the laws and forces by which the existing universe could take shape and exist. Earlier and more modern philosophical speculation on the origin of the world as, for example, in the minds of Epicurus and Descartes, posited a vortex out of which came by a seemingly miraculous co-operation of mechanism and chance the ordered and differentiated and law-abiding universe we know. Science can know only in terms of a continuity of process; every event must be seen as the necessary outcome of preceding events and conditions. Manifestly, therefore, creation as absolute origination is not a scientific concept, for it postulates the appearance of a world with no antecedent events or physical conditions with which it is intelligibly continuous.

Creation means the free and unconditioned act of the Person who is Spirit. Freedom likewise is not a rational or a scientific concept, but it has a deep affinity to creation. Creation is the act of free spirit. Such creativity as man exercises is through the freedom God has given him as spirit, but it is a conditioned freedom—conditioned by the already existing world and by God. But the free creative act of God is not conditioned by anything "other" to himself. To say that God is conditioned by his own nature is meaningless, for it only means that God does what he does; this is not "conditioning" in the proper sense of the term.

Creation means that there is no pre-existing stuff or material out of which the world is made. It also means that there are no "eternal" laws or principles by which God must make a world. It means that God, the Spiritual Person, is absolutely prior to all else and the free Creator of all. Rationality, principles, laws, are descriptive of the character of a world already created; "reason" appears only within a system and is valid in that system. Manifestly there can be no rational proof that the world was or is created; God is known as Creator by faith.[2] If man did not possess some degree of creativity, that is, freedom, he could not have this faith. The very idea of creation would never arise. But it does arise; in crude or refined form it is almost universally present in the minds of men. The creation myth is common among primitive peoples. But these "creations" never represent absolute beginning; they are primitive accounts of the origin out of some already existing but relatively indeterminate or meaningless world. The philosophical idea of creation makes God the "first cause" of the world. But this is a dubious doctrine. Kant pretty thoroughly eliminated it. It is dubious because the idea of cause is ambiguous. Efficient causes operating in an existing world are intelligible, although they tend to become quite complex and are not now useful in science. An efficient cause is simply the force which moves a body. It is mechanical in character, the "push" of present event to bring about the succeeding event. But God cannot be the first cause of the world because God is not a "force" or a "push"; nor is he an "event"; there is not any "first" in the succession of causes. God is the Creator, not the cause of the world, and creation is the exercise of a power which has no cause, but is itself the free and sufficient act of the Spiritual Person.

There are alternate ways of thinking of the existence of the world, chiefly the doctrines of emanation and of eternal existence. The idea of emanation found classic expression in Neo-Platonism, but is a common form of speculative cosmology. According to Plotinus, the world represents an outgoing from the One. Some inner rebellion or disturbance within the One caused a "fall" or an emanation from that complete and otherwise perfect One. This fall or emanation continued to lower and lower levels until it encountered the dark element of matter and the visible world came into being. We are not concerned here with the nature of salvation which, in brief, is the return of the fallen divine particle

[2] The "existence" of the world also is known by faith.

through all the stages formerly traversed until it is again secure within the One—"the flight of the alone to the Alone." We are rather concerned with the conception contained in this system of the origin of the world; it is an emanation from the One which can hardly be called God, or anything else, for it transcends and includes all meanings. This is a doctrine of the world as an unfolding of and departure from the One. There is a residual inconsistency in any such doctrine and that is the assumption of the existence of "matter," a sort of negative, resistant something which, when the emanation from the One in its lowest descent encounters it, co-operates to constitute the visible world.

There is also the idea of the world as eternally existing. This is the assumption of Aristotle. There is no beginning but a process that never began and will never end. This cosmology posits a series of spheres. The outer sphere is moved by the attraction of God who, himself, is not only not Creator, but is not even conscious of the world. He is the Unmoved Mover, but he does not move by doing anything, still less by willing anything in regard to the world. The world is moved by its own desire for the perfection—a purely rational perfection—of God who is himself the first principles of Reason. The "*eros*" of the outer sphere for God is the eternal origin of the primary motion of the universe which is then communicated to lower spheres. The spherical form of the cosmos makes possible eternal and rational motion; eternal because motion about a circle or a sphere has no point of beginning or end, and rational because complete and self-contained.

The scientific view of the world is somewhat akin to this conception. Scientific knowledge always assumes a past essentially the same as the present and a future which develops wholly out of the present. Here also there is no beginning or end, but a sequence of events causally or rationally continuous with what has gone before and what will come after. The world of natural science is essentially an eternally existent world although science as such does not posit eternal existence speculatively. Certainly science has no place for and can find no meaning in the idea of creation.

As has been indicated above, the first ideas of creation are mythological. Philosophical speculation tends, one might say naturally, to the doctrine of emanation. But there are speculative-mythical ideas of creation, the chief of which is that of Plato. In the *Timaeus* Plato puts forward, frankly as a myth, his account of creation. It ought to be said that "myth" does not mean a purely fanciful idea or one devoid of truth. It means rather an explanation that goes beyond the rational. The reason for the myth is that pure reason cannot alone and of itself account for creation. Unless one, therefore, is going to accept (and it must be by faith whether with Aristotle or modern thought) the doctrine of eternal existence, it is necessary to introduce some super-rational element or action to give a full account of the existence of the world. This Plato was not afraid to do. However, he did not abandon the use of reason, or the categories that philosophical thought had so critically evolved, especially those of a mathematical character. Accordingly, Plato posited three eternal elements: (1) the rational Pattern from which pure forms geometrical in character were derived, (2) a Demiurge or creative God, and (3) a Receptacle, or Matter, which was inert and resistant to the rational forms but to a sufficient degree receptive of them so that the visible world might be formed. The Demiurge created the world by taking the geometrical "forms" from the pattern, arranging them in a certain way and impressing them upon the Receptacle. The Demiurge was dependent upon two other pre-existent factors, the Pattern and the Receptacle. This has a certain similarity to the accounts of creation in Genesis where God works with an undeveloped world or chaos and brings it into the order that we know as the world. In both cases the important and effective power of creation is in the will of the Deity, and this is a non-rational power. The seventeenth-century rationalists faced the question, Why did God create this particular rational world? They realized that any number of equally rational worlds (which simply means *orderly* worlds) are possible, given the basic elements and a creative will. The solution to this problem proposed by Leibniz was that this is the "best" of all the possible and equally rational worlds. But this "best" is not itself a rational but a moral criterion. A strictly rational treatment of the matter must face two questions, the answers to which cannot be given in terms of reason: (1) why does any world exist at all? and (2) why, among all the infinite possibilities, is just this world the one that does exist?

The Christian doctrine of creation was formed in the presence of the Aristotelian, the Platonic, and the emanation theories. It affirms that the world was created by God, *ex nihilo*. *Ex nihilo* means literally "out of nothing." But this "nothing" is not a negative metaphysical stuff; the affirmation means that God brought into being the whole existing universe by an act of absolute creation. Nothing, either of material or of rational principle, exists before God. God alone is the one eternally existent Being and Agent. He creates by his Word. Put in another way, the absolutely original reality is Spirit; or, more exactly, Spiritual Person. From the creative act of this Person exercising the creative power of Spirit comes the whole cosmic order within which, as existent, all the laws and orders of reality exist and can be discovered and known by the mind of man. This is the Christian doctrine of God as Creator. It is therefore a nonsense question to ask, What was God doing before he created the world? Or, When did God create the world? There was no "what" nor "when"; there is no "before" the world was created. The act of creation as all acts of freedom is not an act in time; time is the form of the act as it brings into existence that which was not. The creation of the world itself is a constant act, the non-temporal source of the whole space time order. This is not known rationally but by faith.

Perhaps this can all be summed up by the simple assertion that the Absolute First is God. Neither a rational Pattern, nor a Receptacle is co-eternal with, much less prior to, God. The high doctrine, the doctrine of God as Creator, posits nothing besides God until God himself by his free act gives being to a world. When that cosmos appears all its character and laws, all its creatures including the rational mind of man, appear within the existent world, and depend upon its creator for their nature and existence. Rational thought finds its way laid out and must limit itself to that way. It cannot know, much less can it prescribe rules to, the Creator. But by faith man knows directly and simply the God who is both within and above the world. He knows God because God reveals himself. The history of man's religious progress is the story of the increased clarity and meaning in man's response to the self-revelation of God.

CHAPTER VII

THE LORD OF CREATION

GOD AND THE WORLD

God creates the world. This means that the world is not God, and that God is not the world. It means, also, that a certain degree of independence is given to the world. Yet the world is "under God." It could not exist of itself; its existence depends upon the eternal creative act of God. And its dependence means that its own process is conditioned by that creative act. The rule or control of God over the world consists not in his enactment of general laws or principles, but in a creative administration under which the infinitely various movements and operations of the world take place. "In wisdom hast thou made them all" (Psalm 104:24). Within this "wise" and immanent control the world is free to "be itself" at every point and at every stage of its development. The rule of the creative Spirit is not, however, simply permissive; it is also dynamic and intelligent (*logos*), and in an ultimate sense it is purposive (personal). Instead of fixed forms and unalterable conditions the rule of God has openness and flexibility, as does personal control by any free being. This is what delivers the world from mere mechanism and chance.

Inconceivably long stretches of time are required for the formation of an ordered cosmos, and for the emergence of life, sentience, and mind. But this time process arises out of the purpose of God. This is the difference between "will" as such and "purpose." The act of will is an instantaneous act; purpose comprehends the process of time and change. It is purpose that gives meaning to time; perhaps we should say that purpose creates time. So the

world is a time process because it is created according to the
purpose of God. This is a concept that never found development in Greek thought. There is a hint of it in Plato's creation
myth when he says that God was good and wanted to confer
good upon others. But the rational world order of Aristotle
knows no purpose. It is a *teleological* world order. There is an
ultimate end (*telos*) toward which the world yearns (*eros*), and
that is God himself. But in this teleology there is no purpose. God
not only has no purpose for the world; he is not even conscious
of the world. He knows only himself. It is the desire (*eros*) of
the world for God that starts and maintains the world process
but *eros* is not purpose. The Greek concept of *logos*, with all its
variations, lacked this element of purpose. Greek thought never
rose to the true conception of the Person. The Prologue to the
Fourth Gospel states succinctly the transition from *logos* to Person. The *logos* became flesh; this is the transition from rationality
to personality. It is the *Son* who takes over; nothing more is
heard of the *logos* in the Fourth Gospel, which is the epic of
the Son. "No one has ever seen God; the only Son, who is in the
bosom of the Father, he has made him known." Now there is
purpose as well as *logos;* and *logos* is swallowed up in this purpose. God not only created the world through the *logos* which
is now known to be the Son, but he also loves the world, and sent
the Son to save it.

Christian theology early became bound to the concept of *logos,*
which is essentially rationality, and has never fully freed itself to
think in terms of the Son, of personal reality. The mythology
and the metaphysics of the "Word" have obscured the spiritual
and personal character of God's act of creation and even his act
of redemption. I am consciously and purposefully, in this book,
shifting the basis of theology from *logos* to the spiritual or personal reality of God and man. God's government of the world
and of man is to be conceived of primarily in these terms. God
creates the world in wisdom; he loves the world. These are
personal terms; they are ultimate. In his love God sent his Son
that the world might believe in him and be saved. The purpose
of the creation is embodied in Christ; it means for man "Christ
in you the hope of glory," and it means for "creation" that it "will

be set free from its bondage to decay and obtain the glorious liberty of the children of God" (Rom. 8:21).

God rules the world in freedom, and the area of its realization increases with the appearance of higher forms and more spontaneous organisms. In the realm of physics and chemistry freedom seems limited to mere indeterminacy. But with organic life appears spontaneity, and in animal life increasing individual autonomy, especially in the higher animals. Eventually there comes a creature with body and brain and consciousness which is at least potentially human. The distinctive power and quality which make this creature man rest in his ability to know and respond to the personal presence of God. This response is not primarily cognitive; it is not a matter of the creature knowing that God is there and that he can now have some profitable relations with Deity. It is a practical and personal knowing, the recognition of the Other with which or whom man has to do, to which or whom he is essentially yet freely related, upon which or whom he depends for the necessities of life and for the form of his human existence (which is also wholly a social or tribal matter). By virtue of this all-important relation man is called on to control and direct his conduct according to the demand or requirement of that Other; it could hardly be called the "will" of the Other, for at this stage man does not know even himself as a "will."

It is, however, in this situation of demand and response that man comes to eventual consciousness of himself as in some degree free and responsible; in other words, he comes to be and to know himself as in some sense a person. Thus, both the creation of man as man and the consciousness of his own humanity are in response to the mystery of a Presence. The knowledge of God in this elementary sense is the source of man's knowledge of himself as man. The history of man's developing conception of his own humanity goes hand in hand with his developing conception of God; indeed the one *follows* the other development. Man's first knowledge of himself as a free, responsible *person* is a reflection of his knowledge of God as Person. Instead, therefore, of man making God in his own image, or "personalizing" God because he first knew himself as a person, just the opposite is true. Men pondered upon the meaning and mystery of God long before they became concerned with the mystery of their own being. And the development of a high conception of God precedes the attainment of a truly personal knowledge of man by himself. Man's highest aspiration for himself always takes the form of seeking to be like God. Heroes and kings are deified. The Old Testament exhibits this from the beginning and in ever more worthy manner. Adam and Eve were driven out of the Garden of Eden lest they eat of the tree of life and become like God. Later their offspring built a great tower on the plains of Shinar so that they might climb up to the abode of the gods and so become gods. When the prophets came they called the people to be righteous because God is righteous; "you must be holy because I am holy." The discipline and ordering of human life from the center of free response which makes man human derive from this demand of God, or the gods, and the aspiration to be like God.

There is danger in this aspiration; too often it takes the form of a desire to grasp the prerogatives of deity, especially those of power and immortality. The Greeks were keenly aware of this; *hybris*, or presumption, was one of the great dangers and evils of human life. It is a long way from the ambitious effort of the tower of Babel, to the disclosure that true godlikeness is found in love and self giving. Jesus linked the promise, "you shall be sons of your Father in heaven," to the command, "love your enemies." His own godlikeness was in humility and service, and in the cross.

So the creation of man begins with the awakening in the creature of a sense of the presence of God and of the desire to be like him, and to share in his freedom and power. It is out of this beginning that there emerges the moral person and the power of spirit. But this is not a "natural" development; it in some sense goes against "nature." It is natural for man to want to have the power and the immortality attributed to the gods; but it is against nature for man to discipline himself inwardly in the righteousness of a holy God and to submit his will to One who not only demands self-denial, but who cares for all men, and requires of his human children a righteousness which is not a means to an end,

and which makes man the servant of his fellow-men even beyond
the natural limits of family, or tribe or nation. The "natural man"
must go through a profound inner transformation to know and
serve God truly. We might call it a re-integration of the inner
life, but a better word is "regeneration." It is a shift of the central
focus of life from "nature" to "spirit." "To set the mind on the
flesh is death, but to set the mind on the Spirit is life and peace"
(Rom. 8:6). In this rebirth the creation of man is completed; this
is the fulfillment of his elementary desire and aspiration to be like
God.

Some of the Church Fathers, notably Irenaeus, frankly called
this the deification of man; God became man that we might
become God. This was inferred from the doctrine of the incarnation of God in Jesus Christ. But through all the subtle thought
and ponderous terminology of the christological controversy, the
Church held still to the position that man remains man and God
is God. In Jesus Christ God is incarnate but the man Jesus is still
man and the incarnate God is still God. This is the logical paradox
of the idea that Jesus Christ is the God-man, and is "one" Jesus
Christ. But there is also in the incarnation an explanation of the
creation, a disclosure of the intent of the Creator. Jesus Christ,
the true man, the man God from the beginning had been seeking
to bring into being, is the revelation of God's "eternal purpose
which he has realized in Christ Jesus our Lord" (Eph. 3:11).
This is the "mystery" that has been hidden through the ages and
is now made manifest, "Christ in you the hope of glory." The
humanity completed in Jesus Christ and shared by the community of faith in him is the "manifestation of the sons of God"
that Paul speaks of in Romans 8:21.

God's government of the world is therefore seen to be itself
creative, or the continuity in time of his eternal act of creation.
And the essential character of his rule is freedom. God rules the
world in freedom. This is involved in the irreducible independence of the created world. The degree of freedom at the beginning is small, simply the indeterminacy of movement that seems
to exist in sub-atomic entities. But it increases, as has been said
above, in organic and animal life and come to its fullest expression
in man. God gives to the particle freedom to make its random

movement; he permits mechanisms to be mechanical without interference; he honors the spontaneity of organisms. Thus God lets the created world be itself at each stage of its development into more complex and more spontaneous forms. Yet he exercises over it all his ultimate power of control. God is "almighty" and this implies not an infinite coercive force but the power of Spirit which operates in freedom. This is the power both of creation and control over a world that is not God, that is both dependent and independent.

We can find analogies of God's government of the world in man's control of nature, in his use of machines, in his use of animals, and in his exercise of authority over other men. From earliest times men have "ruled" nature in some degree. We use plants and animals, but we make use of them by allowing them to be themselves. We plant a certain tree or cereal or flower where it will grow. We can water and fertilize and prune it but we do not interfere with the growth process itself. Even when we graft or cross breed, we leave it to the living plant to accept or reject the new departure.

In man's use of animals, there is a still larger degree of dependence on the free action of the creature controlled. A well-trained dog is a marvel of free obedience. A horse must be respected and given a great deal of freedom to serve best the purposes of his human master. Dogs and horses have intelligence as well as sensitiveness. Sometimes the human master trusts himself to the sagacity of the dog or the horse and literally depends on its free action. Long training and the long association have won a free service that could never be forced.

This kind of co-operation between master and servant is lost to a generation that depends so much upon machines. Yet even the machine must be ruled by giving it its proper freedom. In fact, the mechanisms which man creates are becoming more and more automatic. Interference with any part directly is disastrous. To get good service from a machine it must be free from any such interference. Otherwise, the machine would be useless. Man respects the structure and operation of the machine which he has himself made and recognizes its autonomy within the limits he has himself set.

The problem of the personal control of mechanism appears in sharply defined form in deism. In the deistic doctrine the world is created by God; this is the affirmation of traditional Christian faith. But the created world is conceived of as a perfect mechanism; this is the product of Cartesian rationalism. The essential responsibility of God is discharged by the creation; having made the world perfect and self-sufficient God becomes not only an absent Deity but also an unemployed Deity. But also derived from the Christian tradition was the belief in miracle. What is a miracle in a world which is a perfect mechanism? It can only be an intervention in the regularity of the world mechanism by the God who is outside the world. Despite the abandonment of deism as a theological doctrine this meaning of miracle still persists. In the present-day world the order of nature is conceived in scientific terms, and its invariable regularities are called the "laws of nature." But whether it is the divinely created mechanism, or the laws of nature, any act of God is thought of as an intervention, an interruption of the regularity of the normal flow of events, a supernatural intrusion into nature.

This is a very artificial conception of the nature of spirit and its control of nature. We think more truly of the real world of which we and our own actions are certainly a part if we take freedom and mechanism to be polar opposites, neither having power or reality apart from the other.[1] Pure freedom and pure mechanism are both abstractions in the created world. The organic unity of the two is found in man himself. Every observable act of a man can be known in terms of the mechanisms of nature. But the ultimate control of his conduct lies in his own freedom. This does not mean that man can do anything he wants to do; he is conditioned by circumstances, by the relatively fixed orders of nature, and by his own abilities. But within these limitations he can "express himself" if it is only to protest that which he cannot prevent, or aspire to that which he cannot do. In between these two impassable obstacles there is a greater or less scope of action which he can take. Life, for the most part, offers real possibilities. Often the consistent following of a chosen course of action increases the scope of possibilities. The chief organ of

[1] This is what John Wright Buckham called a "contraplete."

creative freedom is the power of imagination. Free action is not just the choice between two or three open options; it is also the creation of new options. "Possibility" is not a fixed and limited order; it is an expandable realm. By imagination man in a sense goes back to the beginning of his life problem and makes a new start with new formations, new methods, and often new and better conceived objectives. Among other things man can create new mechanisms—of thought or of material apparatus.

The "man" who does this is man as spirit exercising a certain freedom and creativity. How does he do it? If one means by this question, just where is the part of the mechanism which spirit can grasp, as our hands grasp the steering wheel and our foot presses the accelerator, the answer is that there is no "part" marked "control." Spirit does not direct mechanism by push buttons. "Spirit" is the whole man; it is the whole man in his power of spirit who exercises such control as he can over an organism which is only in one pole of its being a mechanism. This opposition of freedom-mechanism represents only theoretical extremes. The terms have meaning when viewed as the polar extremes of the action of a real man who is the infinitely complex unity at least partially and in outline described above. "Freedom" is an act involving and dependent upon the powers of reason, life, and the approximate mechanism of the bodily complex. "Mechanism" is the form of physical process which becomes actual in man only by the power of organic life, consciousness, reason, and spirit.

In his freest act man controls the action of himself, mind, soul, and body, not by "pressing a button," for example, the pineal gland, or by any direct manipulation of a crucial control part in a bodily mechanism, but by a free motion of the whole person. In any exacting and critical observation of this action, physiological, psychological, or mental, there will be found no interruption of the continuities of "nature." The free act is a wholly incarnate one, and the act of a visible person can only be seen and known in the order of existence of which he is a part. If a man acts from the most simple animal selfishness, his observed act is no more a part of nature than if he acts from the most completely self-transcending love for another. Neither the selfishness nor the love can be observed directly in its own essential nature. The giving of one's life in love for another freely and deliberately no more interrupts the organic life, the chemistry, or the physiology of the man than does another's snatching of a loaf of bread to satisfy his hunger.

In somewhat similar fashion God rules the world of nature, not by interrupting its "laws" (of which he is the author) but by controlling the process of nature in most regular and orderly ways. He is freer than the human spirit. He is absolutely free. All that he does, after it is done, appears to observation as natural. The free control is never apparent—except to faith. And what faith sees is not a miracle, in the sense of an unnatural occurrence, but an act of judgment or grace, a divine mastery of the course of events that reveals his goodness.

When the question is asked, does God rule the world only "in general" allowing the world to be itself as has been said above, or does he determine specific happenings in nature or in history for ends that can be discerned by man, it must be acknowledged that such specific action is certainly within the power of God, as the immanent, free power of creation and control. The criterion of judgment, however, as to whether any specific event or complex of events is so determined is not an interruption of the regularities of nature or the setting aside of human powers of choice and action. God rules the universe all the time. No limit can be set to what he can do; whatever he does, directly or through whatever agencies, once done, is part of the natural and historic sequence that can be known to man. One man may see "the hand of God" in events that have no such significance to others, which is not to say either that the man who sees is deluded, or that those who do not see are blind. We are all blind to many things, but there may be an act of God directed to a certain individual or group which is not our concern at all. When we come to discuss the moral government of men this point will have further elucidation. But here the thing of general importance is to recognize that even in the most regular, natural events, God is not absent; his rule therein is purely permissive. And when most clearly to faith God acts in human affairs the "order of nature" is not disrupted but used by its true master, God. If one does not

believe in God, or in any real freedom in man, this whole position, of course, is mistaken. But if one does believe in God, and
this is a basic Christian belief, and in the freedom and responsibility of man, then the divine government of the world as here
presented is surely both reasonable and intelligible.

GOD AND MAN

So far we have been concerned with the lordship of God over
the created world and but incidentally with his sovereignty over
men. We now turn to this most important aspect of the divine
government. God's rule over men is both direct and indirect. The
more indirect the rule, the more it is to be conceived in terms of
nature or law; but the direct rule is wholly in terms of freedom.
God rules man through the order of nature; he also rules through
a social order; finally he rules in direct personal control. A rationalistic theology will try to find in nature the full and definitive
nature of God's action among and in men. The moralistic theologian will find that rule in terms of legal enactment and moral
command. Consistent with the position maintained throughout
this book, I want to say that both these orders—nature and society
—represent indirect ways by which God exercises his government of man. But it is in the direct and personal form of power
that God ultimately exercises sovereignty over the individual
man; and this rule is a rule of perfect freedom.

  1. God rules man through nature; for man is a part of nature.
He must act according to the "laws" of nature or not exist at all.
He must feed his body and find or make conditions within which
that body can live and thrive. This means shelter, avoidance of
natural and human enemies, a certain degree of co-operation with
his fellows, rest, etc. He cannot breathe under water; he cannot
walk on the air; he cannot renounce the eating of food. He must
develop skills, and observe the natural requirements for the
growth of plants and the breeding and use of animals. Man may be
lord of nature but, as Francis Bacon pointed out, he first must
know and abide by the ways of nature. Now, there is a great
element of moral control in this discipline of nature. It is the
point where man must learn and practise an elementary limitation

of his desires and sometimes a denial of them. Accordingly there
are certain "virtues" that God teaches man through nature; courage, caution, self-restraint, temperance, patience, and even a certain kind of honesty, that is, acknowledging things for what they
are. Nature makes man a realist.

This does not mean that a faithful observance of the laws of
nature, or the development to high degree of the virtues she in-
culcates will guarantee any man life, prosperity, or happiness. For
nature, in relation to man, is ambiguous, both helpful and harm-
ful. And human existence in nature is and always will be precarious. Lightning strikes the good man as well as the bad man.
Famine, flood, and disease show no respect to the virtues of men.
Too often the man who openly violates what seem to be the
moral teachings of nature flourishes like the green bay tree even
though he may not die in the odor of sanctity. Too often the
man who most perfectly exemplifies the virtues of nature suffers
from disease and accident, and often from the hate and rivalry
of his fellows. Nature has provided only the broadest and most
general terms of control over the race of men, and gives no guarantee that any individual or tribe or nation will be secure and
prosperous simply by observing her demands. On the other hand,
men may go a long way in reckless disregard of what seem to be
the requirements of "nature" and still survive and even prosper.

2. God rules men through society. The tribe, the nation, the
state impose controls over men. Mores, or custom, moral standards, laws by a governing authority, all these are forms of the
almost infinitely diverse and often subtle ways by which the
social mass defines and determines conduct. Early civilizations
were ruled by a consensus expressed in proverbs; this was the
ancient order as reflected in the Old Testament; it still has a large
place in oriental civilizations. The formulation of basic rules of
moral conduct such as are found in the Ten Commandments, and
more elaborately in the Mosaic legislation, is a codification and
formal expression of the same kind of control, now explicitly alleged to derive from Deity. Philosophers seek for rational moral
principles, which are general, and valid laws for man beyond the
specific requirements of any particular culture.

So important are these social controls that man could not be man and human society could not exist unless general and real respect were accorded to them. These laws, like the laws of nature, are not perfect in operation. They actually exercise a relatively loose control over men and groups of men. Often the man, good by all the canons of human morality, suffers disease, misfortune, and death; and often his very goodness makes others envious of him and eager to do him hurt. And, strangely enough, while society imposes these controls upon man, any very conspicuous righteousness tends to make a man envied, derided, and hated. The opposite also is true. A friend of mine, watching a political procession in which a notoriously unmoral person appeared, observed the acclaim with which he was greeted. A priest, standing beside him, said, "There is a bit of the rascal in all of us." Many crimes go unpunished; many wicked live to a good old age. Many of the most virtuous suffer affliction. The psalmist said, "I have been young and now am old; yet I have not seen the righteous forsaken or his children begging bread" (Psalm 37:25). The author of this psalm might have learned much from our generation or even from his own if he had looked at it a little more critically.

Neither the order of nature nor the governing power of human society is to be identified directly with God. Both are "established orders" and furnish a rough and approximate set of controls within which man must live and to which he must in some degree conform if he is to be man. This unmeasured margin of variability represents the "independence" of creation. Only indirectly, therefore, and in a most general sense does God rule man through nature and society. The great fallacy of naturalism is the claim that in nature as nature are to be found the true canons of human conduct and goodness; and, somehow, a vindication of those canons must be found in natural process. On the other hand great harm has been done to Christian faith by the direct attribution to God of the kind of moral control society exercises over man through its moral codes and even its laws.

To conceive God's righteousness as justice, to think of God's demand upon man in terms of law, even moral law, is to transfer illegitimately categories that apply to human societies and authorities to God. This was the "legalism" of Judaism which Jesus and Paul and the early Church renounced, but which returned almost in full force in the Roman Catholic Church and is by no means absent in the main branches of Protestantism. Protestants who earnestly affirm Luther's declaration that salvation is solely by grace and faith (*sola gratia, sola fidei*) still say that the law must be upheld; that God's rule over men is through his law *and* his grace. Strictly speaking, it is improper to speak of God's "justice" if we mean the justice of a human society administered through specified codes, and involving a measured reward and punishment. The most contradictory thing one can say is that he lives by the "Christian code." The whole system of justice, of laws, and of rewards and punishments represents a necessity in man's dealing with man. But only indirectly, imperfectly, and never simply do they approximate God's government of man.

The direct government of God over man is personal, or spiritual. This is the relation in which freedom is fully realized. God requires of man free obedience. If that seems paradoxical, then it can be put from man's point of view; man can serve God only by his own free act. This is the essence of the personal or spiritual relation. In the realm of personal relations God's rule is like his act of creation: "He spake and it was done." It is "power devoid of coercion." It is true authority accepted freely, and obeyed willingly. This is, after all, the ultimate nature of any man's authority over his fellowman. Any sovereign rules more by consent than by coercion, despite the fact that all governments must use coercion. Even a military authority, to be fully effective, must be freely accepted by the majority. The more successful a commanding officer is, the more freely and willingly his commands are obeyed. He does not have to "pull his rank" to get obedience. This is the difference between obedience and submission. At the higher levels of command, the orders are given in terms of general objectives; field generals have wide scope of judgment. They are "generals." On the lower levels the orders are more precise, until with the drill sergeant coercion and precision are dominant.

Much of the actual government of man by God is through the indirect media of nature and society. Religion first takes the form of invariable precision and coercion in rite and custom. Religious progress leads to modifications of this literalism; reason and moral

conscience are appealed to in the higher religions and men more
freely and understandingly serve God. But the full freedom of
God's reign over man comes only when God is revealed as Love,
and his service is defined by the two great commandments. The
law of love is not a coercive law, but a law of freedom. It cannot be obeyed, unless it is obeyed freely! This is the true Christian meaning of divine sovereignty. It is a doctrine for spiritual
maturity, and hard to attain. Historically Christianity has operated on lower levels. Men fear freedom, and they fear even
more to grant it to others. That is why legalism and literalism
remain and will remain in varying degrees in the Christian
Church. But the fact remains that what God seeks from man is
a direct relation of love and free obedience, not to laws or
precepts but to himself. This is the "foolishness of God" that is
wiser than the prudence and wisdom of men.

3. In his direct, personal dealing with man God seeks a free
response, but the restraints and compulsions of nature and of
human society furnish a discipline that men need on the way to
maturity both as individuals and as societies. "The powers that be
are ordained of God" although they never fully express and ad-
minister God's will. When, however, God's essential and direct
authority over men is conceived in terms either of nature or
society, "law" becomes a barrier between God and man, and a
distortion of God's righteousness. The real reign of God over
man is ultimately spiritual or personal. What God requires of
man is more than obedience to a law; or justice toward his fellow man; he commands man to love, and love is an act of freedom. God's judgment is not a final trial before a Judge who
knows perfectly the record of each man's life, and sentences each
one in perfect justice. The imagery of such a final judgment has
too much dominated Jewish, Moslem, and Christian belief. Jesus'
use of this dramatic conception (Matt. 25:31-46) was directed
toward a very un-legal lesson; namely, that the basis of God's
judgment of men is not their moral perfection or their religious
orthodoxy, but whether they had or had not shown kindness and
helpfulness to their fellowmen.

The judgment of God upon men is not to be conceived as
consequences or *penalties*. These two ideas belong respectively

to nature and to human society. Man is a part of nature and is subject to "consequences" in his dealings with nature. Certain actions, under certain conditions, have certain consequences; that is what might be called the methodology of nature in its disciplining of man. But it is impersonal; as God's judgment, it is general and indirect. "He makes his sun rise on the evil and on the good, and sends his rain on the just and the unjust" (Matt. 5:45). He also sends death to those on whom the tower of Siloam falls. The consequences of human conduct in dealing with nature are non-moral and non-spiritual. They never directly represent God's judgment.

But neither do the penalties imposed by social authorities of any kind, whether it be public censure or punishment imposed by a court of law, directly constitute God's act of judgment. This human order of moral control is the proper but limited realm of "penalties." It is man's attempt to restrain and to a certain degree to constrain men by moral and legal requirements. Its sanctions are rewards and punishments. Its broad principle is justice. Justice is the imposition of an impersonal rule upon the acts and relations of persons. We have just been showing that the justice is only imperfectly attained. This is due to the limited wisdom and knowledge of men, for justice is always both defined and administered by men. It is also due to the impossibility of apprehending every wrongdoer and bringing him before any judgment seat, whether of public opinion or of a court of law. But a more important thing theologically is the fact that justice itself is a thing that applies only in the relations of man with man, and not in the relations between man and God. Justice is the ideal for the administration of moral laws and sanctions in human society; it is an essentially human concept. When applied to God's dealing with man it inevitably distorts and falsifies. God wills that human governments rule with justice, but justice is not the character of God's dealings with man, except indirectly as he governs man through man. I once heard Emil Brunner say that Martin Luther did a great disservice when he translated *dikaiosune* (righteousness) into German as *Gerecht*, an essentially legal term. A wholly artificial but very disastrous problem is created when we oppose God's justice to his love or mercy. The solution to this problem is not to speak of God's justice; justice is a term that describes a horizontal relation of man with man, not the perpendicular relation of man with God. Justice is the moral equivalent of rationality, and reason and justice are limited each by its own "universe of discourse." "Rationality" applies only to the internal order of a created world (nature); "justice" applies only to the moral order of humanity. The judgment of God, as has been said above, is only indirectly, and never simply, embodied in either nature (consequences) or in morals (penalties). God requires of men justice in their dealings with one another; it is the formal basis of social existence. But it is by no means all that he requires. His full demand is that men love one another.

God's sovereignty over man, the creature made in his own image, is both judgment and grace. This is his direct personal and spiritual relation to man as Lord, and as Redeemer. Both as Lord, or Judge, and as Redeemer, the Christian conception of God has been misunderstood and parodied. On the one hand, God the Lord has been represented as a stern and relentless Judge, as one who is jealous of his own honor and prerogatives, as an "oriental despot." Doubtless much Christian preaching has given grounds for this indictment. On the other hand, God has been pictured as a soft-hearted, indulgent heavenly Parent whose sentimental regard for men is such as to unfit him to be the moral governor of the world. This latter representation was a scandal in earliest times. The cross, representing the good man suffering punishment for the sake of undeserving sinners, was "a stumbling-block to Jews and folly to Gentiles [Greeks]" (I Cor. 1:23). There is more offense to the religious and moral conscience in the "soft" side of God than in the "hard" side.

Theologians who see God as Judge and Savior must reconcile "justice" and "grace." How can God be a God of love, and also a just Judge? How can justice and mercy be reconciled? How can God be at once just and merciful? The wrath of God as manifestation of his judgment seems to drive men from him while his grace draws them to him. Indeed, it seems shocking even to speak of the wrath of God. For is he not a God of love? Both the Christian believer and the theologian seem involved here in an insoluble dilemma. A current popular tendency is to discard the whole idea of wrath and judgment, and to speak of God as pure love, to the point of completely sentimentalizing God; rejecting the whole idea of his "hardness" and frankly accepting his "softness" even though it means unmoral indulgence. But the theologian cannot abandon the idea of divine judgment without denying the God both of the Old and of the New Testament.

Light will be thrown on this problem when we remember that God is a God of truth *and* of love. Anders Nygren has done an incalculable service to Christian doctrine by showing so clearly the difference between *eros* (desire) and love as *agape* (self-giving). *Agape* is the uniquely Christian word. God is not *eros* but *agape*. This illuminates and clarifies our understanding both of God's love for man and of the love that constrains the Christian to serve his fellowman. But the issue still remains between God's love, even as *agape*, and his wrath. Can the God of *agape* also be a God of wrath? Fundamental as *agape* is to the nature of God, it needs to be supplemented by truth; for God is a God of truth as well as a God of love. Indeed in God as Spiritual Person is the perfect unity of truth and love. These two principles ought not to be set over against each other. They do, indeed, create a tension, even in God. But it is the creative and redemptive tension that is found in the life of Christ and in the cross.

Because God is truth, he knows us for what we are; this is his judgment. God cannot lie; he cannot say we are righteous when we are not. God renders "just" judgment because he sees and knows us as we are. But this is not an impersonal judgment; it is wholly personal. It is the judgment of the God who cares for us infinitely. God's love is a personal passion of concern; it is not a general benevolence expressed in principles. But in just the degree to which God infinitely cares for man, the judgment of truth that he makes of each man is wrath. However, wrath is not hate but the negative expression of love. The wrath of God is the passionate condemnation of the sin in man which separates man from God. This is inevitable if the ultimate relation of God to man is spiritual-personal. The wrath of God, therefore, in all seriousness and reality, is his resistance to the sinner whom he loves and whose responsive love and obedience he seeks. If God's reign over

men were that of a remote, just God serenely making dispassionate judgments, "wrath" would be an irrelevant term to apply to
him. But this would not be the personal God of the Christian
faith; it would be the Absolute of the philosopher. The whole
issue of the spiritual-personal character of the Christian God is
involved in this matter of love and wrath, a pair that cannot be
separated so long as God is God of truth and man is a sinner.[2]

The distinction between love as *eros*, or desire, and love as
agape, or self-giving, is significant here as in other connections.
The opposite of *eros* is hate; so we can set *eros* and hate over
against each other. But the opposite of *agape* is not hate but
wrath, which is not a true opposite but a negative form of love
itself. This is seen in the fact that the true opposite of *eros*—
hate—is destructive of its object. Jesus made hate equivalent with
murder. Whatever or whomever we hate we want to destroy.
But this is not true of *agape*. The wrath which one feels toward
the person he loves is not destructive but redemptive. So a mother
passionately opposes her child in his lying, or meanness, or
cruelty. Because she loves him she cannot tolerate his being like
that; she may keep her temper, and use the best pedagogical wisdom in dealing with the faults, but her resistance to the boy as
he is is passionate just because she loves him. If our love is *eros*
we cannot both love and hate the same person at the same time.
The two may alternate, but they cannot co-exist. But if our love
is *agape*, we can both love and be angry toward the same person
at the same time, and we often are. God loves, but he does
not hate.

The judgment of God is his wrath, or anger, his personal "hot
displeasure," his fierce condemnation of us as we are. This is a
direct personal matter. It is the divine punishment. But we must
hasten to say that this "punishment" is not to be equated or
identified with the *consequences* of nature or the *penalties* of
human society. Natural calamities are not divine punishments.
Men who have a guilty conscience may be shocked by such

---

[2] Cf. Emil Brunner, *The Mediator*, Philadelphia, 1947, p. 478. "To reject the
idea of the wrath of God also means to reject His love...God is angry
because He is personal, because He really loves."

calamities, seeing them as deserved punishment, and being moved
to confession of their sins and repentance toward God. Neither
are the judgments which men make upon us a sure sign of divine
disfavor. They may well awake us to the fact that we are sinners
and prompt us to seek God in penitence, although they too often
stir resentment and the impulse to self-justification.[3]

The judgment of God in wrath is essentially and wholly personal; in our sin we turn away from God, we deny him or rebel
against him. He does not strike us down with some disease, or set
men against us. He simply and terribly "turns his face away." He
withdraws from us. Or, to change the figure, if he looks upon us
it is with anger and condemnation. The personal relation with
God which is our life has been broken by our sin; he is against us.
Yet we cannot really get away from him; our very existence as
spiritual persons consists in relation to him. And we cannot be
indifferent to God; even less can we be so than to the earth upon
which we stand. God will not let us go. He will not simply thrust
us away and ignore us. But this is not because he needs us as we
need him; it is because he loves us.

Someone may say, "Then the judgment of God is only his
personal feeling toward us. That is unfortunate, but so long as
there is no substantial punishment in the form of natural loss or
injury, and no penalty such as fine or imprisonment, and perhaps
not even the disfavor of our friends, we can go on without being
too much disturbed about it." Meanwhile the rational moralist
will say, "If this is all the judgment of God is, then it is a pretty
weak thing; it is almost as though he had no real power and exercised no real sovereignty over the world. This is a demoralizing
sentimentalism; the government of God must be more stern, and
his punishment for sin more swift and visible. This is the scandal
of the cross; it shows the weakness, not the strength of God."
There are two things to say in reply to this indictment. The first
is that, as pointed out above, God in his indirect rule of men

[3] Cf. W. E. Hocking, *The Coming World Civilization*, New York, 1956, p. 7.
"The state of today is at a loss for a satisfactory—shall we say technique?—
in dealing with crime....It can apply the penalties. But is cannot punish...
only the good man can be punished. And he would be better without the
penalty—he is punished by the judgment."

THE LORD OF CREATION

through nature and its consequences, and through human society and its penalties, has set bounds and provided a rough but effective means of control and discipline over mankind.

But for the personal being, all natural and worldly goods are less than the love and fellowship of other persons, men and God; and the most terrible punishment is rejection by other persons, men and God. So, a man may provide for his wife all the comforts she may desire, and may do everything the formal duty of a husband may demand; but if his heart is turned away from her, he has struck her the ultimate blow. On the other hand, though he may fail through misfortune or sickness to provide at all, and indeed need to be provided for, if he still loves her, she can find peace and strength in the unbroken bond of love. This personal relation is hidden behind many impersonal, conventional forms, but it is the real life of man. Even more is it the real relation between God and man. The Creator rules the creation, God is the Lord of history, but both the creation and the redemption of man are accomplished in a direct personal act of God. The real predicament of man, which we shall discuss later, is this alienation from God which is the essence of his sin, and the terrible state of having the God of infinite goodness and love turn his face away, or look upon man in anger. No natural calamities or human penalties are so terrible, nor can they so strike at the heart of human existence.

But the rule of God over man is not only judgment, it is also grace. Grace is the positive manifestation of his love. Luther calls wrath the *opus alienum* (the alien work) and grace the *opus proprium* (the natural work) of God. Grace is the positive expression of God's love, and even wrath is redemptive because God loves the sinner. The heart of the Christian revelation might well be summed up in the affirmation of Paul in Romans 5:7, that "while we were yet sinners, Christ died for the ungodly." This is the stumbling block of the cross for the Jews, and the foolishness of God for the Greeks. The story of the grace of God is what is called in theology the doctrine of redemption, so we now turn from the discussion of God as Lord to the exposition of his work of redemption. God is Creator and Lord of the world; he is the sovereign Ruler of men; but he is also the Savior of men. The incarnation of God in Christ is revelation; but it is specifically revelation of God as Savior. We must therefore turn now to Jesus Christ and think of his person and work as the incarnation of God and the Savior of men.

CHAPTER VIII

GOD IN CHRIST

CHRISTIAN FAITH is faith in Jesus Christ. Thus the ultimate object of Christian faith is not a doctrine nor a rational interpretation of the world, life, or religious experience. All of these enter in to the specific form of Christian faith, but the objective and controlling reality is not an idea but a person, the Person of Christ. Knowledge of Christ is not derived from knowledge of the world, nor from a profound analysis of the human spirit; it comes through the historic event of Jesus Christ, and the testimony of those who knew him; it is historic in character. But it is also a knowledge of faith. Those who saw and heard Jesus Christ "in the flesh" knew him as the revelation and the act of God "by faith." Their knowledge was thus deeply personal, and it was from the beginning the knowledge of a community, a community of faith. Jesus in his teaching ministry is seldom found talking with an individual; he addresses mainly chance gatherings of men, that is, he spoke to men as they are in common life. His appearances after the resurrection were, with one exception (Paul), to groups of those who believed in him. He did not choose and instruct *a* successor, but twelve apostles (missionaries) who bore corporate witness to his teaching and witnessed to his reality as the risen Lord. His disciples are not separate individuals but a "congregation," a Church.

The "faith" of the Christian community was faith in the present and active God whom they knew in Christ. It is the faith of those who never saw or heard Jesus, but who believe in him through the witness of the apostles, believe not because of the clarity and completeness, or the rationally convincing character of that witness, but because of their response of faith to the God who is immediately present. Their faith, therefore, is the same as the faith of the apostles; it is a response to the self-revealing act of God in the historic life of Jesus Christ.

Faith in Christ is faith in his teachings, faith in him as "a teacher come from God" (John 3:2), as one who had "authority" (Matt. 7:28). He spoke simply and vividly about the deepest matters. Much of his teaching was occasional, response to a question, or teaching addressed to a group gathered without previous planning and announcement. He did not teach any "system." It would be hard to say what he taught in terms of our present-day departmentalizing of knowledge. He certainly did not teach science or philosophy. He did not even teach ethics. And it is remarkable that not only did he not teach religion; most of the comments he had to make on religion were critical and some of them caustic. The religion he observed, especially in its official representatives and interpreters, was to a large extent a barrier between men and God.

The subject with which Jesus dealt constantly and directly was life, the life of man with man and the life of man with God. It was wholly practical teaching; in it Jesus was briefing men for life, for both the immediate act of the present, and for the ultimate meaning and destiny of man. He followed the usual forms of teaching in his day, forms still common in the Orient—precept and parable—and he was master of both. The authority with which Jesus taught was both the authority of truth that shines by its own light, and the authority of the prophet, one who speaks in the name of God. In the name of the living God, Jesus said, "It was said to them of old times ... but I say unto you," and thus radically reinterpreted the orthodox tradition. The "I say unto you" is the quiet assumption of primary authority to speak of God and man, and to speak for God to man.

Jesus held these teachings to be of the greatest importance. The sermon on the mount closes with a parable, the parable of the two builders, and Jesus says, "Everyone then who hears these words of mine and does them will be like the wise man who built his house upon the rock, ... And every one who hears these words of mine and does not do them will be like a foolish man who built his house upon the sand" (Matt. 7:24, 26). Faith in Jesus Christ is, to begin with, faith in him as the teacher sent from God, who taught the truth about man and God, and the true nature of the relation between God and man, and between man and man. No theological development of the meaning of Christian faith can dispense with or treat lightly this body of teaching given so occasionally and fragmentarily, and in such diverse ways. It remains the origin and point of reference for both Christian doctrine and Christian ethics.

Faith in Christ is also faith in him personally as Lord. The teaching is inseparable from the teacher. He said to his disciples not only, "Do what I say." He also said, "Follow me." His disciples (learners) are also his followers (doers). The truths Jesus taught are not only illuminated by his life; they are embodied in his life. Their truth is living truth because he lived it. He said, "Love your enemies," and he loved his enemies. He said, "Take up your cross and follow me," and he went to his cross. He said, "Except a grain of wheat fall into the ground and die it will bear no fruit," and he died that he might bear fruit. He paid the price of ultimate leadership; he went before and did all that he demanded of his disciples. So his demands were justified: "You call me master and lord, and you say well for so I am"; "Give up all and follow me." It is remarkable that the one who spoke these words, and made these demands upon his followers was completely devoid of what we ordinarily call egotism and self-seeking. The words of the prophet were applied to him, "A bruised reed he will not break, and smoking flax he will not quench." He was "meek and lowly." Evidently the fifty-third chapter of Isaiah is fulfilled in him. Yet it was this meek and gentle man, who sought no possessions, or glory, or power in the world, who said to his disciples, "If any man would come after me, let him deny himself and take up his cross and follow me" (Mark 8:34); who spoke with the authority of God in the demands he made upon men, and in the forgiving of sins to those who put their faith in him. "My kingdom is not of this world." His kingdom is the Kingdom of God.

The Christian, therefore, believes in Jesus Christ as Lord and

Master. This is the point at which religious faith transcends all
secular and rational ethics. This, in particular, contradicts the
whole Kantian tradition, the very foundation of which is the
autonomy of the "rational moral will." No "other" can command
such an autonomous will; that would be heteronomy! But Jesus
Christ is an other who will have as disciples only those who sur-
render their wills to him. But this is an inadequate way of putting
the matter. It is not a matter of two wills, Christ's will and mine,
or yours. It is two persons. If life is to move within the limits of
the Kantian system, or any rationalistic or naturalistic system, we
do have the "will" contending with "nature" or some other element in man and his environment. This way of viewing goodness
has even led to the doctrine of God as a Good Will struggling
with a Given, or a surd, element in his own nature, as in the religious philosophy of E. S. Brightman.[1]

Both Kant and Brightman believed that they were setting forth
the real meaning of religion and specifically of the Christian religion. But what they and many others have actually done, indeed
the whole import of nineteenth-century philosophy of religion, is
to substitute for the objective personalism of Christian faith a
subjective rationalism, the principle and method of which are
analysis of the unity of consciousness. But the "will" is not an
autonomous agent within the human person, naturally rational
and good, that tries more or less successfully to discipline and
order the appetites and impulses of "nature." "Will" is simply a
word to designate the determination of a person to act. As said
above, it is not the will that is free, but the whole person. Christian faith deals, and has always dealt, not with some "faculty" of
man such as the will but with the whole man, the person. Jesus
Christ called men; he did not just challenge wills. It is not, therefore, a submission of our wills to his that he seeks, but our obedience to him, our trust in him, our following him. If we use the
word "will" it ought to be used as a verb, not as a noun. Christ's
will for us is what *he* commands *us* to do and to be; this can be
expressed as he himself summarized it, in the requirement to love
God and our neighbor; it can be seen elaborated and illustrated
by his whole body of teaching and by his life. We follow *him;*

[1] E. S. Brightman, *A Philosophy of Religion,* New York, 1940, pp. 336ff.

he is our Lord. Tennyson's well known lines are cast in the language of that philosophical tradition that sets the will over against something else, not someone else. "Our wills are ours we know not how; Our wills are ours to make them thine." This is a half truth continuing a mischief with the Christian faith that ought to be discarded. What we should say, rather, is something like this (which is not poetry, but theology): "Thou hast made us free, but we do not know how to use our freedom, and so have come into bondage to sin. But thou hast sent to us one whom we acknowledge as Lord, and so find the freedom that we had lost." It is ourselves in our wholeness, including the act or decision which we call "will," that we make his.

He is our friend, but not as an equal. "You are my friends," said Jesus, "if you do what I command you" (John 15:14). It is one of those absurdities we find in Jesus' conduct that he could wash his disciples' feet, and then say, "You call me master and lord, and you say well, for so I am." Another such saying goes to the root of the matter, "I am among you as one who serves" (Luke 22:27). No lowliness or humility, however, is ever allowed to hide his assumption of unconditional authority over those who believed in him. Nor did he ever accept a disciple upon any other basis. The complaint of religious leaders that he had called himself the son of God and so had made himself "equal with God" (John 5:18), was quite justified. That is just what he did. He demanded an unreserved obedience that man can give only to God. It is this person, Jesus Christ, who is acknowledged as Lord by the Christian. Who he was and what he did are of supreme importance. He suffered under Pontius Pilate, he was crucified; he died and was buried; he rose again and is the living Lord of men. The life of the Christian is frankly heteronomous; another rules it. The supreme duty of the Christian is to obey him and to follow him. "It is enough for the disciple to be like his teacher, and the servant like his master" (Matt. 10:25).

But belief in Christ is more even than believing in him as Lord and Master. It is belief in him as Savior. "You shall call his name Jesus, for he will save his people from their sins" (Matt. 1:21). We may freely accept his teachings as true; we may accept his own estimate of them in the parable of the two builders. But this alone will lead us to despair; the very completeness and perfection of his teaching condemn us, for we have not the power to follow it, and everything hangs on that. So we see only one end for the house that we have built; the storms of life and death will sweep it away. The perfection of a superhuman goodness, truly set forth in the teachings of Jesus and lived in his life, leads us to moral despair.

But, we may say, these teachings are richly fulfilled in Jesus Christ himself, and he is our Lord. We can follow him and he will help us. But the man Jesus is not here; the Master left his disciples to live their own lives. As an historic person Jesus looms large as the one who attained. But he is not here to meet us at close of day and comfort us for our failures, and in the morning to send us forth with new courage born of his touch and word, and with his personal presence. This kind of "heteronomy" Jesus was not willing to exercise. He not only could not always be with his disciples "in the flesh"; but it was expedient, he said, that he go away. This historic presence must be given; it must also be taken away. "If I do not go away, the counsellor will not come to you" (John 16:7). The moral authority and the earthly presence of Christ as teacher and Lord, must be transformed into a direct relationship with God which is mediated by his death and resurrection, and by the "coming of the Holy Spirit."

The "autonomy of the rational moral will," which is freely surrendered in the disciples' unconditional obedience to Christ as Lord, is replaced by something much greater, a personal relation to God immediately present within the believer as Holy Spirit. This is true freedom, not a theoretical freedom of the will, but a real freedom of the human spirit, of the person, in a redeemed and transformed relation to God. This is what Christ does as Savior. He does not give to his disciples the power to be morally perfect or sinless; but he does bring them to repentance and the forgiveness of their sins. He brings them into a new relationship with one another, and into communion with God. He saves men from sin and death.

Jesus Christ is teacher, Lord, and Savior. This is the Christian confession. But here he stands in the place of God. He does what only God can do. So from the beginning Jesus was acknowledged as the Messiah, the Christ, the Son of God. Paul summed up the meaning of Christ in the phrase, "God was in Christ reconciling the world to himself" (II Cor. 5:19). How can the man Jesus be the Son of God? How can Jesus Christ be God? How can God be incarnated in a man? The Christian Church has always affirmed that these statements are true. They were first made not as theological propositions, but as religious affirmations—affirmations of faith. In the New Testament we see this faith clearly expressed, most consciously in the Pauline and Johannine literature. There is no doctrine of a Trinity, no theory of the person of Christ; but there does appear the formula: "Father, Son, and Holy Spirit" (Matt. 28:19). The benediction perhaps most commonly used throughout the Christian world was first used by Paul at the end of the second letter to the Corinthians: "The grace of the Lord Jesus Christ and the love of God and the fellowship of the Holy Spirit be with you all." The striking thing about this benediction is that Paul puts the "Lord Jesus Christ" first. At the end of the first letter to the Corinthians he simply writes, "The grace of the Lord Jesus be with you."

It is this faith that precipitated and precipitates questions which lead to the formulations of two doctrines: the doctrine of God and the doctrine of the Person of Christ. It is the truth of these two doctrines that we must now seek. They represent respectively the theology and the christology of the Christian faith. The first was formulated in what is known as the doctrine of the Trinity at the councils of Nicaea (325) and Constantinople (381). The christology got its final form at the council of Chalcedon in 451. Orthodox Christianity has held to these two formulas, although with wide diversity of interpretation. There has also been a persistent revolt against them in what may be generally called the arian or unitarian movement. The doctrine of the Trinity affirms that Father, Son, and Holy Spirit are three Persons but one Substance. Or, as originally stated in the Greek language, there are three *hypostases* (persons) in one *ousia* (substance). You do not confuse the persons nor divide the substance. The Father is not the Son, the Son is not the Holy Spirit, the Holy Spirit is not the Father, etc. The council of Chalcedon declared that there is one Lord Jesus Christ, a complete divine

nature and a complete human nature united in one Person. The
two natures are not to be either mingled or separated. Here the
warning is not to divide the person or to confuse the natures.
Unless one has followed with some care the course of thinking
that issued in these two creeds it is all likely to be confusing,
especially since in the one, "person" is used for the plurality and
distinctness, while in the other, "person" represents the ultimate
unity.

It is not my intention to go into a discussion of even recent
developments in the interpretation of these two basic doctrines,
but rather to make some comments on the use of terms, and then
to set forth the meaning of both doctrines in terms of the spiritual person. The origin of orthodox theology and christology is to
be found not in speculative thought but in the religious faith and
worship of the new Christian Church. We have already seen how
the early disciples in practice identified Jesus Christ with God.
They were already believers in the one God of Jewish faith,
whom Jesus called Father. But a new aspect of deity became of
commanding importance at the very beginning of the Christian
Church, namely the Holy Spirit. The day of Pentecost is the real
beginning of the Church; there the Church was created and au-
thenticated by an ecstatic experience of the Holy Spirit. The book
of Acts is the book of the Holy Spirit. The Spirit not only moved
missionaries to make their witness, but it (or he) gave specific
direction to Philip, to Peter, and especially to Paul. The Spirit led
Peter and Paul across the boundary between Jew and Gentile
and validated their preaching of Christ to the non-Jews. Paul's
final argument for the reception of the Gentiles into the Church
was that God had given them the Holy Spirit. The early Church
was without official clergy, liturgy, and theology, but it had the
Holy Spirit. After baptism the baptizer laid hands on the con-
vert and said, "Receive the Holy Spirit." Thus for these first
Christians the Holy Spirit was real and potent; they "lived by
the Spirit."

These Christians were monotheists, in contrast to the polytheism that was almost universal in their world. But they worshipped God the Father, they acknowledged God the Son as
Savior, and they knew the personal presence and help of God

the Holy Spirit. The theoretical problem of three "persons" being one God does not seem to have been then or later any problem for practical religion. The word "person" of course was not known, nor was any such general term employed. The form in which non-Christians criticized the Christian faith was the charge that they worshipped three gods. The official formulas adopted at Nicaea, Constantinople, and Chalcedon, despite a persistent arian (unitarian) movement and the separation of the Nestorian Church, provided a definition of orthodox belief that has been held by the greater part of the Christian world down to the present time. Roman Catholic, Eastern Orthodox, and Protestant bodies generally accept these creedal definitions or declarations.

However, there arose in the nineteenth century a new method and approach to the interpretation of religion in general, and specifically, of course, of the Christian religion. This was a result of the Enlightenment, and more distantly of the Renaissance. The essence of this movement was the assertion of the competence of human reason to know, and a repudiation of dogmatic authority, first in art and politics, then in the knowledge of nature, and finally in matters of religious belief as well. Culturally and traditionally Europe was Christian. The Protestant Reformation, although it had denied the power of the Church of Rome to define authoritatively the Christian faith, had held to the essential creedal forms of that faith, never questioning, for example, the two doctrines we are now discussing. Within the Protestant countries of Europe, especially Germany and Britain, there were or there arose universities where freedom of philosophical and theological thought prevailed—to a degree, of course. We have mentioned in Chapter II the rise of rationalism which assumed to give knowledge of God by pure reason; and also the "Kantian revolution" which destroyed this boast of objective rationalism and produced the period of subjective rationalism. This latter period was interested in religion *as* religion, and the philosophers derived theories of the nature of religion from an analysis of the religious consciousness. The three main lines of this development, as has been shown above, followed, respectively, Kant, Schleiermacher, and Hegel. Thus the nineteenth century produced what Karl Barth called neo-Protestantism. This religious development not only rejected the dogmatic theology of the Church, Protestant and Roman Catholic, but it also denied the claims of the rationalists to know God by pure reason. In place of dogma and objective reason it put "experience." It accepted the empirical method of science, and the doctrine of evolution. The essential problem of this philosophy of religion was to validate belief in God as a personal, creative Spirit. Its position was that of Theism, as against materialism, naturalism, and atheism. Liberal Protestant thought, so far as it had a theology, was theistic. So at the turn of the century Charles Carroll Everett was lecturing at Harvard on "Theism and the Christian Faith."

Thus the heritage of modern Protestant liberalism is the belief in a personal God which is called Theism. The God of Theism is personal. He is also One. For this form of religious philosophy the doctrines of the Trinity and the Chalcedonian christology are of only historic interest. The issue is not the three Persons and their unity in the one God, but the validity of belief in *a* Personal Spirit who is not simply a generalization from the nature of the world, but in some sense transcendent to and even Creator of the world. The defense of this belief in a personal God is based, indeed, upon religious experience, but its methods and materials are derived from idealistic philosophy. Personal Idealism is a philosophical position; its fundamental assertion is the existence and reality of the one, supreme, personal God. Strictly speaking, and technically speaking, this is unitarianism. There are not three personal Gods, but One. And the two-nature doctrine of the person of Christ seems meaningless because "personality" has the same essential definition whether attributed to man or God, the only difference being the degree of completeness or perfection. God is the perfect, infinite Person; men are imperfect, finite persons; this is God's "nature," this is man's "nature." When, therefore, a man appears in history who is perfect in his personal life, he reveals in this perfect personality *the* nature, not the *two* natures of both God and man, that is, personality in its perfection. In this theology of Personal Idealism both the problem of the Trinity and that of Chalcedonian christology disappear.

But this was too facile a solution of the real issue. It is not union of the "nature" of God and the "nature" of man that is involved in the Christian faith; it is God, the Spiritual Person who is distinct from and transcendent to all men, and Jesus of Nazareth, a human person who is said to be the Son of God, or a man in whom God dwelt. God is an Other for Jesus; Jesus is an other to whom God comes, or whom God sends, or in whom God is incarnate. This is the real faith of the Christian. Both the ancient creeds and modern Personal Idealism fail to cope fully with this fundamental fact. The failure of the ancient creeds was due primarily to a deficiency of adequate categories. What the theologians were trying to say in abstract language was that the faith of the Christian Church was true; but they were trying to express the truth of the faith in abstract terms. The faith all accepted, namely that God the Creator was incarnate in Christ and present to the believer as Holy Spirit. Incidentally, there was no dispute about the Holy Spirit; the essential issue was the real and unequivocal deity of the Son. When the theologians, now heirs of Greek philosophical thought, tried to say that this Christian faith was true and also that there is one God, they employed terms developed in a critical philosophy of nature. *Ousia* and "substance" represent the metaphysical base and origin of all reality; they are essentially physical terms. They are also rational terms; "rational" and "natural" are co-ordinate terms, so "being" (*ousia*), the ultimate category of reason, is also "substance," the metaphysical subject and support of all that exists. One word is Greek, the other Latin, and both are used to mean both the conceptual and the metaphysical ultimate.

The other term in the trinitarian formula was *hypostasis* (Greek) or "person" (Latin). (Literally, *hypostasis* is exactly the same word as the Latin "substance." [2] This is just an added element of confusion in the terminology employed.) It was the Latin word "person," however, which in Western theology represented the three: Father, Son, and Holy Spirit. The doctrine asserts, then, that there are three "persons" but that together they are one God. What is a "person"? Volumes have been written on this question; this one is, in a way, another of them. I hope it

[2] "Person" and "substance" are, of course, Anglicized forms of the Latin *persona* and *substantia*.

does something to clarify the issue, or at least not add to the confusion. As a matter of fact, none of the councils ever defined the term. Nor has the Church, Catholic or Protestant, undertaken to do so. However, "person" as used by the creed makers certainly did not mean what Boethius defined a person to be, namely, "an individual substance of a rational nature." Nor did it mean the unity of consciousness as in modern idealism. Still less did it mean the "psyche" of psychology or psychosomatic medicine.

If one may venture to demythologize the language of Nicaea and Chalcedon, and also to dephilosophize it, one may say that what the word "person" meant was that there are three fundamental acts or relations of God, all of which are fully accepted by the Christian faith, *and* that it is one and the same God who acts in each instance. God creates and governs the world: God is Father. God is incarnate in Jesus; God is the Son. God dwells in the man of faith as an immediate presence; God is Holy Spirit. But it is the same God who in all these acts or relations manifests himself.

This certainly would not have satisfied the ancient theologians, nor the orthodox theologians of any later time. The three "persons" are "hypostatized," and doctrine has made much and still does make much of the relation of the Father to the Son and of the Son to the Father. A literal pre-existence of three "parties" in the Godhead, as well as the hypostatizing of the threefold act of God in Creation, Redemption, and In-dwelling has been taken to be essential to the full validity of the Christian faith. This leads close to tritheism, and even seems to eventuate in that situation. The "social trinity" of many present-day Anglicans is really a doctrine of three Gods united in perfect communion.[3] A less literal kind of hypostatic distinction betwen the three persons is derived essentially from Augustine. Augustine suggested many sets of three, such as the sun, its light, and its heat, as more or less remote analogies of the Trinity, but found in the complex unity of consciousness the nearest analogy (although it must always be remembered that he refused to accept this as really disclosing the mystery of the Trinity). He finds in the mind memory, will, and love. "Memory" seems to be just the basic

[3] For example, L. Hodgson, *The Doctrine of the Trinity*, New York, 1944.

consciousness. I am, I will to be, and I love my being and my willing to be. But here are not three "persons" as Augustine was quick to assert. Today theologians bent on preserving the trinitarian faith point out that God is love, and if this is his eternal nature, then there must always have been a Father to love and a Son to be loved. Here are two persons of the Trinity; the third person is the love between the Father and the Son.

I have difficulties at two points with this argument. One is the hypostatizing of the relation of love, i.e. between Father and Son. Love is certainly personal but it is not *a* person. On the other hand, why must God be Father and Son to be love eternally? We may say that man's sin is self-love, that he loves himself. If man can love himself and does so, why cannot the eternal God love himself? Aristotle's very rational God spends eternity in self-contemplation. Is self-love any more difficult than self-knowledge? If it is necessary for another person (the Son) to be present in order that God should be eternally love, then is not the argument of Tennant valid that the world is as necessary to God (if he is to be Creator) as God is to the world? It seems to me that neither of these arguments is valid, and that they reduce the life of God to terms of finite existence.

Let us then make a new approach to the whole matter, not in terms derived from the knowledge of nature or of finite persons, but in terms derived directly from the life of the spirit. An insight of St. Paul seems to have been overlooked in this theological venture. The interpretation I shall make might be considered a sort of theological homily on these words of St. Paul: "For what person knows a man's thoughts except the spirit of the man which is in him? So also no one comprehends the thoughts of God except the Spirit of God. Now we have received not the spirit of the world, but the Spirit which is from God, that we might understand the gifts bestowed on us by God. And we impart this in words not taught by human wisdom but taught by the Spirit, interpreting spiritual truths to those who possess the Spirit" (I Cor. 2:11-13). The "natural" (psychic) man, says Paul, does not share in this wisdom. I do not think that we have to do here with some form of mysticism or irrationalism, but directly with the nature of spirit, or what I have called the spiritual person, the one who acts, who sustains relations with other persons, whose nature and acts cannot be truly represented in the categories of "nature" or "reason," taking those terms in their technical sense. The "mind of Christ" is not the rational intellect, but the knowledge of spiritual actors (persons) and their relations of love and grace, of sin and redemption.

The conception of "Spirit" which was central with Paul seems to have been almost completely ignored by early theology, and later theology also, and the theologians have created doctrine in terms of what Paul called the wisdom of this world, despite his warning that in this wisdom the world "knew not God." It is true that "Spirit" is not defined or theoretically discussed in the New Testament any more than "person" is, but the New Testament is full of the Spirit. In the formulation of the Nicaean creed the Holy Spirit is included as one of the "persons," but as a "poor third." The interest lay wholly in Father and Son. Perhaps there is no element in Christian faith which is so vague for most Christians as the Holy Spirit. I once heard a layman explain it as the holy "disposition." I have heard more than one minister of the gospel confess that the Holy Spirit had little if any meaning for him. Recent writers on the subject usually begin by pointing out that this is the neglected point in Christian theology.

Yet Jesus said, "God is Spirit." This has often been hailed as a profound utterance. Certainly all Christians would accept it. God is Spirit, the one God who creates and rules the world is Spirit. Personal Idealism was certainly on solid ground when it contended for the existence and reality of God as Person. But that position seemed to be too much defined and expounded in relation to the world of "nature." And the nature of personality is defined in terms of subjective rationalism (called idealism) as the unity of consciousness. As suggested above this made meaningless the idea of three persons in the Godhead; but it also stopped with the nature of personality, its functions, qualities, etc., and it ignored the supremely important thing, the relation of person to person. Thus the direct reality of the Christian faith was clouded, for that faith is not concerned with the idea of personality, with its inner structure, etc; it is concerned with the act of *the* Person, God, and with his dealings with us human persons. This is concrete not abstract, practical not theoretical concern, and not for "personality" as such, but for this person and that person, and above all for *the* divine Person, God. The Christian faith is concerned with the *act* of human persons, sin; with the demand of God for obedience; with the act of repentance, which is not just a change of mind (*metanoia*), but a "return" to God. It glories in love and grace and forgiveness, and in reconciliation. This Christian terminology was either dropped entirely or else interpreted "spiritually" (of all words, using the spirit to repudiate the spirit!). That is, the basic words and ideas of the actual life of persons and their relations were replaced by the abstractions of principle, quality, and function.

Christian faith is not a doctrine of personality; it is faith in God the Spiritual Person, and in his creative and redemptive acts. It is the faith of human persons, made in the image of God, but "gone astray" and needing salvation. It is faith in the Man whom God sent to be the Savior of men, and in the reconciliation of man to God which he effected, not by the sublimity of his teachings, but by his death on the cross.

These observations are needed as an approach to the exposition of the Trinity in terms of the spiritual person. Let us remember that "person" indicates the *subject:* the ultimate subject of action and passion; the subject of thought and action; the responsible subject of relations with other persons. And "spirit" or "spiritual" indicates the wholeness of the person, and what it "is," the "heart" of the person. The living God of Jewish and Christian faith is Spiritual Person. He is One who acts, is related, loves and suffers. The language of philosophy, oriented to a rational absolute, must deny most of these things to God. The Absolute is unrelated, inactive, and of course does not suffer; neither does he (it) love. But the Christian God is wholly obscured by such an Absolute. He is Person; he is Actor; he is Creator; he is Redeemer; he is Comforter. He is Spirit; he is perfectly one with infinite diversity of powers and relations; he is free to create out of nothing and to love, even where there is nothing lovable. All this is involved in the simple statement that God is Spirit, for Spirit is not immaterial substance, impersonal quality, diffused radiance; Spirit is

the reality and completeness and power of Person. The Person
acts by the power of Spirit.

A certain confusion appears in the two things that Christian
theology says of God: (1) God is Spirit, and (2) the Holy Spirit,
the third person of the Trinity, is God. This would seem to lead
to the awkward assertion that the Spirit has a Spirit, or that one
of the "persons" of God who is Spirit, is the Holy Spirit. And yet
no one seems to be troubled by this language; perhaps because it
is traditional; perhaps because the idea of Spirit is so vague that a
looseness of language is justifiable, and even inevitable. But it
seems to me that if we mean by Spirit both the wholeness *and* the
heart, or the inwardness of the Person, these two statements are
not only intelligible, but thoroughly consistent, even complementary. Thus the statement: God is Spirit affirms the perfect
unity of God, his "simplicity" and wholeness, and his freedom to
act in infinite and unmeasured creativity. And the statement: God
is Holy Spirit affirms the power of the Infinite God to be personally present to each and every human person who in faith and
obedience will receive him. The risen Christ created this possibility for men, that is, the possibility of knowing God as immediate and personal presence, the Holy Spirit. "Inwardness" means
simply immediacy of presence. It is only as spirit that one person
can be thus "inward" for another; God the Holy Spirit seeks
such inwardness with each and every one of his human children.
It is a "relation" which is natural to Spirit; indeed it expresses one
basic meaning of Spirit, the other being the wholeness and simplicity of the Person as Agent.

In the light of this discussion of the meaning of Spirit, and of
the affirmation that God is Spiritual Person, we may discover the
essential religious truth of Christian faith which the creed at-
tempted to express while using the essentially inadequate and
misleading categories of a natural-rational philosophy. We can
say unequivocally that there is one God, one divine Person who
is Spirit. What then does it mean to say that God is "three"?
There is a real "trinity" in the acts of God as well as in the religious experience of the Christian Church. But it is the one God
who acts. The Christian knows God as Father (Creator), as Son
(Redeemer), and as Holy Spirit (Comforter). God as Creator is

mediated to man through the creation; that is he deals with man, and is known by man in and through the wonders and powers of "nature." God as Redeemer is mediated to man through a man, Jesus Christ. We might say, through history, for Christ is the central truth of history. God performs his gracious act of forgiveness and salvation in Jesus Christ, the man. The reconciled man has immediate communion with the Creator-Redeemer God. This is God as Holy Spirit. But there are not three "Persons" in the meaning we have given to "Person." This, I think, is what the Nicaean theologians were really feeling for. But whether it was or not it seems to me to be the truth of the self-revelation of God in Christ and its reception by the community of faith. Whatever acts and relations God performs and sustains to this or any other world, the three which are essential in Christian faith are these acts of God as Creator, Redeemer, and Comforter. But it is the same one Spiritual Person, God, who is the subject of them all. This is what it comes to when we demythologize and dephilosophize the doctrine of the Trinity, and when we venture to use the language of Spirit in thinking and talking about God and his dealings with men.

The theological problem of the Trinity arose from the acceptance of Jesus Christ as the Son of God and Savior. Despite the elaborate theoretical form of the discussion the main point is the reality and validity of faith in Christ as Savior. Only God can save; if Christ is Savior he must be God. As Son of God, Christ must be God; not a divine being in any sense second to the Father. The apparent absurdity of Christendom being split over an *iota*, the letter "i" in Greek, is not as absurd as it sounds. The question is whether the Son is of like substance with the Father, or of the same substance (*homoiousios* or *homoousios*). And the ultimate importance of this question is not theoretical but practical; if Christ, the Son, is not unequivocally God, then he is not Savior. The issue of the controversy, of course, was that the Son is declared to be of one substance with the Father. But he is a different Person. The Son is Jesus Christ, God incarnate.

But this decision raised what is the central theoretical question of the Christian faith, the question of the Person of Christ. So theology, beginning with an affirmation of faith about Christ,

made the long and troubled journey in the higher reaches of
theology issuing in the doctrine of the Trinitiy. But that point
having been made, it returns to the previous question: the nature
of Jesus Christ. It had been established that the Son is God,
unequivocally. But Jesus Christ is universally acknowledged to be
a man, the man who suffered under Pontius Pilate, and so on.
The Trinity said God is One, and also, God is Three. The christology said Jesus Christ is a man, and Jesus Christ is God. Now
a doctrine of the person of Christ, paralleling or comparable to
the trinitarian theology, must be worked out. It must not in any
manner or degree deny the humanity of Christ. It must not in any
manner or degree deny the deity of Christ. It must hold to the
universal faith in the One Lord Jesus Christ. Here two—God
and man—must be affirmed in One—Jesus Christ.

What the council of Chalcedon said—and this is still orthodox
Christian doctrine—is that Jesus Christ is one Person (*hypostasis*)
in whom two natures are perfectly united, although each nature
remains complete and distinct. Naturally there were many attempts to explain how these two natures could be united in one
person, but all were rejected. Some tended to qualify or deny the
humanity; some tended to absorb the humanity into the deity.
One, Nestorius, seemed to make such a distinction between the
natures that it resulted in two persons. He refused to say that
Mary was the mother of God (*theotokos*). But all these explana-
tions were rejected and Christendom received the heritage of a
doctrine of Christ as a Person in whom two natures are perfectly
united but also perfectly distinct.

I should like to repeat the comment that the fundamental difficulty of method here lies in the use of categories which are
essentially physical-rational in a realm where personal and spiritual realities are being dealt with. Most orthodox Christians accept
this christology and do not try to explain it. And this is not to be
condemned or wondered at. Every philosophy or theology comes
at last to a mystery or a given, or a "first principle" that is simply
accepted. Philosophy does not like to use the word "mystery"
but theology tends to glory in it, sometimes too much. On the
other hand there have been rationalists who have simply denied
the doctrine and have found the significance of Christ in other

terms, religious or moral. The modern developments which led to liberal Protestantism, as has been shown above, made both doctrines irrelevant, but left us without the reality of a personal God dealing with real human persons. The faith of the Christian Church is that God is revealed in Jesus Christ, that God is incarnate in Christ, that Jesus Christ is the Savior. The thing that is lacking in the liberal doctrine is the positive acknowledgment of God present and active in Christ, so that these affirmations of faith may have clear theological expression. The humanistic and idealistic presuppositions of liberal theories distort the true picture just as much as the rational-natural categories of the orthodox doctrine. Neither objective nor subjective rational terms can express the reality of the incarnation.

The orthodox doctrine defines the incarnation as the "hypostatic union" of God and man in Christ. Further development of this idea has resulted in the strange idea of *anhypostasia,* or the impersonal humanity of Christ. Roman Catholic theology, with characteristic thoroughness and rationality, holds this as official doctrine.[4] Briefly it is this: There is one Person; this Person is the Son, the second Person of the Trinity. As God, he has the full and complete nature of God. But in the incarnation a complete human nature was assumed by the Son and united to the divine nature which was his eternally. In Jesus Christ, therefore, there is no human person, or *hypostasis.* He is not *a* man. The "subject" of his human nature is God the Son. So it can be affirmed that Jesus Christ is fully human, or that his humanity is complete, but that he is not *a* man. The subject of both natures is the Son, who is God. Accordingly God does not suffer in his divine nature in Jesus Christ, he suffers in his human nature. He performs miracles as God; he hungers as man.

Protestants, orthodox or liberal, ought to take account of this doctrine of impersonal humanity. It is the ripe fruit of a method consistently pursued, the scholastic method or rationalism in theology. In this system there are two distinct categories (1) *hypostasis,* or person, or subject, and (2) nature. "Nature" itself is really a dual term; it includes (a) an individual "subsistence,"

---

[4] Cf. George D. Smith, ed., *The Teaching of the Catholic Church,* New York, 1949, vol. 1, chap. XI.

and (b) the general characteristics of humanity. That is, it was this particular "nature," Jesus of Nazareth, which the Son assumed. So there are really three terms: (1) person, (2) subsistence, and (3) nature. It is not said that God, the One God is incarnate in a man, Jesus of Nazareth. There is no union of the one God and any one man; there is union of the natures of God and man, or of humanity and deity. This is a generality, an abstraction. Few Protestants will accept this doctrine, yet it is a logical outworking of the Chalcedonian formula.

The great defect of this doctrine lies in the fact that it does not represent a real union of God and man; it is not a true hypostatic, or personal union. A personal union is a union of persons. A personal union of God and man is the union of a human person and the divine Person. This is most certainly what the Christian faith originally means. Jesus is *a* man, sent of God. He is *the* man chosen by God. He is *a* human person. He is one who can say "I" and address God as "Thou." In the Fourth Gospel, which is intent on setting forth who Jesus Christ is, he says, "The words that I say to you I do not speak on my own authority; but the Father who dwells in me does his works" (John 14:10). This is not one nature speaking of another nature; it is one subject, a man, speaking of another subject, God. It is clear that while he might be acknowledged as the Son of God, as Savior, or even as God, Jesus Christ was for the early Church a man. The Church left it to the theologians to explain how this could be, and the theologians did the best they could with the categories at their command, but the categories were both inadequate and ultimately misleading.

However, if our conception of the spiritual person is sound, it is possible to express the Church's faith in incarnation in terms that are both adequate and true. We will use spiritual words for spiritual things, which Paul counsels us to do. Charles Cochrane says that Christian theology found a "new starting point" in the idea that "while the properties of matter are such that two bodies cannot occupy the same space at the same time, the special characteristic of spirit lies in its permeability." [5] To put this simply,

[5] Charles N. Cochrane, *Christianity and Classical Culture*, New York, 1957, p. 367.

two persons being spirit can be one without ceasing to be two. Or, in Dean Inge's words, "Personality is of such nature as to be distinct but not separate." (This is what I call the spiritual person, not the "personality" of idealism.) The Cappadocian fathers and Hilary of Poitiers, and others, speak of the coinherence of the persons of the Trinity, that is, their mutual inwardness and inclusiveness of each other. Other terms for this oneness of three are *circumincession* and *perichoresis*, Latin and Greek respectively. The idea here expressed is that individuality is not absolute. At the roots of spiritual being we are literally members one of another. It is certainly true that your body is not my body, that your mind is not my mind. Personal Idealism stopped here and declared that personalities are absolutely external to each other. This is in a way true if the personality is simply the unity of consciousness. Here individuality is dominant, although even here it is not absolute, for we do share our consciousness with others. But consciousness is *private;* the "person" in its full reality as spirit is *essentially* open. It exists as a relation to other persons, God, and other men. We have asserted that the creation of the *humanum* was the call of God and the response of man, and that the existence and nature of man are found in responsible relation to God and man. This is one of the great contributions of Emil Brunner to Christian anthropology.[6] It is impossible, therefore, to speak of a complete human nature as distinct from God, for the basic element in human nature is man's relation and response to God. It is true that in men generally this relation and response are only dimly realized and that all men through self-will reject God and so are sinners. It is true also that all men need to be saved from what they actually are to what God created them to be. But man as sinner still is man because he is related to God. Orthodox theology had made the divine and the human natures absolutely different and mutually exclusive. Here the difference is maintained but the *relation* which is constitutive for man is affirmed, and it is not an external relation.

The incarnation means that Jesus of Nazareth, by his own free response, from childhood was one with God, was a true son. He grew in wisdom and stature and in favor with God and man, but

[6] Emil Brunner, *Man in Revolt*, New York, 1939, chap. V.

God always dwelt in him unhindered by disobedience. God the divine Person is always the central Reality of the life, first of the boy and then of the man. By coinherence the man Jesus and the personal God are one. One what? Perhaps the best answer is "one life." This is the language of I John. It is certainly one man, one human person. But this man is what he is because God, the divine Person, is one with him, is "in" him as he is "in" God. (John 14:10: "I am in the Father and the Father in me.") This is true hypostatic or personal union, union not of two natures but of two persons. But one of these persons is God, the original and creative One by whose power all human persons exist and are human. The other person is the man Jesus who is like us in all things, yet without sin. Now sin is precisely the spiritual alienation of man from God, the rejection of God, and his existence under the wrath of God. So, although the sinner's existence as man is dependent on the relation with God, it is a relation of separation and enmity. In Jesus Christ we see the true man, the normal man, the man whose life is one of full and free obedience to God and complete inner unity with God. God is present and active in Jesus Christ. What is done in this human life is the doing of God, not by the displacement of the freedom of the man but by the exercise of that freedom in obedience. What the incarnation means is that God is not far away; that he is near; that he seeks full freedom to dwell within his human children. It is the rest of us who are out of step in this case. The person of Christ is completed in the personal God and becomes a transparent medium through which man can, by faith, see God. His life is the life of God in history.

CHAPTER IX

THE REDEMPTION OF MAN

CHRISTIAN FAITH is faith in Christ; it is faith in God as known in Christ; it is faith in Christ as the Savior of men. We have seen that confession of Christ as Savior was the material point in the faith of the early Church. George Foot Moore, Harvard's great scholar in the field of the history of religion, used to say that the right way to know any religion is to consider it as a way of salvation. This is certainly true of Christianity. The central doctrine in Christian theology is the doctrine of redemption. It determined the theology of Nicaea and the christology of Chalcedon. The two major theologians of the nineteenth century, Schleiermacher and Ritschl, assumed this doctrinal center. Schleiermacher defined Christian faith as faith in Christ as Redeemer; Ritschl's great constructive work was on *Justification and Reconciliation*. It has often been pointed out that the Eastern Church is concerned primarily with incarnation, and the Western Church with redemption. But the two doctrines are two sides of one shield.

Despite this historic development, the later nineteenth and the early twentieth centuries saw increasing emphasis placed on "creative" religion,[1] while "salvation" became a secondary interest. The word itself was seldom used. "Social salvation" was respectable, but salvation in the historic sense, as the act of divine grace and as of central importance in Christian faith, was left to the fundamentalists and the fringe sects. But the terrible experiences and the profound frustrations of the last few decades have re-

[1] Cf. E. W. Lyman, *The Meaning and Truth of Religion*, New York, 1933, pp. 11ff.

vealed to men generally the desperate predicament of man both as
an individual and as a race. Man never had greater power in the
technological sense, or more elaborate knowledge of his own
psyche than he has today, but his total situation seems to be getting more threatening both politically and psychologically. The
evil in human life does not seem now to be incidental; somehow
it appears as a basic condition, what is called in theology original
sin. It is not strange, therefore, that there has been a revival
of historic Christian faith and especially of the doctrine of redemption.

But it must also be admitted that both the common and the
theological conceptions of salvation generally held have been such
as to cause many devout and intelligent Christians, as well as those
not holding the Christian faith, to reject the whole idea. Salvation
commonly has been viewed as the result of a man getting into the
right Church, and holding to correct dogma. It has been thought
of in both magical and moralistic terms. The magical side is that
which has to do with technical correctness theologically, eccle-
siastically, and ritually. The moralistic side is represented in the
idea that a man wins or earns his salvation—gets into heaven—by
his virtues and his good works. Along with such conceptions has
gone a crudely individualistic interest; salvation has meant that
"I" am to be saved. Personal ambition for success in this life has
been extended to the yearning for "glory" in the next life. The
gospel song, "O that will be glory for me," was a frank expression
of this simple self-interest. Thus, on both intellectual and moral
grounds the idea of salvation became repugnant to many people.

Theologically the dominance of essentially commercial and
juridical doctrines of atonement repelled and still does repel many
who are aware of the need of salvation, but cannot believe that
God deals with man in such fashion as these doctrines describe.
I have already stated that conceptions of justice, punishment, and
reward and the inevitability of natural consequences not only do
not directly apply to the dealings of God with man but that, if
so understood, they tragically misrepresent the whole God-man
relationship. If rational-natural concepts distort the idea of God,
it is equally true that juridicial-moralistic concepts do the same
thing for the doctrine of redemption. At no point in our under-

standing of Christian truth is it so necessary to preserve the personal-spiritual point of view as in our formulation of a doctrine
of redemption. In the New Testament many metaphors are employed to communicate the wonderful news of salvation through
Christ; the Jewish sacrificial system, the paying of debts, the
buying and selling of goods, the imprisonment of a criminal, the
victory over an enemy, the healing of a sick man. Paul used most
of these metaphors, but he never identified the fact of salvation
with any one of them. There is a relatively simple theme running
through the whole New Testament account of salvation and that
theme is the gracious act of the Heavenly Father in forgiving
men their sins and receiving them back into his fellowship and
favor. This is essentially a purely personal matter; it is in these
terms that the Christian gospel of salvation can be most truly
expressed and understood.

God's act of creation is inseparable from his act of redemption.
Just as God's rule of the world is a creative and immanent sovereignty, so in his dealings with man creation is completed in
redemption. Schleiermacher saw the appearance of the Redeemer
in history as the completion of creation. But it is the appearance
of the *Redeemer;* it is not just the coming of a complete and
perfect man; it is the initiation among men of the work of redemption. Redemption is the final achievement of creation. God's
creative act is, from the beginning, redemptive. The redemption of man, therefore, is for God re-creation and for man
regeneration.

Paul's scheme expresses this relation of creation and redemption. "The first man Adam became a living being; the last Adam
became a life-giving spirit" (I Cor. 15:45). In the Fourth Gospel
Jesus says to Nicodemus, "You must be born again." Paul writes,
"If any one is in Christ he is a new creation" (II Cor. 5:17).
Note: not a new being but a new creation. This biblical and
theological conception of re-creation or regeneration has support
both in the psychology of the individual and in the history of
the race. Early writers on the psychology of religion, James, Coe,
Starbuck, and others, found a normal co-ordination between adolescence and conversion; certainly the period of adolescence is a
time of psychological, perhaps we should say psychosomatic,

reorganization. The racial parallel to this psychological "conversion" in religious faith is treated profoundly in a review article
by Jacob Taubes which appeared in the *Journal of Religion* in
April 1954.

> In the mythical stage of religion the divine presence can be experi-
> enced without recourse to ecstatic meditation or philosophical specula-
> tion... the abyss between the human and the divine has not become
> manifest in man's consciousness.... Religion in the classical sense of
> the term presupposes that the mythical harmony and unity of man,
> universe and God is broken and man left isolated from the other
> elements.... Man's alienation from the divine marks the crisis of the
> mythical consciousness, be it expressed in general skepticism or in the
> emergence of monotheistic religions. (p. 123)

The Christian doctrine of redemption deals with a "lostness"
of man which is manifest in the development of the individual,
in the religious history of the race, and, one might add, in the
light of the present-day dilemma of man, in the demonic aspects
of social and political existence. Christian faith does not deny or
discount any of these problems of man's personal and racial struggle. But it does hold that the underlying and ultimate terms of
man's lostness and of his possible redemption—his actual redemption in Christ—are found in the relation of God to man and of
man to God as Creator and Redeemer. This is a personal-spiritual
relation and transaction. It begins in the goodness of God; it embraces the sin of man, God's forgiveness, and man's reconciliation
to God. Man's "lostness" is due in the first instance to the natural
conditions of his existence. Reinhold Niebuhr pointed out in the
now famous book, *Moral Man and Immoral Society*, that our
social sin is due in large part to the fact that we lack both knowledge of the sufferings and needs of others, and imagination to
make them real to us, and that group loyalty creates group
conflict. We shall see that there are similar influences and conditions that tend powerfully to make for individual sin.

Man's "lostness" is complex. It can best be described as alienation; from God, from others, and from self. It is both moral and
existential; man needs to be saved from sin and also from death,
for no matter how the moral problem might be solved, man is
mortal and the total enterprise of his life is cut off by death. In

both morality and mortality man needs salvation; that is, both present a threat to human life with which human power cannot cope. Each, in its own way, threatens to destroy him. It is not that there is no goodness in man; in many men there is a high attainment of goodness. But there is also an evil which man of himself cannot overcome. It is not that mortal men do not live; the intolerable thing is that they do live, and that the vision of life in fullness and completeness lures them on. But its lure is an illusion, for either by slow decline or by sudden interruption death comes. Thus each generation of men and each individual is stirred and lured on to the highest human attainment only to face this ultimate frustration. Neither the good that lures us nor the joy of life fully realized is attained or attainable for mortal man. This is not the predicament of "modern man" any more than of medieval or ancient man. It is the predicament of man.

Such is the predicament of the human person. Man in his wholeness (spirit) sins; this spiritual person dies. There is no part of man, call it soul or spirit, which is free from sin or which is not mortal. The whole man sins; it is the illusion of the Ritschlian theology, and of many religious philosophies, that the spirit of man is naturally good. Ritschl took over Kant's "rational moral will" from philosophy and made it the "spirit" in his theology. So the "problem" of man and especially of religion is the conflict of nature with spirit, and the work of religion is to give spirit victory over nature. But back of this modern religious philosophy lie the great idealisms of India and Greece. Platonism and Vedantism identify the spirit with the Idea, and the Idea is the Ideal. The Ideal is the Divine; the soul of every man is a part of the Divine. For the platonic West the souls are many; for the vedantic East they are One. Both West and East recognize the moral problem, and both have doctrines of cycles of existence and of reincarnation in which the evil can be purged out or the bad karma overcome. But the ideal, divine character of soul or spirit sets it over against the world of appearances, phenomena or "unreality." In any case the soul is by nature immortal and essentially good.

But Christian faith follows its historic source, Judaism, in the acknowledgment that man is mortal, and that the whole man sins.

The doctrine of "total depravity" does not mean that man has no good in him; it means that there is no "higher" element, spirit or soul, which is pure and which is naturally opposed to the evil of the body. "Total depravity" does not mean that all men are totally bad. It means that the whole person is involved in the sin which is a part of every man's life. The whole man, the person, needs to be saved.

Redemption is a work of healing, restoring, and bringing to completion the whole man. This includes the body. The body created by God is not evil; its health and well-being are involved in redemption. The healings of Christ indicate his concern for bodily health. Even more inclusive is Jesus' concern for the bodily well-being of men indicated in the account of the temptation. The first temptation he faced was to make the feeding of the hungry his main objective. He was tempted because he was keenly aware of the suffering of the poor. He rejected this appeal, not because he did not want to see men fed, but because just feeding men did not save them; for "man shall not live by bread alone." His own act in seeing that the multitude was fed reveals at once his compassion for their hunger, and his unwillingness to confine his mission to even the most urgent economic needs of men. The brief list of petitions in the Lord's Prayer includes one for "daily bread." Salvation in the Christian sense includes the "saving" of the body so far as it can be saved, without making this the ultimate or determinative objective. So the Christian minister visits the sick, and the Christian Church is concerned about the physical well-being and economic security of men. The twenty-fifth chapter of Matthew can never be forgotten or ignored.

Redemption is also a work of health and restoration in the realm of mind and soul. The thoughts of men and the affections of men are involved in salvation. Honest thinking and truthfulness in speech, and faithfulness and wholesomeness in the affections, are ends and aspects of redemption. The "saved" man is one who is "pure in heart." It is at this point that faith and prayer can to a large degree directly effect the realization of redemption.

Redemption means for the wholeness of man as spirit, eternal life. But eternal life is not the survival of some pure and naturally immortal element; it is a gift from God the Redeemer. And it means life not in a rarefied, abstract, intellectual, or ideal form. It means life in fullness, a fullness which the complex totality of the person in this world represents more truly than does the idea of a spiritual essence. In the Christian faith this is the promise of resurrection. Man is a creature; he does not exist by his own power of life or being; he dies, and the God who created him and who has redeemed him, bestows on him the gift of eternal life. The redeemed man is thus not only a morally transformed person in that the qualitative fullness of life is realized; he is also a living person upon whom God has bestowed life eternal. To have the qualitative fullness of life and not to have life itself would be a strange and irrational destiny; to find for a moment the ideal realized, and then to die. Yet that is what the emphasis of idealism seems to be. John Dewey, in his Terry lecture, sets "existence" over against ideal values, and says that the true religious spirit is interested solely in the values. "Existence," even the existence of God, can only add "force to establish, to punish, and to reward." [2] Of course, the word "existence" is ambiguous; what Dewey apparently means by it is "matter of fact" existence. In that sense God certainly does not "exist," but as the Spiritual Person who creates and redeems, God certainly is. And the man whom he creates and redeems, also is and will be, not as a matter of fact, but as spiritual person living in the fullness of life which God bestows.

MAN THE SINNER

Man is a sinner. Sin is a religious concept. It has to do with man's relation to God. Men are immoral in relation to one another; a man may do wrong to his neighbor; but we sin against God. "Against thee, thee only have I sinned, and done that which is evil in thy sight" (Psalm 51:4). The returning prodigal exclaims, "Father, I have sinned against heaven and before you" (Luke 15:21). Whatever the form of man's evil act, the practice of vice against his own good, or the doing of wrong to his neighbor, it is sin against God. Apart from the God-man relation, sin ceases to

[2] John Dewey, *A Common Faith*, New Haven, 1934, p. 44.

be sin. A purely secular or rational ethics will have to do with vice, immorality, evil, but not with sin. Sin is offense against the holiness, the goodness, the love of God. That is the reason why there is an immeasurable evil in sin. By sin man projects his evil action into the realm of the infinite, he implicates himself in a quality and extent of evil beyond his power to cope with or overcome. Sin is against God; and God, as the Party of the First Part, must deal with it on his own terms and according to his own will and nature. Man can sin; only God can save man from sin. Reconciliation can come only by grace of the one offended. This is true in all personal relations, those between man and man as well as those between man and God. And salvation is first of all reconciliation.

THE CONDITIONS OF SIN

There are certain conditions of man's existence that are not evil in themselves—indeed they represent what it means to be a man in the created world—but which present the possibility and occasion of sin. They do not make sin causally or rationally necessary, yet they make it inevitable that man will sin. Essentially these conditions are (1) creatureliness, (2) individuality, and (3) nature. Man is a creature; he is an individual; he is a part of nature.

1. To be a creature means to be dependent upon the Creator for existence. But man is a creature endowed with freedom and imagination. Both freedom and imagination direct his vision and desire to the infinite. The creature in the highest aspirations of his spirit aspires to the infinite. But the infinite is God. In his heart the creature spurns the position of dependence and permanent inferiority; he would be "as God." He does not want to accept the limitation put on his freedom by God; he wants the power and the glory to be his own by right and by achievement, and not a gracious gift of God. This presumption is symbolized by the tower of Babel; it is the *hybris* that Greek thinkers saw as man's great offense against the gods. The part of the creature is to obey; this is the moral recognition of the existential fact of creatureliness. Humility is required of one who exists by the will

of another and who is dependent on that Other for the ultimate direction and destiny of his life. Obedience and humility; this is what man must learn as a creature. But obedience "from the heart" is a lesson hard to learn. Man's very self-confidence, the assumption of competence for his own needs which is an element of his humanity, tends to make him restless under authority, even the authority of God. Men first learned obedience as sheer submission to force; the compulsion of society or of persons who represent society. This is the kind of obedience or service that they then offer to God or the gods; they cringe before the gods as they kneel before human authorities. Or they bargain with the gods to avert their wrath and secure their favor. But to know God as Creator and true Lord, to accept with humility the status of creature and to render free and loving obedience to God, this is a rare and difficult thing. The next step beyond a cringing submission may be either defiance or indifference. Of the two, defiance is better than indifference. There is a certain magnificence in human egotism; it is *hybris* or *superbia*. It is indeed the pride that goes before destruction, but it reveals a sense of the divine and exalted nature of existence, even though it be a man snatching at the prerogatives of deity.

But indifference to God means the flattening out of life. This is the great curse of a secular civilization, under which the so-called Christian civilization of the West is now living. The glory is departed when men become so preoccupied with their own doings that they are no longer aware of a greater One, the Creator; when the creation has been demoted to an order of nature, and man rides high on his conquest of that order. He will probe deep into the atom, and far into the reaches of space, but all he finds is a mechanism. There is no spiritual depth in the sub-atomic world, and no divine heights in interplanetary or even interstellar space. This scientific quest may well be thrilling for those actually engaged in it, and exciting if sometimes terrifying for the rest of us who are spectators; but as a total activity of man it can easily awaken false hopes and visions of a better future.

For there is nothing in the deeps of the atom better than the obvious aspects of nature; there is nothing higher in the stars than man, with open mind and responsive heart, can find on the surface

of the earth. And the power and prosperity that technology puts
at the disposal of man still leave him restless, harried, and alienated from the real meanings of life. It is hard today for the citizen
of either West or East to be truly humble, and to give free and
loving obedience to God the Creator. This is the "lostness" of our
present time. Today it is not only a Pharaoh, or a Caesar, or a
Napoleon who is guilty of the sins of indifference and *superbia;* it
is whole populations. And no religious revival, no frantic calling
on God to protect us from the Communists, will avail to save us
from sheer flatness of life without real humility and obedience.
We are already lost; our salvation will come not by some greater
technical achievement, but by re-learning the lessons of humility
and obedience.

2. To be an individual is both a fact and an achievement. We
are individuals *per force.* Even in the most socialized and totalitarian order men are still individuals. Primitive man has his name,
civilized man his identity. To be an individual involves a certain
degree of self-confidence, self-respect, and self-interest. The first
lesson for a child to learn is to care for himself, to be responsible
for his appearance, his health and his own safety. We try to make
children conscious of their appearance, to train them in habits of
cleanliness and decency. We warn them about crossing a street
without looking both ways, and about taking up with strangers.
That is, we instill in them as part of the responsibility of being
individuals a certain self-awareness and self-concern. We want
them to become self-reliant adults. But this tends to cultivate the
self-centeredness which is one of the basic evils of human life,
and self-love which is the chief obstacle to our love of God. Thus
a natural condition tends to sin. A necessary training in responsibility for their own lives, safety, and success, prepares our children
for the sin of self-centeredness in maturity.

3. The other condition of sin involved in being human is the
fact that man is a part of nature. "That which is first is the natural." The natural basis of man's existence as spirit is biological
and psychological. Man is an animal; his soul is first the *anima*
that he shares with all living creatures. He is a hungering, desiring,
passionate creature before he is a rational mind or a spiritual
person. But in his full existence as man he is still all of this. His

appetites and passions are, first of all, the *eros* of nature. This raw
power and instinct of life is slowly disciplined and conditioned
until rational thought and moral will develop in rough and broad
dimensions. The spiritual response to a transcendent God and a
transcendent goodness in sensitive individuals and in small communities troubles and slowly modifies this earthbound humanity.
It is hard for the prophet or seer; his one protection is the superstitious fear of a certain mystery that enshrouds him. Thus dread
of the power exercised by the shaman provides a certain degree
of immunity for the prophet when he comes or the priest who
seeks to lead men into true knowledge of God and reverence for
his will. Such is the rise of the spiritual reality of man. It is made
out of natural and socially fashioned stuff. The spiritual man can
never freely and simply live by the light and power of his faith
in God; he is always involved in the whole heritage of humanity.
There is, indeed, this ambiguity in man. He is nature; he is spirit.
Historically the natural is first; it must not be renounced and rejected but disciplined, molded into a morality, and redeemed as
spirit. But man never ceases to be a natural creature and the highest attainments of his mind and spirit are constantly and with
infinite subtlety tempted and beguiled by the elemental *eros*.

These are the basic "conditions" of sin in human life: creatureliness, individuality, and nature. They are not themselves sinful or contrary to God and his rule in the life of man. They *are*
man as God has created him and so are good. This is the sense in
which it can be said that man as a part of God's creation is essentially good. But the sin of man arises in the exercise of these good
powers of his being. It is the freedom and imagination, the sense
of an infinite possibility which lures man into the ambition to be
"equal with God." It is pride of self-sufficiency that arises from
man's necessary assumption of responsibilitiy for his own life, that
in practical terms causes him to make himself the center not only
of his own life but of the universe, and makes him a rival of God.
These are the special temptations of the strong man, the leader,
the one who feels and claims the higher powers of his humanity.
But all men live by the natural passion of life and are constantly
pressed, driven, and beguiled by the appetites and desires of
the animate creature. Sheer instinct and omnipotent mores first

restrain and control this natural desire. But as man advances and
life becomes more complex and free, the life force becomes increasingly a power to corrupt and destroy the humanity which it
has helped to bring into being.

Thus man is a divided kingdom; he is created good, but the
powers of his created being constitute threats and temptations to
his full existence as man, and furnish occasions of sin against his
Creator. This is the polarity of man's personality; this is the meaning of Paul's "natural man" and his "spiritual man," terms which
represent a dominance in human life of the one pole or the other.
The spiritual man is not the pure spirit separated or separable
from the natural; nor is the natural man the animal devoid of the
spiritual. They represent, respectively, a human person under
dominant control of God, or of nature. The natural man is sinful
because he rejects God for the sake of natural satisfactions. He is
the "bond servant of sin." He lives in the flesh (*sarx*). He cannot
please God. The spiritual man is the one who disciplines and
even denies the natural passions in order that he may serve God.
He is the servant of righteousness. The natural goodness of the
creature is preserved in the spiritual man. This is redemption. The
"flesh" is at enmity with God when it masters man, but it is the
servant of God through redemption. Man in his natural life of
pride and self-seeking sins by using the good powers for evil
doing; he uses the gifts of God to dishonor and deny him. As the
Catholic theologian would say, in the sin of man the "matter" is
furnished by God, the "form" by man. There is this close implication of God in the sin of man; the very powers and materials of
man's life by which he sins are the good creation of God. Man's
sin is a desecration and dishonoring of God's works, of his creation, of God himself.

THE ACT OF SIN

The actions of men are always specific; they are *acts,* each one at
a particular time and place. Insofar as the actions of men are sinful, therefore, they are specific sinful acts. So we speak in the
plural of our sins and we might well add, "which are many." But
that which is sinful in our actions is the common element of our

disobedience and faithlessness toward God. We can therefore speak properly of sin, in the singular. In the immediately practical utterances of Jesus it is sins we hear about; he was direct and concrete in his teaching. Paul, however, and John also deal with the basic fact of disobedience and faithlessness, and accordingly write about sin. This is what we do when we theologize. We are concerned about the general and ever present factors and relationships of our multitudinous sinning. So we may examine the act of sin.

The sin of man is an act of freedom. Unless a man acts freely it is not his act. Not that man always does, or ever does, exactly what he wants to do or all that he wants to do. This is, indeed, a rare thing for most of us. But it is involved in our being responsible and therefore free persons that we are free in our ultimate effort, and this element of freedom extends in varying degrees to all our actions. The first and absolute obligation of man is to obey and serve God. Such faith and obedience is possible only as a free act. But man is also free to disobey, and his disobedience is an act of freedom.

Sin, also, is an act of knowledge. It is not only that man must have moral freedom to sin; he also has rational freedom and is responsible for his own judgments as well as his acts. He knows what he is about, and is able to plan and execute the action of his own design. This is not only the knowledge of right and wrong; it is also the knowledge of "nature" by which man exercises control over his environment and to some extent determines his own future.

Man's humanity lies in his possession and exercise of freedom and knowledge, and in the planning and ordering of his own future. The possession of full humanity is certainly not sin; however, it is this that makes sin possible. This insight into the human condition is clearly and vividly expressed in the first chapters of Genesis. Most obviously, of course, in the result of Adam's (and Eve's) awakening to moral consciousness not through obedience to God, but through disobedience. This is. the elemental fact of man setting his own will against the will of God, and of the universal bad conscience of mankind.

But there is also the sin that arises from what we properly

call man's rational knowledge. In the Genesis story this knowledge is represented directly by the fact that God gives Adam the right to name the creatures, animal, bird, and fish. To name is to classify and the elementary form of rational knowledge is the power of generalization, or of classification. This is the beginning of scientific knowledge, and here it is a gift bestowed on man by his Maker, and constitutive of his role on the earth. The commission is made still more specific when God gives dominion over all the creatures. Power over the world is given with knowledge of the world; this is seen in the Genesis account as a basic power and function of man as God created him. Yet it was because of this knowledge of right and wrong, and knowledge of the creatures and the world itself that the human pair were put out of the garden and thrust into a life that was doubly cursed. The bearing of children was to be in pain and the ground was cursed for their sake. Man must exercise his dominion over the earth by dint of hard labor, and at the cost of much suffering and disappointment. All this labor and suffering are somehow due to the freedom and knowledge that make him human.

But from the same source also comes the sin that seems universal in human existence. That freedom which is the power of spirit is strange and paradoxical. But there is a logic involved; to *be* free a man must assert himself as the ultimate source and authority of his own act. But actually to do this sets one formally against God. For if I act on *my* authority I am not acting in obedience to God; therefore, in my freedom I am usurping God's place; I am a rebel against God. But it is this primary assertion of personal freedom that constitutes man as man. This is not a matter of openly recognizing God as the ultimate moral authority, and then consciously and deliberately defying him and doing one's own will. Such a melodramatic defiance of God is possible, but only for a very highly sophisticated mind. The exercise of personal freedom with its implied rebellion against God is hidden in the concrete conditions and conceptual context of our lives. It may be justified by a rational philosophy or decked out in the mythology of some form of totalitarianism; in both cases the self-sufficiency of man is asserted or assumed. But however it occurs, in the individual or in the race, it is "natural" to us because we are human.

Thus man begins his conscious dealings with God as a sinner, as one alienated by his act of freedom, an act that he must perform to be a man, and which yet sets him in opposition to God. This situation is modified in many ways, and kept under the control of moral and religious teachings, but it remains an underlying fact of human existence. It is not only the sophisticated thinker who has this inner problem, but all men. Man universally comes to full moral consciousness in the consciousness of sin. The shame of Adam and Eve is a mythological representation of this fact. The philosophical statement of the fact is concisely put in the words of Taubes quoted above (p. 148): "Man's alienation from the divine marks the crisis of the mythical consciousness, be it expressed in general skepticism or in the emergence of the monotheistic religions." "Skepticism" seeks to escape from this dilemma by denying any absolute authority in the moral life. It can find none, of course, in "nature." The monotheistic religions acknowledge that authority in God from whom their assumption of freedom has alienated them, and seek in responsible dealings with God to find reconciliation with him. Knowledge of God is knowledge of the way by which his favor may be won, or his grace enjoyed. This is why religion basically is a way of salvation. Primitive man turns to the gods to help and deliver him from the dangers of unknown powers in nature; in "classical monotheism" man turns to God for deliverance also from an evil that is within himself. The Christian gospel declares that God in Christ has himself taken the initiative in the redemption of sinful man.

The other "power" of spirit that constitutes man is knowledge —rational knowledge. This is primarily knowledge of the world in which we live, and it is knowledge by means of which we live. For reason is first practical or utilitarian in character. We seek knowledge in order that we may live and that we may live well. As over against moral knowledge, the knowledge of right and wrong, which was the first source of man's "fall" in the garden, we may characterize this as "economic" knowledge. Put simply, this is knowledge of how to make a living in the world, and either avoid or cope successfully with threats to our security. It was on

account of this kind of knowledge that the mythical Adam and
Eve were put out of the garden. This represents man being forced
to take responsibility for his own support and the ordering of his
own life. Thus man begins to "come of age." He is thrust out of
the paradise of dependence into the cold world of independence,
at least into the necessity of making his own way in the world.
This is doubtless for his good, but man quite generally has had to
be forced to it. I remember a motto in the front office of a firm
for which I worked as a young man, "Jehovah never did a better
thing than he did when he thrust Adam and Eve out of the
garden and said, 'Now children, get busy.' " Thus we make a
virtue of necessity, and stir in our youth an ambition to stand on
their own feet and make their own way in the world.

This is, nevertheless, a prolific source of sin. Man doesn't just
forage, or go out to hunt and fish when he is hungry. He uses
what knowledge he has of the fish, and animals and birds, as well
as the plants that grow in the earth, to regularize his source of
food supply by developing herds and by domesticating animals.
He very early stirs the soft earth with his pointed stick and sows
seed, looking for a harvest. So man is launched on the toilsome
and precarious undertaking of planning for his future, of making
his living. He barters, carries merchandise on his camels, sets sail
across the waters, and widens the scope of his economic effort
and increases the hazards of his existence. Here is man living by
his own efforts and his own wits. He knows success, he knows
failure. He dimly understands that God or the gods are the
ultimate powers that give the world its character of nourishment,
and may turn against him to destroy him. When he reaches that
"classic" religious faith in which he knows the One God as both
moral authority and Lord of the world, and when he has acknowledged in his own heart that both obedience and thanksgiving are due to God, this rational competence in planning for
and achieving his own economic and social security beguiles him
in two opposite and contrasted forms of sin.

There is the temptation of success. The man of physical
strength, with skill and knowledge, becomes a successful hunter,
and herdsman or farmer. He has the "know how." He is strong,
he is courageous, he is competent; therefore, he prospers. He may

have begun with petitions to God for help, and God apparently
has helped him. But he begins to see that his success is really
due to his own knowledge and effort. He really does not need
God. He becomes in his own mind master of his own destiny.
This is the temptation of the able and successful man to forget
God, to ignore him, even to consider dependence on God a
weakness to which he will not be subject. This is neither an
ancient nor a modern sin of man. It is a basic sin of *man*.

There is also the temptation of failure, or of the fear of failure.
This produces the anxiety that besets the man who must plan for
a future: a crop, an increase of the herd, the success of a trading
expedition. When man takes over consciously the making of his
own way all kinds of dangers and uncertainties assail him. The
farmer sows his seed; then he must wait. The rains may not
come, too much rain may come; birds or animals may eat the
young sprouts, blight may strike the growing plants. Just before
the harvest time, the dry wind may sweep over the field and
scatter the precious seed on the ground. And the price may fall
at the time of selling. These are the kinds of uncertainties that
fill the farmer's heart with concern, worry, and anxiety. Similar
and even more complex uncertainties bedevil the merchant and
the professional man. We do not have to wait for the *Angst* of
the sophisticated modern intellectual to know how man's very
power to plan and to work out his own living becomes a source
of care and anxiety that can destroy him. Now we have not the
man puffed up and neglectful of God because he doesn't need
any divine help. We have the opposite, the man sorely tempted to
lose faith in God altogether. For he has prayed as well as worked;
he has known that God is the Creator and Ruler of nature. He
has acknowledged that his real security is in God. But this anxiety
overshadows his faith and corrodes it. When the harvest comes
and all is well, he may look back and be ashamed of his lack of
faith. But when the harvest fails he is tempted to complain, or
to say, "There is no God," or "God does not care," and so to
make his service of God a bargain, and see it as a bad bargain
at that.

Thus these two forms of sin arise from man's rational knowledge and the power it gives him over nature and his own future.

If he succeeds, he sins through pride and self-sufficiency and the disowning of God. If he fails, or fears failure, he sins through allowing his natural responsible concern for the future to become anxiety, and so loses faith in God completely, as though God were responsible to give success, or as though God could be judged by the economic prosperity that he gives. Both these forms of sin are dealt with by Jesus in the parable (Luke 12:13ff.) of the man who had an abundant crop and who communed with his own soul (not with God), "Soul, thou hast much goods, enough for many years. Take thine ease, eat, drink and be merry." But God said to that man, "This night is thy soul required of thee." Then Jesus goes on to say, "Be not anxious for the morrow," and pointed to the lilies of the field whose beauty God bestows upon them. The answer to this anxiety and faithlessness is to "seek first the kingdom of God and his righteousness." Our age is beset by both temptations. The almost incredible power that man has gained over nature makes prosperity possible beyond the wildest dreams of earlier times; this is by our own knowledge and skill; what thanks are due to God? But the threat of destruction that hangs over us also makes faith in God difficult through the sheer terror that it creates.

THE NATURE OF SIN

We have discussed the conditions of sin, that is those basic features of man's existence as man that are conducive to sin; and also the act of sin, an act of freedom and knowledge. The nature of sin itself is most simply and inclusively defined as alienation from God. Alienation, or the turning away from God and the separation of one's self from God, has many forms and degrees. The most common form is just indifference, living without any thought of God or reverence and thanksgiving to him. Many people who would hasten to affirm that they believe in God are in this way alienated from him. They live, and think, and plan, they love and hate and enjoy or suffer as though there were no God. They do not consciously oppose him or dishonor him; they just ignore him. Now there is no more complete affront to a person than to be in his presence and to ignore him, even per-

haps talking about him as though he were not there. This affront
to a human person we seldom see directly; but it is a common
practice toward God. This is a practical atheism more sinful than
the theoretical atheism of the man who cannot honestly believe
in the existence of God even though in many ways his life may
express a real faith in and obedience to God. The practical atheist
is like the greedy child who snatches a gift and turns away to
enjoy it without a word of thanks. Or like the dowager who
speaks to a friend about her secretary as though she were not
present, demoting her to the status of a human gadget.

A more obvious form of sin, and one in which we all indulge,
is just plain disobedience. We know the will of God but we do
not do it. This is due to all sorts of things; we are dominated by
desire, we are momentarily forgetful, we beguile our consciences
with specious reasoning, we are gripped by passion or fear. In
short, we are human. We are children of God; yes, but we are
very disobedient children. The most sincere servant of God must
come to the end of the day with the confession, "Almighty and
most merciful Father, we have erred and strayed from thy ways
like lost sheep . . ." This is a chronic and recurrent alienation that
constantly needs the healing of God's forgiveness.

When we speak of "rebellion" against God, however, we are
dealing with a more sinister form of alienation. It may be a
dramatic defiance of God by the man who really believes in God
but finds his rule intolerable. Such defiance may result from a
tragic misconception of God, or from an almost equally tragic
misunderstanding by a man of his own nature. At any rate it is
a near pathological condition that needs both theological and
psychological treatment. The more common form of "rebellion"
does not involve the conscious thought of God; the rebel may be
theoretically a believer. He believes that God exists; he may have
some formal dealings with God. He may in fact consider that the
basic difference between himself and the Communist lies just in
this, that he believes in God and the Communist does not. Or he
may be a theoretical atheist, a man who cannot honestly believe
in the existence of God, whether he has some alternative conception of ultimate reality or not. But whether theist or atheist,
theoretically the rebel is one who exalts his own will to the place

of an absolute and irresponsible authority. This is *superbia* in its pure form. There are big men and little men who thus defy God by absolutizing their own desire and will. They also defy society, and even the kindlier impulses of their own lives. No one would ever have the right to identify any individual as such a rebel, unless it was himself. Perhaps the only authentic witness to this open rebellion against God is that given by someone who has turned from it in repentance, and confesses it as his own sin.

Thus the sin of man, most generally described, is alienation or separation from God. That alienation may take any of the forms outlined here, and often more than one. But sin, in any form, is against God; it arises only in the God-man relation. Man is a sinner because in some form and to some degree he is against God, either passively or actively, either consciously or unconsciously. It is this alienation from God that is the deepest and most destructive evil in human life, because the life of man the creature is life in relation to God the Creator. When that relation is wrong, nothing else can be really right. It is a form of death, for death is essentially separation. The old phrase, "dead in sin," is expressive of this condition.

The alienation from God is also alienation from other human persons. Love for neighbor is knowledge of God (I John 4:7, 8). It is the concrete form of our love of God, as the epistle says (v.20): "If anyone says he loves God, and hates his brother, he is a liar." To look upon our neighbor and to act toward him without love is to be alienated from him; thus we put him at an infinite distance. But we cannot do this without also rejecting God. It is love or alienation; it is God *and* neighbor, or it is the rejection of *God* and neighbor. Alienation from the neighbor through sheer disregard or through hate, means opposition to God and alienation from him. The *act* is directly toward the neighbor; the alienation from God is prior to the act and makes it possible. One has already forsaken God when he hates. Sin against God opens the way to wrong against the neighbor. Alienation from God brings alienation from others.

This is also alienation from self. What we are is inseparable from our relations to God and other men. We cannot sin against God or do wrong against other men without in some sense

destroying ourselves. The alienation from others in disregard or
hate, the rejection of God, denies the deepest reality of our own
self. We are "separated from the ground of our being." More
simply and directly we are separated from God who at once is
the Creator and source of our being, and the One whom we serve
in the love of our neighbor. It is this inner, this "domestic" dis-
unity and conflict that underlie the lack of unity and communion
with the other. Whatever the analogy we use to make this vivid,
the truth of the self-alienation is there. The man who hates or
despises his neighbor, and turns away from God, has denied the
origin of his own personal existence; he is a self-alienated soul.

CHAPTER X

GOD THE REDEEMER

MAN'S ESSENTIAL lostness is sin; sin is against God. God himself is the Redeemer. The "two parties" are alienated; there is no "third party" to effect a reconciliation. It is the one against whom the offense is done that must do the saving, God the Party of the First Part. In the alienation between God and man, man is the offender. The act of sin is not against a code, or a principle, or an impersonal order. If it were, a sinful man might find out what is required to satisfy the formal conditions, and by dint of great effort and patience set himself right again with Deity. But the alienation is personal; another Person has been rejected and offended. This Person is not another human person, himself at fault in other matters and needing help. The Person is God, complete in love and good in all his acts. He is the God of Truth who judges just judgment; his judgment is passionate just because this is a personal matter. God loves man who has sinned against him. Indeed, the magnitude of the offense arises from the fact that it is against the holy love of God. An offense against justice is serious, but it is impersonal and may be set right, as suggested above. But an offense against perfect love is immeasurable; it can only be overcome by the initiative and grace of the One offended.

Alienation can be overcome only by reconciliation, and reconciliation is a personal matter. The initiative is taken by God; in Jesus Christ he comes to man the sinner, calling him to repentance and offering forgiveness and reconciliation. "All this is from God, who through Christ reconciled us to himself and gave us the ministry of reconciliation; that is, God was in Christ reconciling the world to himself, not counting their trespasses against them, and entrusting to us the message of reconciliation" (II Cor. 5:18, 19).

So the whole work of redemption is in the realm of personal reality, the God-man relation, and is historically centered in the person of Jesus Christ. The "gospel" which the Church declares is this gospel of reconciliation and redemption. The work of redemption needs to be seen in the total context and activity of man. Human life is complex and involved in movements diverse in character. Much is done for man by nature; man can do much for himself, but his ultimate deliverance is in the hand of God. *Evolution* is a work of nature in *time; progress* is a work of man in *history; redemption* is a work of God in *eternity.*

Evolution may be taken as a term for the whole process of nature of which man is a part and by which he is largely determined to be what he is. It represents specifically the pre-human creative factor in which God the Creator gives freedom within the broadest conditions for the energy and life of the creation to try out its possibilities. The eternal act of creation is made concrete and temporal in all the clash and conflict, the productiveness and the wastefulness of nature, in the emergence of relatively successful ventures and the discarding of those that fail. Man is a species among other species; by a patient and uncoercive control the Creator brings into existence in nature a creature responsive to his Spirit. Man's own part in this work is first of all response to the Creator.

Progress is the work of man himself. It is the factor that freedom adds to nature. Here time becomes history, a significant movement in meaning for rational and moral beings. History is not some movement that goes on above the course of nature. It is wholly conditioned by nature, and nature is the stuff with which man works in history. But in history the forces of nature are profoundly conditioned by the rational conceptions man has of himself and by his conscious and unconscious striving for certain forms of existence. Man endeavors not only to live and reproduce, he seeks to live in a certain way. He develops mores, which are not determined wholly by nature but also by what man considers himself to be; he reflects upon his past and then projects into the future as an ideal what an idealized past has presented as the way of the ancestors and the will of the gods. He exercises his creative power in the making of tools, utensils, weapons, houses, visible representations of the gods, codes of behavior, standards of artistic beauty and civil law. This is the human world produced by the restless and creative soul (psyche) of man. It is a dynamic world, that is, it is progress; and the course of man's existence in this world of cultural productivity is history. History is human time, or time filled with human effort and significance. To say that this is progress does not mean that there is a straight line of advance to the better and ever better. There are both advance and regression; but it all is significant change in terms of the productive activity of man in time. In this realm man is the creative agent fashioning a human world with powers somehow bestowed upon him by the course of nature, and out of material that he finds at hand, and culturally "expressing" his own conception, vision, and desire. Progress is a possibility and when it happens it is an achievement of man in history. Despite all failures and losses progress remains a human possibility.

Within the context of evolution or nature, and progress or history, is redemption which is a work of God in terms of eternity. As history is not a movement that goes on above nature, so redemption is not a work that goes on above history. History is human time, or more strictly, humanized time. So eternity is the act of God in history. History is an element of depth in time; eternity is an element of transcendence in history. In redemption God acts directly in terms of the freedom and responsibility which man actually manifests in history. The Creator of nature, the Lord of history, is also Redeemer of man the spiritual person.

Nature cannot produce history, much less can it effect redemption. *History* can bring progress, but it has no power of redemption for man, for it is man's own achievement and ineradicably marked with his failures and defects. The claim that nature *can* redeem is expressed in the idea that man evolves into his true destiny. This is the hope set forth by LeComte du Nouy in *Human Destiny*, and in a much older work by Joseph LeConte, *Evolution and Its Relation to Human Thought*. The same theme runs through Griffith-Jones's *The Ascent Through Christ*. These

serious and imposing attempts to find in the process of nature itself the redemption of man share too much nature's disregard for
the individual; they are developed in terms of the race and not
the individual. They also lack the elements of freedom and transcendence which are the essence of spirit and of redemption.

History can bring progress but not redemption. Progress is
what man does for himself; redemption is what God does for him.
The modern doctrine of progress has various roots and elements.
It is, in some cases, a simple and uncritical transference to history
of the idea of evolution. It is also profoundly conditioned by
Hegelian rationalism which issues in the theory that history is the
concrete unfolding in time of the Idea, and that it is a "necessary"
movement of dialectical advance. This, transferred from the ideal
to the material order, is the structure of Karl Marx's doctrine for
which history is an inevitable movement in terms of economics
and through class conflict to the paradise of the classless society.
A more engaging rationale of progress derives from the doctrine
of Hegel conditioned by the empirical method, and the social
idealism of democracy. Its great prophet is John Dewey, who sees
man as his own savior, and the social process operating through
the realization of ideals as both progress and redemption of man.
Unfortunately the ideals that actually dominate man and so tend
to get realized in history are not always the ideals of democracy
and freedom. As we have seen in the past half century, they are
too often ideologies of totalitarian and dictatorial and ruthless
domination of man by self-chosen oligarchies.

Redemption is something done to man and for man by God.
Man does not move on to his destiny by the powers of nature or
through the processes of history. He is created by God; "It is he
that hath made us and not we ourselves." But universally man is
not what God created him to be. Lesser orders of creation may
simply be what they are. The individual animal may be a better
or worse example of a species, but he is wholly and unequivocally
a fox, a deer, or a dog. He does not need to be made such. But
with man it is different; he is not simply man, a better or worse
example of a species. He is an individual; not merely man but
this man. To be truly and completely man, he must be "re-done."
He needs to be re-stored, re-created, re-conciled, re-deemed. Bi-

ologically he may be a valid instance of the species, psychologically he is an instance of the human; but in the realm of
his freedom, as a responsible *person* his conscious spiritual existence begins in an effort to regain what he has never had, to
return to where he has never been, to reclaim what he has never
possessed. All culture and education, intellectual and moral, is a
process of bringing each and every man into the realization of
what he really is. Redemption is the radical form of this realization; it cannot be merely self-realization, for although man is the
individual person he is fully man only in relation, and in right
relation, to Another. But this is a matter of the two "parties." God
is the prior Actor; God is the "Party of the First Part." God is
the Creator; he is also the Re-creator, the Redeemer. Man is not
fully at home either in nature, or in history; he is at home fully
only in God.

The "good news" of the Christian gospel is that it is the will
and purpose of God that all men should be not only created,
but also saved. This is the "eternal purpose that he purposed in
Christ" (Eph. 3:11). This is God's "choice" or "election" for
mankind. God elects no one for destruction. There is no hell
in the purpose of God. Men destroy themselves; they create hells
and live in them. But there is no hell into which God does not go
to save men. This is indeed an affirmation of the Apostles' Creed:
"he descended into hell." It is also the joyous and wondering
affirmation of the psalmist: "If I make my bed in hell, thou art
there." Jesus Christ confirmed this by becoming part of a sinful
and lost humanity. "For our sake he made him to be sin who knew
no sin, so that we might become the righteousness of God"
(II Cor. 5:21). Christ died. But Christ is God, and death is separation from God. How can God be separated from God? But,
again, how can he not be? For in love of the sinner God goes out
to him and dwells with him in redemptive wrath. God goes
through death and resurrection to save sinful man. This is spiritually understandable, but it is not metaphysically intelligible. It is
part of the mystery of God, of his creative act and of his redemption of man. He goes into the sin without sin being his own
act; he lives in hell, because those he loves are in hell.

I met a Christian Chinese woman in Shanghai who lived and

worked among the dwellers in the underworld. She told me that people asked her if she was not afraid for her own reputation. But she always replied that she was not afraid because she was there to serve and to save. She shared the lot of the hell in Shanghai but she did not help to make it; she was there to redeem it. She risked her reputation. So God has risked his reputation in the incarnation. If a human person can so enter into the sin and hell of this world to restore it, why cannot God? Hell is not a place; it is a condition of alienation and separation from God. But even in this alienation men are still dealing with God, and he shows his love toward them in wrath. He is *there*. He is there to redeem. He bears the sin to be with the sinner. But this is what love does, and God is love.

Redemption is a work of love. Love is the "righteousness" of God. His righteousness is not justice. The old problem of the relation of God's love to his justice is a problem created by the misplacing of a conception, justice, which properly belongs in the organized relations of man with man in history. God does not judge men according to a standard of either distributive or retributive justice. His *dikaiosune* (righteousness) is not justice but *agape*. Even among men where the idea of justice is a valid and necessary instrument of discipline and order it is never the full and adequate form of righteousness. Human life needs kindness and mercy beyond all the demands of justice.

The answer, then, to this problem of God's love and justice is that if justice is thought of as rewarding the virtuous and punishing the wicked in proportion to their virtue or their wickedness, then God is not in the business of dispensing justice. We must say to the rational moralist who fears for the moral integrity of the universe, Do not fear; God has provided through nature and human history approximate controls and disciplines. But these have no power to make men good, or to save the sinner. God rules by love and takes the cost and consequences upon himself; this is what the cross means. God rules in freedom; he judges in truth, and he redeems in love. We cannot impose any category such as justice upon this divine sovereignty. God's goodness is not rational or legal; it is the goodness of free Spirit. There is no prior principle by which God must be controlled, no law by which he is limited. He acts in the sovereign freedom of Spirit.[1] He is not constrained to reward men or to punish them according to their deserts. After all, Augustine was so far right; if we are to think of the rule of God in terms of justice, the result is that we are all worthy of eternal damnation. The doctrine of *merit* which is essential in Roman Catholic theology, is a heresy for Christian faith. Martin Luther saw this clearly and he turned Christian faith back to its true center when he declared that salvation is by grace alone. But this, as we have said before, is a hard doctrine to hold. Protestantism has entangled itself again and again in the idea of "merit" and "justice," and rational philosophies of religion have taken for granted a salvation of law or reason.

God's goodness is love *(agape)*. Love is unreserved self-giving. Love makes demands upon the one to whom it is given.[2] To receive the love freely bestowed by God one must also freely give himself to others. Love is not a quantity, or a quality; it is an act. The great doctrine of *agape*, self-giving love, degenerates quickly when it is thought of as the unlimited generosity of God in bestowing benefits and making people happy. Love is a morally powerful thing. It goes beyond mere compassion with which it is too much equated, especially in oriental religions. Love is thoroughly moral; it demands more of man than does justice or any rational moral code. Love recognizes no limit to the devotion of self to the good of others; it has in it no grain of justified self-interest. It represents a freely recognized obligation to others that is never cancelled. "Owe no man anything," said Paul, "except to love one another" (Rom. 13:8). The two great commandments express the whole meaning of faith and the full content of ethics: Love God with all your heart and soul and strength and mind, and your neighbor as yourself (Luke 10:27).

I think, despite the weighty theological tradition of such interpretation, that it is not strictly correct to speak of "self-love." Love *(agape)* is essentially the act of a spiritual person toward

[1] This is the lesson of Jesus' parable of the workers in the vineyard, Matthew 20:1-16.
[2] Cf. Emil Brunner, *The Divine Imperative*, Philadelphia, 1947, chap. XXIII, in which the author sets forth the life of love as both gift and demand. "But although this realization of the Divine Will is a gift, it is also a demand. The gift includes the task." p. 242.

another person; it is the determination of conduct toward the *other*. It is not merely feeling or affection, but action toward another. Strictly speaking, therefore, one cannot love himself, though one naturally has affection for himself. The care and concern for one's self and the persistent drive to achieve one's own good, are the product of nature not of grace, to use theological language. We don't have to be exhorted to care for ourselves. It is true that we need much instruction and sometimes discipline to learn what is good for us. But not to seek the good as we see it. But to have equal concern for the other, and to seek his good with as much persistence and zeal as we seek our own, is the product of love. So when we love our neighbor as ourself, it is not that we love him as we love ourself, but rather that we act with true feeling toward him (love) as we do toward ourself (nature). The self-concern is natural and justifiable, although it needs control and restraint and sometimes denial; but the concern for others is not "natural," it is the transcendence of the natural by the power of love.

The love of God brings us under a more severe judgment than would the most exacting justice. We are judged by his love which he would bestow upon us, that we might really be "sons of God." It is a high doctrine of man to say that he is a son of God. But actually this is our condemnation. To receive the love of God and to make it our own, is to live by love. We know what this means; it means the utter obedience and devotion of Christ, and it means the cross. It means to love our enemies. But this is not a natural heritage; it is a gift of redemption. The unredeemed man is a son of God; but he is a disobedient and lost son, one who needs to be saved. Sonship to God is what God has created us for but which we actually have not accepted. The judgment of love upon our loveless lives is more devastating than any judgment of justice. But the love by which we are judged is also the love that redeems us.

The work of love in man's redemption is the forgiveness of sins. Man sins; God calls him to repentance; when the sinner turns to God in repentance, God forgives him. The alienation is overcome; man is "saved." This is the simple, direct, non-mythological account of redemption. The saving act of God in free forgiveness

of the sinner is an act of *grace*. Grace is the undeserved goodness
of God toward man. "For by grace you have been saved through
faith; and this is not your own doing; it is the gift of God—not
because of works, lest any man should boast" (Eph. 2:8, 9).
In all the diversity of doctrine among the various branches of the
Church there is agreement on the fundmental fact that we are
saved by the grace of God. The World Conference on Faith and
Order at Edinburgh in 1937 affirmed this fact unanimously. There
are different interpretations of the working of God's grace, having to do with "conditions" and "channels." Much of the discussion over such matters would disappear if the relation of God to
man were seen in the essentially spiritual-personal terms which I
have been assuming in this treatment of theology.

The act of grace is a personal act of the personal God. The
forgiveness of sins is an act of grace, because the sinner does not
deserve to be forgiven. It is a free act because there is no requirement imposed on God to forgive. It is for him a sovereign act of
free Spirit. It is the free expression of his own nature and purpose.
It is a true manifestation of his goodness. The goodness of God
does not conform to any prior existing principle. "Principle"
means the "first," the primary authority or reality. But God himself is the Principle (or Principal), the Authority. The answer to
the old question, Does God do what he does because it is right,
or is it right because he does it?, is that God himself is the good,
the ultimate standard of the right; his goodness is love; love is
the free and sovereign act of Spirit. Principles and categories of
goodness are generalizations having to do with human conduct;
they arise in a world which God has made and over which he is
the sovereign ruler. God does not therefore have to account to
any "principle," for he is the Principal and Lord of all meanings
in the realm of goodness. All laws and codes and principles of
goodness are secondary and derivative; the reality and origin of
goodness are found in the nature and act of God. Even for man,
"The whole law is fulfilled in one word, You shall love your
neighbor as yourself" (Gal. 5:14). This is the moral "godlikeness"
of the human person. So God freely forgives the sinner; this is
God's act of grace, it is man's salvation by grace.

The grace of God is "prevenient," which simply means that

God takes the initiative in the reconciliation of man to himself. God loves sinful man even while he is under judgment and subject to divine wrath. The "gospel" is the good news that God is seeking man to save him. This was Jesus' message: "Those who are well have no need of a physician, but those who are sick: ... I came not to call the righteous, but sinners" (Matt. 9:12, 13). This, of course, is the "scandal." God sent the prophets, and he sent Christ; now he sends the Church not to the righteous but to call sinners to repentance. Man is indifferent to the love of God, but God is not indifferent to man in his lostness. God as we see him in the New Testament, and in many parts of the Old Testament, is a seeking, pursuing, suffering God. No conception of God as the Absolute can be allowed to deny this passionate character which is revealed both in creation and in redemption, for both are accomplished at the cost of suffering. Religion generally may be represented as man's quest for God. But that quest is too often a self-seeking, a quest for certain benefits to be obtained from God, security, health, peace of mind. Christian faith begins not with man's quest for God but with God's quest for man, with his calling first Israel and then all men to be his people. The authentic quest of the soul for God is really a response to God's prior calling of man, and indeed to his creation of man. God is always the Party of the First Part. Much religion, even Christian religion, is religion in reverse because it assumes that man himself is the Party of the First Part. But redemption is an enterprise of God, and God's chief problem is to awaken men to faith and repentance. Forgiveness is not a problem for God, for that is what God does himself. The problem is faith and repentance, for this is what man must do.

But if men must do something, if they must believe and repent, then are not these "works" by which man at least partly saves himself? These are indeed works, or acts, free acts of the sinner. They are, however, not works of merit, good things done by which the sinner earns or deserves his salvation. The key idea here is "merit." To accept a gift freely given is an act, but not an act of merit, not an act by which one shows himself worthy of the gift. It is not a "work" in the theological sense, by which man even partly effects his own salvation. The grace of forgiveness is eternally present and complete in the heart of God and it is historically presented in Christ. No man is worthy of it; the acceptance of that grace as grace is precisely a confession of our lack of merit. In this Luther was right; he abandoned entirely the claim to and the very idea of merit in the personal relation between God and man, and his *sola gratia, sola fidei* is profoundly true, because in this personal-spiritual relation of giving and receiving the freedom of spirit is supreme. It is the freedom of God's act of grace and the freedom of man's response of faith and repentance which are not moral acts in the ordinary sense and can have no "merit" attached to them, but are free acts of spirit in a purely personal relation. The moral government of the Christian involves the formulation of principles and rules of conduct and the education of the will. With all this the Church has been properly concerned, but these are secondary to the original and sovereign act of divine grace by which we are reconciled to God and live as his children.

Repentance is not merely a "change of mind" *(metanoia)*, a transaction that goes on within the person of man; it is not just a subjective change that produces good results. It is a "return" to God; man the sinner who was turned away from God in self-will, pride, and self-centeredness, turns back to God, confessing his sin and accepting the forgiving grace of God. The primary fact is the new and saving relationship between God and the man who was "lost." Its inner effects in the forgiven sinner are profound; he is a "new creature," but this is the result of the redemptive presence and act of God. It is reconciliation between God and the man who has been "astray." Two parties are involved, one with the power to restore communion by forgiveness, the other needing that forgiveness to heal a breach that he himself has made but cannot heal. All doctrines of redemption are off center unless they conform to and express this basic fact of the personal act of grace on the part of God, and the personal "return" of the sinner. At this point in Christian doctrine the faith needs not to be demythologized but detheologized, for most theological constructions have lost the sovereign act of grace in a "system" or in the imposing on God of laws and principles presumably necessary to preserve him from irrational or unmoral conduct. The parable of the Prodigal Son remains the most authentic representation of God's act of redemption.

The grace of God has become historically actual in Jesus Christ. It is not primarily a theological doctrine, an idea; it is not only a truth about God discerned by the prophetic spirit, although it is that for Hosea, and Jeremiah, and Second Isaiah. It is historically real and humanly embodied in the person of Jesus Christ. So we can all follow Paul in saying "the grace of our Lord Jesus Christ." It is God's grace, but "God was in Christ." The life of Christ is the life and act of God in man. Jesus spoke God's word when he began his ministry by calling men to repentance. He said to the paralytic, "Your sins are forgiven." These were empty words unless spoken by God, for it is true that "only God can forgive sins." But it is also true that God can speak to men only through a man, or as a man. He did indeed speak *through* the prophets, but in his own proper person he spoke *in* Christ. This is incarnation, Jesus Christ *is* man; he *is* God. The man was seen with the eyes and touched by the hands of his disciples; God was seen by faith and known by his power in the lives of those same disciples, and of all Christian believers. The more technical exposition of this God-man unity which constitutes the complete person of man, is given above. Here we are concerned with the fact that the saving grace of God becomes overtly and effectively historical in Christ. The incarnation of God is his act of grace that culminated in the cross.

But why the cross? Why could not Christ have declared the forgiveness of sins, and given full assurance of God's saving grace without the pain and humiliation of the cross? He might have spoken the words, he might have taught the doctrine without going to the cross. But Christ could not live the life of God in a human society without suffering rejection and death at the hands of men. This, in concrete historic terms, is what the God of love and grace suffers because of and for the sake of sinful men. In the specific context of Palestine it meant denunciation by religious authorities, and execution by the civil power. The religious authorities saw the issue clearly; this man claimed to be the Son of God; he offered not a theoretical statement about the goodness of God; he was the God of grace in his own person. It was Jews

who rejected him; it was also Jews who accepted him as the Son
of God. Only in a Jewish context could the issue be seen clearly,
and taken in full seriousness; only a people who had known God
through the prophetic mind and heart could either accept or deny
Christ.

It is useless to speculate about what any other people would
have done if God had so lived among them. It was only because of
the historic revelation and knowledge of God as Creator and
Lord, in a true personal sense, and also a God of judgment and
grace, that the Jewish community could really be faced with the
fact of the incarnation, and the affront to their religious faith of
the High and Holy One appearing in the form of a servant, the
invisible and almighty Creator moving among them in the common conditions of human existence. But history is full of evidence
that whenever God approaches too near to any society through
godly men he encounters opposition, rejection, and suffering. This
has been true, and still is true, in nominally Christian communities;
in the name of Christ the servant of Christ has often been sent to
the stake or to the gallows. God is not a popular citizen in any
human community, for the saving grace he offers is always preceded by judgment. It is good for worshippers to look upon the
cross; it would be better if they could see and confess that they
have been involved in putting Christ upon that cross. By our con-
tinual sinning we "crucify the Son of God on our own account
and hold him up to contempt" (Hebrews 6:6).

But why does God suffer, for that is the implication of the
cross? It is Christ, the incarnate God, who dies on the cross. We
are told that the cross reveals the sin of man and the love of God.
In terms of the sacrificial system Christ is a sacrifice for the sins
of men making possible their salvation, a perfect and adequate
sacrifice. "He died for us." "He died for all men." The New
Testament and Christian preaching and theology abound in such
affirmations. But the question constantly arises, Why must the
forgiveness of our sins, and our reconciliation to God involve the
suffering and humiliation of the cross? The relation of God and
man is personal, spiritual. The act of grace is direct, free, and
sovereign; why must God suffer in the act? Why do we confess
that the suffering of Christ on the cross is a revelation of the suf-

fering love of God? This is not a question raised by the theologian
in his study; many Christian ministers have asked this question,
and have admitted that they did not really see why the cross is
necessary. Orthodox dogma has furnished an explanation in various terms. The most influential is the Anselmic doctrine of atonement. This represents the death of Christ as literally paying a debt
that man owes to God because of his sin. In a legal and even
commercial way the death of Christ is a substitute for the death
and eternal punishment of the human race. It settles and more
than settles the account and leaves God free to forgive the
penitent sinner.

But in reality there is interposed between God and man no
structure of a sacrificial system, no rational or moral or legal
set of conditions by which God must perform his act of grace.
The essential relation of God to man is personal-spiritual. It is a
relation of love and freedom. Sin is personal alienation from God,
salvation is reconciliation, the personal reconciliation of man to
God. God's act of grace is a free, complete, and sovereign act.
The repentant sinner is fully restored to fellowship with his Father.
This is the meaning of the parable of the Prodigal Son. Doubtless
there were "consequences," physical and psychological, of the
young man's riotous living, and penalties which the clan would
visit upon him and which he deserved; the elder brother is the
guarantee of them. But these have nothing to do with the essential
fact; the son is fully received back into the unqualified love and
care of his father, the reconciliation is complete.

Good, we say, this is quite understandable; but where is the
cross? God is the Father who gives free, instant, and complete
forgiveness; he does not need the agony of his Son and the terrible true life drama of the cross. But this is a hopelessly superficial understanding of the nature of love and reconciliation. Perhaps the deepest truth about the God-man relation as a relation of
persons is the cost of love, and the inevitability of vicarious suffering. Let us put it bluntly: no one can love without suffering.
Agape involves us in the fortunes and sufferings of those we love.
This is true vicarious suffering; the lover suffers on behalf, on
account of the one loved. Parents suffer in the pains and troubles
and failures of their children—if they really love them. A real

friend cannot go freely and joyously on his way while his friend
is in trouble. Love makes one vulnerable to all kinds of suffering;
as a friend of mine said during the unemployment of the 'thirties,
"For one to have a family means giving hostages to fortune." It is
always true. For one to have a friend is to give hostages to fortune; for one to love his fellow man is to commit himself to
vicarious suffering.

But God is *Agape;* he is the source of love in men. He supremely is the One who suffers in the agonies, the afflictions, and
the sorrows of men. This is the revelation of God in Christ. In
Green Pastures Gabriel, looking over the parapets of heaven,
sees the man in the city below carrying a cross, and he asks, "Does
it mean that even God must suffer?" Yes, that is what it means.
And the deepest suffering that God must bear because of his love
is the suffering inflicted by the sins of men. This is the cost of
forgiveness, of reconciliation. God has already borne the cost of
reconciliation when he forgives, and he forgives the moment the
sinner turns to him in repentance. This is a purely personal,
spiritual matter. There is no formal system of sacrifices, no obligation of justice, no principle of morality that intervenes. God
forgives man; that is all and that is everything. The bond of fellowship between the man and God is restored unconditionally.
This is salvation, it is life eternal. There is no residue of accounts
to be settled. As a member of society the man must come to terms
with what is roughly justice as understood in the time and place.
As a part of nature, there may be consequences to deal with. But
these have nothing to do with the fact that God has forgiven him.

And the cross? It is the visible manifestation in history of the
suffering God ever bears because of the sins of men, and conquers
by his forgiving love. He triumphs over both the sin and the
suffering. It is the cost—to God—not a price paid to anyone or to
any system, of his free and unconditional act of grace in reconciling us to him. All this is in purely personal terms, in the terms
of a relation between man and God, between the sinner and the
God of grace. The ambiguity of such terms as "cost" and "paying
the price" has given support to the idea of a commercial transaction, or of a legal requirement met. The Anselmic theory is
frankly substitutionary; Christ paid my debt on the cross and I

go free! But Christ did not pay any debt, he did not settle any account. He bore the cost of divine love for sinful men, the love that forgives and cancels all accounts. Even if he had not said on the cross, "Father, forgive them," his suffering and death would have been the visible manifestation of the cost to God of his redeeming grace and his redeeming love.

The real analogy in human life of this act of vicarious suffering is the reconciliation of an offender to the friend he has wronged. In all such reconciliation the one who bears the cost of the reconciliation is the one wronged. For in the offence the injury has already been experienced. Let us say that someone, in jealousy, has lied about his friend to prevent him from being given a much needed scholarship. The thing is done; it can't be undone. The injured man is not destroyed, but a real obstacle is placed in his path; the confidence of certain persons has been lost never to be regained. A disappointment and hurt have been inflicted, especially when he learns that it was his friend who told the lie. It is a personal injury. Let us say that the wronged party is not bitter; he has exposed his heart through friendship, and the "friend" has betrayed him. This is the real hurt, the real injury. When his friend, however, sincere in his repentance, comes to confess the wrong and to ask forgiveness the whole burden of reconciliation rests on the one who forgives. He has already suffered; he has borne his cross. If he forgives, it is a free, unmerited act of love. No such wrong can be "atoned for" in the common meaning of that term, that is, be paid for either by any suffering the wrongdoer might be willing to undergo, nor by any extra kindness he might do for the friend he had betrayed. But there can be reconciliation, because reconciliation is the free assumption of the suffering inflicted in the past, and the free forgiveness of the offender. No personal evil can ever be undone; it must be forgiven. And there is a divine forgetfulness in forgiveness. "I will forgive their iniquity," says the Lord, "and I will remember their sin no more" (Jer. 3:34).

This is the way of God with man. It is the way of Christ. It is the way of Christian life. This is what it means to take up one's cross daily and follow Christ. The "cross" is not the bearing of pain or poverty or sicknenss; it is the acceptance of suffering at

the hands of others, and then forgiving them. This is the power
of reconciliation working in all human relations. It is the cost
borne by the injured in the restoration of broken ties. No family
can exist as a true family without constant forgiveness, and the
bearing of the cross. It is the essence of the Church to be a fellowship of the forgiving and the forgiven. Jesus tied this practice
of forgiveness directly with our reception of God's grace, "For
if you forgive men their trespasses, your heavenly Father will also
forgive you; but if you do not forgive men their trespasses,
neither will your Father forgive your trespasses" (Matt. 6:14, 15).
Thus are real enmities overcome, the enmity between man and
God created by human sin, and the enmities between men. God
in Christ bears the cross of suffering on behalf of those who sin
against him; he then freely forgives all who turn to him in
penitence. But it is a cross that he ever bears; for every time we
turn to him asking forgiveness, we confess that we have again
inflicted upon him a sorrow that he will expunge from the record
in his act of forgiveness.

Shall we then say that we do not understand the cross, that
we cannot see why it has anything to do with God's love and
forgiveness, and with our salvation? As the historic manifestation
of the law that all reconciliation is at the cost of suffering on the
part of the one offended, the cross permits us to understand more
fully the nature of God as Spiritual Person, *agape* as free self-giving love, and man as made in the image of God and life eternal
as life in the love and fellowship of God and with one another in
him. This is the realm where the meaning of the cross is found,
and most metaphors obscure rather than disclose it.

CHAPTER XI

THE KINGDOM OF GOD IN HISTORY

"Now AFTER JOHN was arrested, Jesus came into Galilee, preaching the gospel of God, and saying, 'The time is fulfilled, and the kingdom of God is at hand; repent, and believe in the gospel' " (Mark 1:14). The kingdom of God is the life of man under the sovereignty of God. This is an eternal kingdom; that is, the time or the place, or the structure of life and event is not the essence of it, but man living in full and free obedience to God. We should only provisionally interpose any other terms between man and God; saying, for example, man doing *the will* of God, or man living by *the spirit* of God, or even man living by *the love* of God. All these statements are true and meaningful and we rightly use them to express and elaborate the meaning or meanings of the simple and fundamental affirmation—man living in obedience to God. The will of God is God acting and demanding, the spirit of God is God in his freedom and power, the love of God is God in act according to his nature, as what he is. But God the Spiritual Person, the single and only One, is in his act and power and nature directly, that is personally, the Lord of men, and man finds redemption and life in direct personal obedience to and joy in God. Attributes are adjectival; God the Personal One is subject; the kingdom of God is the simple all-encompassing reality of man under God, of man in God; this is eternal life.

The redemption of man takes place in history. The temporal life of man is the scene of God's act of redemption, and it is the locus of man's life in his kingdom. Here is the reality of the life of man with God; the kingdom of God is "in your midst," that is, in time or in history. "Thy kingdom come, thy will be done in earth as it is in heaven" is the first petition in the Lord's Prayer. But history is the realm of man's activity and relative competence. History is what man does in time, in the environment of nature and with the energies supplied by nature. In man the *psyche*, the energy of life, becomes a rational consciousness, and culture which is the product of this "living soul" arises. There is, in culture, both the life energy which man shares with all sentient animals, and also the power of reason. There is also the "sense of presence" so that man is both awed and sustained by the spirits which, either as demons or deities, encompass his life in mystery. The mystery is not merely the unknown; it is always somewhat known because the spirits are akin to man; only they enjoy prerogatives, freedoms, and powers which are denied him. But though denied him they still create in him a restless aspiration. The intellectual growth and the creative imagination of man thus are nurtured in a more than human world, or in a superhuman world, which is still continuous with this world, and upon which man depends for his ordinary well-being.

As we have pointed out in Chapter V, it is the power of soul, or *psyche*, by which man produces the works of culture and makes history. But the man who lives in history is not just a living soul; he is also rational mind and spirit. The beginnings of his human freedom are seen in the element of creativity and inventiveness in primitive culture. It comes to fulfillment in the birth of conscious rational activity and moral responsibility which are represented in the Genesis stories. These accounts of the beginnings express poetically, or mythologically, the paradox; man is stirred to productive and creative activity by the sense of the supernatural; but the aspiration shows itself in disobedience to God and in *hybris*, the presumption of trying to "be God." Thus culture and religion, as Tillich says, are united by an inner bond.

However, both culture and religion represent at the outset an uncriticized activity of the human soul. The criticism came for Western man, and perhaps we should say for *man*, for both have a universal human reference, from two directions and more or less at the same period; development of the critical reason through the study of nature in Greece, and the prophetic movement in

Israel which set up universal standards of truth and morality and which brought both popular religion and the common culture under judgment. Much has been said and written in recent times about the tension between the Greek and the Hebrew heritages. But it is a creative tension; both movements show man coming of age, responsible both to a nature of incorruptible law, and to a God of incorruptible righteousness. Thus reason and conscience gained a valid and absolute grounding. Man cannot think as he pleases; nor can he do as he pleases. Man is *responsible* to inviolable standards of reason and goodness. If he pays respect to nature as it is and reverence to God as he is, human life opens out into infinite possibility.

But these powers awakened by the integrity of nature and the majesty of God are deeply involved in the heritage of soul as irresponsible life and sentience. Few men actually pay the price of rigorous intellectual discipline, and attain even a general sense of the inviolability of truth. Few men take seriously and know personally the majesty of divine righteousness. The philosopher in ancient Greece is scorned, or made to drink the hemlock; the prophet in Israel is stoned. The vital energies of the soul are only partially curbed by reason or directed by conscience. Culture is a great field of struggle between the divine capacities of man and the surging demands of his passionate nature. This is an old story. Culture is a morass in which are islands of beauty; its passion of creativity both exalts and corrupts man. The reason is made servant of the natural desires of man and religion is made to serve human ambition. Culture and religion which are products both of man's reason and of his faith in God, are earth-bound and ambiguous, containing seeds of their own disintegration. History is the work of man, and man is not God. Man is not the true lord of history; that is, he does not have the wisdom or the power to make a world that is truly rational or good. It is true that we have a heritage; that there is progress. It is also true that there is in that heritage much evil, and that there are forces of degeneration which always threaten and often destroy the good attained. One thing that is often forgotten in calculating the possibilities of progress is that the world is being constantly replenished with a new generation. The whole treasure of history must be handed on

to the new humanity that is constantly arriving. So far no system
of education has been devised to accomplish this so that the gains
may be preserved and the losses wiped out. It is always the older
generation that does the educating and that generation itself is
only half aware of what it is about, and often blocks the growth
of the better things and fosters the evil. Human culture is always
in a precarious state; it is always a mixture of the good and the
bad; it is always promoting growth and producing corruption.

So to a large extent with religion. Religion is a work of man.
It is not gods that are religious, but men. Religion is a human
response to the divine; it is what man does when he comes under
the sense of a divine power and demand. The ultimate reference
is God, but the content and expression of religion are products of
the human mind and soul. Religion is not *per se* good; it shares
the ambiguities of culture, for it is not wholly but largely a part
of culture. The points at which this identity is challenged have
been indicated above; namely the criticism of the rational mind
and of the prophetic word. Religion needs constantly to be re-
formed; it is perhaps the most intransigent defender of ancient
evils. There is no virtue or salvation for man merely in being
religious; there may as well be evil and damnation. Both reason
and the prophetic word can be employed to convict men of the
evils in religion as well as in culture; let us say the evils of a culture religion or of a religious culture. However reason suffers
from a fixed limitation in its power to reform religion or culture.
Reason as a critical faculty came to its own in ancient Greece. Its
point of ultimate reference was nature, even though it used religious and anthropomorphic language and ideas. Its instrument was
the process or law of articulate thought; that is, thought expressed
in language, the Greek language. It soon arrived at the two limits
of such a rational activity; on the one hand, the concept of nature
as a fixed and mechanical order; on the other hand, the concept
of reason itself as a fixed logical system in which any given meaning is defined strictly and exhaustively in terms of other rational
meanings. Along both lines thought finally arrived at the One
which is eternal, immovable, unchangeable, and unrelated, because
it is itself the Whole. This is the dead end to which pure reason
always comes and always must come; it does not give the truth

about anything for truth is found in the intelligible relation of parts within a whole. Indeed strict rationality is the order within a system; it does not apply to any possible relation of the system with other systems, the whole with the other whole.

Empirical reason broke away from this impasse and became a disciplined instrument by which the phenomena of nature might be classified and its process traced out in general laws. That is very largely what it is today since science has superseded philosophy and philosophy is to a considerable extent the handmaid of science. But science is not occupied with any search for truth about the universe in an ultimate sense. It contents itself with an ever widening discovery of the structure and operation of nature, and with the ways by which these natural resources can be employed for human ends, and sometimes for inhuman ends! Science, thus, is largely and perhaps essentially technical, instrumental and utilitarian. The results of "pure" science are taken over into the realm of operations which both "prove" the validity of the results and make them useful to man. Now, there is nothing in this that can do much for religion; it can expose false factual claims and irrationality in doctrine; it can replace the "spirits" by the laws of nature. But religion was not produced by man's knowledge of nature and even primitive man has a considerable knowledge of nature. It is an expression of man's consciousness of a supernatural presence, of God who has power over both nature and man. Reason, as natural science, may say there is no such "presence" to be observed and known. Naturally, there is for natural science, no supernatural. But man is more than a scientist and he still lives in the consciousness of God. He has inherited profoundly developed religious systems in which the meaning and destiny of his life have been defined in terms of God and eternity. Any particular man may say, with Freud, that religion is an illusion which is passing. Theoretically this may be true. But the religious man with more or less conviction will still be religious. He may reject the word "supernatural" for that smacks of superstition and ignorance. He may say instead that there is a transcendent Reality which sustains the phenomenal world. This is more acceptable, perhaps, to the cultured mind but what it means is that the natural is dependent upon the supernatural. In quite simple and adequate terms, God creates and sustains the world. At this point religion survives not by the grace of reason as science, but to a certain degree in spite of it.

But if reason being ultimately oriented to nature cannot deliver religion from its faults, errors, and incompleteness, the prophetic word being oriented toward the transcendent God has no such limitations. The real reform of religion in Israel came through the prophets; its complete deliverance in principle from the earthbound culture of men came in the incarnation when God came into history, when God indeed became the redemptive power in history. In Christ God directly judges human life—both culture and religion—and redeems man. This is the coming of the kingdom of God. History, apart from Christ, is still the aimless even if grand accomplishment of men. Both religion and culture, however, are subject to the ultimate futility of natural vitality and finite reason.[1] The Christian community is a community of faith and life in Christ. Its ultimate reference is not nature or the world, but the risen Christ, the God who was incarnate in Jesus Christ and who is present as Holy Spirit in the Church. The Christian community is in the world but not of the world; it is an historic community but its indwelling life is the eternal God.

We have pointed out that man sustains three main relations: to nature, to history, and to God. The life of the redeemed man and of the redeemed community is still the life of creatures who are part of nature. Their spiritual deliverance does not absolve them from the hazards of existence in the natural order, nor give them special guarantees of safety and success. Christians share with all other men the advantages that come through the advance of knowledge; also the heightened tensions and the new dangers introduced by technology. The life span is extended, medical care and aids for failing vision and hearing help in the declining years, an antiseptic civilization frees us from many infections, from flies, fleas, mosquitoes, etc. This is what science with its orientation to nature has done. It is a long delayed fulfillment of the command to replenish the earth and subdue it. There is, however, the

[1] Both Gautama and St. Paul were aware of this futility. Gautama sought deliverance in the extinction of desire; Paul found redemption in the new creation in Christ (Rom. 8:19-23).

sinister side of this conquest of nature, the threat of nuclear destruction. The replenishing of the earth, largely due to the increased life span, together with the destructiveness of war reminds us that life is still precarious. Nature is grandly neutral as regards the moral aspects of human life, and the hopes of men for a better life on the earth.

The life of the Christian and of the redeemed community is also life in history. Redemption is the act of God in history and the life of the redeemed is part of the life of the human race, biologically, economically, socially, politically. The kingdom of God is an eternal kingdom, but in this life it is a kingdom within the temporal existence of man. Many attempts have been made by individuals and by small communities to "withdraw from the world," and to preserve purity of life apart from the rest of society. This is certainly a possible and legitimate option and many have found approximate satisfaction in it. But these individuals and communities still must eat and find some shelter from the weather, and even the hermit must deal in some fashion with other men. The recent closing out of the Amana community suggests that all these efforts are partial and provisional ways of evading involvement in the common lot of man. For the greater part the Christian is confronted with the problem of being in the world, participating in all its normal activities and relationships, fulfilling duties social and political, and still "seeking first the kingdom of God and his righteousness." That is, the Christian must accept wholeheartedly the human condition and be a man in history.

CHRISTIAN MORALITY

History is the realm of morality; morality is order in social existence. To live together men must have common standards by which conduct is controlled. Mores, moral codes, laws, principles, ideals appear in the developing moral life of man. Man must work out, discover, or create these laws and ideals. Morality has its place in the relation of man with man in history; it is not the nature of the relation of man to God in religion. The baseline, long ago discovered but difficult to define in precision and in detail, is justice. Justice is a goal partially achieved in any reasonably stable society. It means, in most general terms, that each man does his part and gets his rightful share in the common life. This is not "equality" in the ordinary sense, but there is a certain underlying sense of a valid claim that each man has and of an inescapable duty; a worth and a responsibility that pertain to man as man.

The relation of God to human morality is fundamental but has been quite variously understood. In primitive religion it is simply that the gods sanction and sustain the mores. In more advanced religious societies God is regarded as the author of a code, such as the Ten Commandments, or the Code of Hammurabi, or the Laws of Manu. In more speculative and philosophical religions morality is taken to be a cosmic law, karma, or the idea of the Good. Thus the problem of ordering man's life in history is projected into the realm of the divine and the absolute. Roman Catholic ethics assumes the moral law as the natural law in the realm of human relations. Kant kept the absolute character of this moral law but snatched it from the gods and the order of nature and located it in the free action of the will, defining religion then as obedience to the moral law conceived of as a divine command.

Certainly God the Creator is not only Lord of the world but also Lord of history. He is profoundly concerned about human righteousness. Not even the primitive man is fundamentally wrong when he assumes a divine sanction for the specific mores of his tribe. Nor is the philosopher wrong when he assumes a universal law or principle; God is for the right always and everywhere. But the actual form of life developed in any primitive society is the direct resultant of the conditions in which men live and the necessities of an effective common effort. In its detail it is a natural and human device. The universal principle of rational ethics is a generalization of the human mind which makes intelligible and rational the meaning of goodness. There is nothing any more essentially divine in this rational idea than there is in the concrete mores of the primitive. Both represent a human formulation of the good which certainly has the sanction of the Creator God, but equally certainly cannot be directly identified with his will or claim the absoluteness of his goodness.

The Christian faith was early—by Jesus, Paul, and John—and

clearly formulated in terms of an ethic as well as a religion of love *(agape)*. God is revealed in Christ as love; the life of Christ is that love incarnate; the death of Christ is the visible cost of love completely lived among sinful men. The forgiveness (redemption) of men is the work of that love of God which costs him the vicarious suffering of the cross. The redeemed community is a fellowship of those whose lives are ruled by the love which is of God. The ethic of Christianity is the ethic of love. It is not necessary here to quote again the two commandments, or the thirteenth chapter of First Corinthians, or the fourth chapter of I John. Love is the true service of God (religion); love is the true righteousness of men (ethics). Thus religion is continuous with morality. The common element is the free compulsion of love. But love is not a rational law or a formal principle; it is the nature of God, and it is the true relation or law of personal existence. It is a free act of a free (spiritual) person. It is the creator and power of true community among men and between God and men. To be a true person is to live in love with other persons. This is *agape* not *eros;* it seeks the good of the other as one's own good, not enjoyment of the other necessarily and certainly not indulgence of one's natural passion with the other. Love seeks together with all who will share in it the service of God who is love. This is the kingdom of God, on earth or anywhere else.

This is the Christian absolute—love. But it is a basic motive and intention, not a detailed code. The Christian possessed even approximately by love lives in a society in which codes, rules, principles, and even laws are needed to define personal and social conduct. Assuming the purity of love, and that is the internal problem of the Christian individual and the Christian community, Christian conduct must still patiently, intelligently, and responsibly deal with all the demands of social existence. Christian ethics is inevitably involved in continuous discussion to discover the best way to embody the basic impulse, as well as in continuous prayer for light and leading, for forgiveness and restoration by God. The ultimate light and power of Christian living are from God; the specific form and act of Christian behavior must be in terms of human conditions and with serious regard for human endeavors to do the right.

We have been instructed for a generation and greatly to our profit by Reinhold Niebuhr in the relativity and ambiguity of all human goodness. This ambiguity makes it impossible for man ever to claim for his actual character or conduct the absolute goodness which is found in love, even though he truly loves. For man as part of nature and of history is necessarily moved by natural desires and passions, and driven by the ambitions that produce human culture. These passions and ambitions are all basically good, but they are not absolute goods. Every appetite and desire of man, even though it is vital for his existence and well-being, needs control, restraint, and sometimes suppression and denial. The pressure of society without and the voice of conscience within every man must constantly struggle with desire. This is an endless and inescapable struggle. All efforts to escape it or transcend it have failed. For the individual and for the race the struggle is renewed every day by reawakened desire, and there is that constantly arriving new generation always starting from scratch with a lusty even if lovable and innocent demand for satisfaction of its appetite for life. Our forefathers thought they must "break the will" of the child. More recently it has been suggested that desires should be satisfied even at the sacrifice of morals. These are drastic and false ways of trying to escape the patient labor and wisdom and responsible discipline that are an inescapable part of human life.

The task of moral discipline can be performed with rational sternness and inflexibility, or it can be sidestepped by letting children "express themselves." But there is a better way, the way of love. Children need authority; they need to be taught obedience; they need guidance and control. So, indeed, do we all, even in our adult years. But authority and control must be exercised in integrity and intelligence and love. There is a certain gift conferred upon man by love, the gift of understanding. Love overcomes the self-interest and the tendency to self-justification, and frees us to sympathize with, to understand, and to deal patiently with those whom *we* must discipline. Love, in the end, will cause us to demand more of those we love than will any lesser morality. It will cause us to point them in the way of unselfishness and even of self-sacrifice. The ingrown self-interest of the individual and the family and the class will be constantly challenged by this discipline of love. But insofar as such training succeeds it will free those subject to it from the worst bondage of human life, bondage to self.

In the competitive life of society, in politics and professional life, in short in the common life of man where culture is created and where progress is made, the Christian seeking to live by the law of love finds himself part and parcel of a struggle. "Love is patient and kind; love is not jealous or boastful; it is not arrogant or rude. Love does not insist on its own way; it is not irritable or resentful; it does not rejoice at wrong, but rejoices in the right. Love bears all things, believes all things, hopes all things, endures all things" (I Cor. 13:4-7). How can a man succeed in business, in a profession, in politics if he is under the control of love? The merchant says as effectively as he can, Trade with me. The professional man says, I can serve you best. The politician says, I am the best man to fill the office. Each one is frankly self-seeking, even though he also seeks the common good. There is a native self-assertion, a self-confidence, an ambition which creates and sustains this competitive struggle. It is the social equivalent of the natural passions and desires without which we could not live and be men, but which must be subject to constant discipline, restraint, and sometimes denial. In this self-assertion and ambition is the power that creates the good of human culture. But it is a restless and often lawless thing. All societies, especially the more dynamic ones, face constantly the problem of containing this human energy which threatens ordered existence. Human society is always in a state of unstable equilibrium. The self-expression and self-assertion of ambition cannot be denied for it is the raw energy of human progress. It can to a large extent be controlled by strong government, although it is always threatening to corrupt government itself, and too often it succeeds. Education and propaganda in the ideals and standards of the nation and the community are powerful; but they also may be used to exploit and enslave men. There come times when it seems that the public well-being requires us flatly to go against the admonition of love to "bear all things, believe all things, hope all things and endure all things." We must for the sake of the common good refuse to tolerate, or believe in, or endure evils in the common life. We must act sometimes drastically to uproot and destroy things that are wrong. Such is the responsibility of an informed and free citizen.

It still remains true that the health of human society lies in the possibility and the actuality of men, even in this vast social and political struggle, fulfilling essentially the description of love that St. Paul gives. The apostle doubtless had in mind not the modern highly developed and competitive struggle that we live in; but he knew all the elements of it in the simpler life of his time, and was by no means unacquainted with the ambitions of men in high places. What we must learn to accept is that the self-assertion of the strong man and the ambition of the aspiring man are elements of the creature that God has made, and are involved in his fulfilling the mandate, "replenish the earth and subdue it." The struggle will never end, in this life. Mankind will never arrive at Utopia. The life of love must be lived in a world that denies it. But this is the life of the Christian; this is the kingdom of God on earth; a struggling kingdom, threatened by enemies without and weaknesses within; yet this is the reign of God. "It is your Father's good pleasure to give you the kingdom" (Luke 12:32). But the kingdom will be constantly given to us in the midst of this struggle.

There is both a this-worldly and an other-worldly aspect to the life of the redeemed man and the redeemed community. The service of God certainly is within this world; it is equally certain that it looks beyond this world. We enter by faith into eternal life in this world; that is the life of love, the kingdom of God on earth. But the full power and meaning of eternal life go beyond this world or any world or worlds, and are found only in God himself. "Heaven" is not another world; it is not "a world behind the world," to quote Paul Tillich again. It is personal existence in God which is the life of love, the kingdom of God. As such it is as much in this world as it is out of this world. But it is not "of this world" or of any other "world"; it is of God. This means that the true life of man with God is a personal reality and order in which love is the substance, rather than any finite order or structure of existence in any world, and all "worlds" are finite.

God, the Creator, has infinite power to create worlds or to make life complete without any world. This is what we mean by the essential other-worldliness of Christian faith and life. By the indwelling power of God Christian love creates its own world. This is the demythologized meaning of the eschatological hope of the Church; not an end to time or history, but the act of God and the gift of God both within time and beyond history. Christian morality is the temporal form of life in the eternal kingdom, the kingdom of God.

THE CHURCH

But if it is true that the kingdom of God is in this world and that Christians live in the common life of culture and history, it is also true that Christian faith produces its own form of historic existence, a world which is within this world and yet which denies the dominant self-interest of the world. The Church is a "new creation," created at Pentecost; its members are the company of those who believe in the crucified and risen Christ, the immediate power of its origin and continuance is the Holy Spirit.[2] The early Church knew itself as the "new Israel," the true "people of God." The presence and power of Christ dwell in this "people." It is his body. Paul in chapters nine to eleven of the Roman letter contrasts this new historic community with the people of Israel, God's "chosen people" in times past. Membership in this community is not by birth or by political citizenship; it is by faith in Christ. It is thus open to all men. It is not a new community within Israel, but an open fellowship destined some day, according to the divine purpose, to include Israel. Even the great doctrines of grace and salvation by faith which Paul develops in the Roman letter are elements in this universal spiritual conception of the new people of God, and the obvious purpose of the whole letter is to give theological justification for the carrying of the gospel to Rome and beyond, that is, to the world. The two extremes, the individual and the universal, meet in this community of faith in Christ: the individual, for each man by faith is "born"

[2] Cf. Emil Brunner, *Die Lehre von der Kirche vom Glauben und von der Vollendung* (*Dogmatik* III), Zürich, 1960, pp. 20-33.

into it; the universal, for all men regardless of race or nationality may by the act of faith become members of the community of which Christ is the head. More than that, all men have sinned and are under judgment of the holy God; all men, through faith and the acceptance of God's grace in Christ, are saved and enter into the kingdom of God.

The Church is first and essentially a religious community. It represents a radical advance and reinterpretation of the nature of the religious life conceived both as a form of human fellowship and as the service of God. The relation to God is a relation of faith and grace rather than of law and merit. This is the "new covenant." It harks back not to Moses but to Abraham, who "believed God and it was counted unto him as righteousness." Baptism into this religious fellowship is baptism into Christ; God is known as he reveals himself in Christ. The central act of worship and communion with God is the Lord's Supper, in which the simple elements of bread and wine represent the body and blood of Christ, and by the partaking of which each one spiritually partakes of Christ. Thus the Church was—and is—a "heavenly" company, the earthly, imperfect form of the eternal kingdom. As a human fellowship it is the direct, personal community of love. Doing good to one another, repenting of wrong done, and forgiving the offender, preserving the fellowship by "speaking the truth in love"—these are the basic characteristics of the human community that is the Church. Paul describes, idealizes, and drastically criticizes the Church from the standpoint of this, its true character. A character, it need not be said, never very convincingly exhibited in any of the little congregations created by Paul's missionary labors; nor by the actual Church at any time or in any place. That Church without spot or wrinkle, or any such thing, exists only "in heaven." The "heavenly company" that is the actual Church is judged by its own Head, and were it not also redeemed by his grace it would completely cease to be.

This community constituted by faith in God and his redemptive grace, and existing in direct personal love and fellowship of the brethren, is the original, God-created reality which Emil Brunner calls the *ecclesia*. It is not so much a religious reality as a pre-religious creation of God. As such it has the truth and purity of the works of God. But being a community in history it quickly became a religion. The seer of Patmos saw a vision of the Holy City, the new Jerusalem, and there was no temple there; that is, no religion. Religion, as we have said above, is a human affair; it is what man does. True, it is what man does in his service of God. But it is still what man does and has all the defects of human conception and action. Religion is the expression in time, and in the materials and forms of nature and history of man's response to the self-manifestation of the eternal God. The life of the Church, or the Christian religion, is the very human historic product or result of the revelation of God in Christ. The revelation is not a religious act, for it is God's act, and religion is a work of man and not of God. One might truly say that Jesus Christ is not a religious figure; he is not the founder of a religion, or a teacher of religion. He is rather, as the perfect unity of God and man, the personal reality that produces in history the community of faith, and constitutes in eternity the Kingdom of God. The essence of that fellowship out of which the Church grew is the immediate personal relation of man with God, and with his fellow man in love.

But there had to be from the beginning an institutional life, and organization, and a common language of faith and form of worship. This is the Church in its historic form. This is the origin and development of the Christian religion; it might almost more truly be said, of the Christian religions, for the Church has always been diverse in some degree, and over the greater part of its history differences have been pronounced. Christian religion appropriates and uses to its own purposes the standard elements of religion. Baptism and the sacramental meal were common forms which appear in the Church with a Christian meaning. Prayer, worship, liturgy were already a language of religious expression common to mankind. That is, religion was ready at hand, to be taken and used in the nurture of the new faith. Soon a priesthood, a liturgy, a creed, a hierarchical order of Church government came into existence not by the creation of totally new forms, but by modification of already existing forms of religious expression. Christianity as a religion represents the Christianizing of common forms of religious life. The Eastern Orthodox and the Roman Catholic Churches appropriated quite comprehensively the language, the symbols, the psychological methodology, and the thought forms of traditional religion. Most of this religious heritage was rejected by the Protestant Churches; some of it is gradually returning. Even the most simple common religious life and worship must participate in some form and degree in the religious heritage of man.

The faith of the Church from the beginning had to be interpreted in ideas; this was the beginning of Christian theology, or, more properly theologies. Early expressions of Christian faith used ideas and language taken from current Judaism, from the mystery religions, from Stoicism and Gnosticism, and from the Platonic-Aristotelian tradition generally. But all these currently existing terms and ideas were made to serve so far as possible the main purpose which was to communicate the truth found in God's self-revelation in Christ. The effort was not entirely successful; nor has any theology been able to convey adequately and without some distortion the full meaning of that truth.

Liturgy, government, orders, theology, educational and devotional practices, even the hermit and the monastery, all this complex of worship, organization, and activity that constitutes the Christian religion in history with its own distinctive character, intent, and meaning, represents the peculiar and distinctively Christian use of the general human fact of religion. We must make a distinction between Christianity and other religions, for they represent different and in some ways radically different meanings. But they are all religions, human manifestations of the sense of the divine, of some consciousness of God, and of deep human need for God. They all constitute the human language of faith and human forms of response to the prior presence and act of God. A history of religion is possible; a psychology of religion also, and a sociology of religion. Among the higher religions, where thinkers seek to express the rational meaning of faith, much the same theological ideas develop, and similar theological problems appear. This is all because "religion" is the doing of man, and man everywhere and always is essentially the same. He is the same physiologically, psychologically, and intellectually. He is basically the same morally.

We must make an even more general distinction than that between Christian religion and non-Christian religion: namely, the distinction between Christian religion, which includes all historic forms of the Church, and the act of God in Christ, the Christian revelation. The latter is complete and perfect in its kind. Moreover the presence of God in the fellowship as Holy Spirit means that the historic Church in its spiritual reality is not a work of man; it is not *a* form of religion; it does not share in the relativity and imperfection which besets all the works of man in history. The Church is this "heavenly company" of those who share in the direct personal communion with God through faith, and in love of one another. The forms of the Christian religion are sacred and the acts of the Church are sacramental only insofar as they nurture and express this spiritual, personal communion and fellowship. There is nothing in all the liturgy, ministry, or creedal structure of the Church's life that as a religious form carries unequivocally divine authority or power. Ultimate truth is found only in the act of God in Christ and in the Holy Spirit, the Spirit of Truth, which is the inner reality of the Church.

One further distinction needs to be made if we are to see the full meaning of the Kingdom of God in history, the distinction between the sacred and the secular, or between the religious and the secular. This is a real distinction, but it does not signify the difference between the better and the worse, the higher and the lower aspects of man's life. The secular life is simply the life of man engaged with the environment of nature and within the temporal order of his own existence. The religious life is the life of man as oriented to and concerned with the divine power or powers however conceived. Action in the secular life is direct and "literal" in a world in some degree subject to human control, both the natural and the human world. Action in the religious life is indirect and symbolic; it is an appeal to powers beyond man's control but whose help is essential to man's existence. The distinction is expressed in the two forms of human activity—worship and work. Worship is communion and communication of spirit with Spirit, in freedom. Work is the direct application of force by tools and mechanisms.

The Church as an historic institution is elaborately involved in the secular life, of necessity. A great amount of the activity and

"work" of a local church is the doing of things that are in themselves completely secular; building buildings, training choirs, writing letters, etc. Even the most sacred moment in the life of the
church, the celebration of the Lord's Supper or the Eucharist,
involves much preparation. The bread must be baked, the wine
must be made, the table must be set. On the other hand the life
of the Christian in the Kingdom of God is at every point responsive to the will of God. Both individual and group action either
fulfill or deny the Kingdom. All the secular life of man is "under
God," either a service of God or disobedience to him. This is the
fundamental truth in Luther's assertion that the cobbler at his
last serves God just as truly as the priest at the altar.

Therefore, the Church as the fellowship of faith in history is
not just a religious institution, or the true and absolute form of
the religious life. In its essential reality it is man serving God,
both at the altar and at the shoemaker's last, both in worship and
in work. God alone, revealed in Christ and present as the Holy
Spirit, is the Absolute, the Perfect. This is the "intention" of the
Christian Church, the thing that makes it Christian. Both the
worship of God in the Church, and the service of God in the
world are imperfect and only approximately adequate forms of
human thought and action. We cannot absolutize a theology, a
liturgy, a church order, or a morality. Church and secular life
are under the judgment of God and are dependent upon his grace.
The religious life, *per se*, is not good, not even the religious life
of the Christian Church. The secular life, *per se*, is not bad, not
even the life of the non-Christian. It is all ultimately judged and
subject to redemption by the love of God. The great treasure of
the Christian Church is its knowledge of that love and that grace
in Christ; the great worth of its life is that all that it does, in work
or worship, is referred to this revelation of God. Even though as
a religion it speaks the common language of mankind, and never
completely or perfectly realizes or communicates the truth of that
revelation, it has the gospel which is the historic testimony to it,
and within it dwells the Holy Spirit. But the Church is always
forgetting its gospel, and becomes deaf to the Spirit, and so un-
faithful to its own true reality and mission. To be the Christian
Church is always an end sought but only partially realized.

THE WITNESS OF THE CHURCH

The Church is the witness in history to the self-revelation of God in Jesus Christ. Its first business is to preach the gospel, and to witness through the redeemed life to the presence and power of the living Christ. The Church preaches the gospel first to itself; it is constantly forgetting and needs constantly to be reminded of the gospel, and to be renewed in its faith and devotion to Christ. But it is also the business of the Church to proclaim the gospel to the world. The Church is not just an enclave within the world trying to defend itself from invasion and corruption by the world. It has a positive mandate to declare to the world the saving grace of God and to call men to faith and obedience to him. "You are my witnesses," said Jesus to his disciples. It was to the world that God sent his Son. It was for the world that Christ died. When the Church becomes a self-seeking, defensive company, even if bent on the attainment of a rich and pure spiritual life for itself, it ceases to be the true Church. Not only racial segregation, but cultural and class exclusiveness and parochialism, deny the character of the Church. The true Church has its doors and windows open to the world; more than that it is constantly sending out evangelists and missionaries to make known the gospel. Every congregation is, in fact, a mission "station." Every member is an evangelist. When this is said, and it must be said, it must also be pointed out that the gospel is communicated both by word and by life. The witness of the ordinary Church member will not be through preaching, probably not very much by words, for few have the gift of effective speech regarding the faith. The witness is in the first place habitual participation in the common worship of the Church. This is primarily a matter between the individual and God; it is also a participation in the life of the community of faith. But it is also "public" worship; that is, John and Henry, and Mary and Helen openly before all worshipping God in the name of Christ. This is public confession and commendation of the faith. Habitual and sincere public worship is the basic witness of the lay Christian to the gospel. This is not all; there are many ways in any community in which the weight of any man's testimony can be put behind the gospel, aside from a

life lived in the service of Christ. And intelligent and hearty support of the organized effort of the Church through missions, local,
national, and international, is a living if conventional form of
participation in the mission of the Church to the world.

The witness of the Church, however, goes beyond this, its primary task of the proclamation of the gospel. It involves the constant interaction with the intellectual, cultural, social, and political
life of man. The preaching of the minister, the teaching program
within the Church, and open discussion of the common life are
all involved in this endeavor both to declare what the God revealed in Christ requires of men, and to make as intelligible and as
effective as possible the truth of the faith. The Church is always
engaged with the problem of faith, the honest skepticism of the
human mind. It has the constant task of clarifying the meanings of
Christian faith. This is a matter of theology. No one can be won
to the faith by theological argument or exposition but many can
be enabled to accept it heartily if they can be given a real understanding of it. This is especially important in a time dominated
by natural science and technology. Practically the preoccupation
of the mind with natural processes and with technical developments tends to create a wholly secular way of life. Men feel that
if we could just dispose of the Communist menace man's triumph
over nature would bring general prosperity and happiness. We
probably need God to win out over the Communists, but, that
victory won, we can get along pretty well. The psychiatrist and
tranquilizer pills can cope with personal tensions. If the planet
gets overpopulated, fortunately science has made it possible to
move out onto other planets. Life promises to be exciting in the
space age, once we have got the Communists out of our hair. But
there is an uneasy feeling that maybe we won't get the Communists out of our hair; and that perhaps even the psychiatrist
may not be able to get to the heart of the matter.

The heart of the matter is the heart of man, the man himself;
the creature made in the image of God; the sinner who needs to be
reconciled to God, and to his neighbor, and to himself. The way
of reconciliation, of salvation, is the same today that it was in
ancient or in medieval times; it is the way of faith in God and
free obedience to him. This is both the intellectual and the ethical

answer to the predicament of man, even in the age of technology. After all it is man who is the technician; his chief problem is himself, and that is not a technical problem but a spiritual problem. The Church has the answer to this problem. It has the gospel, the "good news" that this mortal creature who occupies this planet for a few decades is a son of God, even though a willful and thoughtless son, and that his true home is in the Kingdom of God. Perhaps the fact that with increase of technical capacities human life seems to encounter more unmanageable and terrifying evils will increase rather than diminish man's lostness and the conscious need of God. At any rate, the Church must with sympathy and with intelligent understanding make the gospel known to the world in this time as in any time.

Despite the fact that the historic process is in such large measure a product of natural desire and the ambition of men, the Church must constantly confront it with the truth of the Kingdom of God. Even knowing that the world will always be the scene of a struggle between the primary impulses and the demand of God for love and service, or just because it knows this, the Church must constantly make that demand and bring the self-interest of man under the restraints and constraints of the gospel. It can never hope to see this task finished; its ultimate completion is in the eternal kingdom; but this world is the scene of God's redemptive act in Christ and must always be the scene of the Church's testimony to that act. The world is always in need of redemption; it is the mission of the Church to be the historic organ of God's redemptive work.

CHAPTER XII

LIFE, DEATH, AND ETERNAL LIFE

DEATH PLAYS a prominent role in the New Testament. In it death is moralized, rationalized, spiritualized, accepted, and conquered. The treatment is neither morbid nor sentimental. Death is moralized in that it is seen as the limit put upon man within which he must fulfill the will of God and stand before him for judgment. It is rationalized, or made intelligible, because it places man in the order of creation as one who shares the life cycle of all living things. It is spiritualized in that it represents man's dependence upon God for his existence, and is directly a symbol of the separation of man from God through sin. It is accepted: this is the realism of Christian faith. There is no attempt to evade the fact of death, nor to weave a curtain of poetic or speculative illusion to protect the self from its reality and inevitability. But it is met head on and conquered by the power of God in the resurrection and exaltation of Jesus Christ.

Christ, the central figure of Christian faith, died. He "tasted death for every man." The bell tolled for him as well as for every other man. He was raised from the dead, "the first fruits of them that sleep." Paul summed up this identification of Christ with mankind in death and resurrection: "For the love of Christ controls us, because we are convinced that one has died for all; therefore all have died. And he died for all, that those who live might live no longer for themselves but for him who for their sake died and was raised" (II Cor. 5:14, 15). Paul links sin and death as the condition and destiny of created man, symbolized by "the first man Adam" who was a "living being." He puts in contrast with this "natural man" ". . . the last Adam, who became a life-giving spirit" (I Cor. 15:45). Here is the New Testament contrast between the *psychikos* or natural, and the *pneumatikos* or spiritual man. Through Christ, the life-giving spirit, come both righteousness and life. Paul even assumes a causal relation between sin and death; through the sin of the one man, Adam, death came into the world. This mythological account contains a valid truth, namely, that man's mortality and his sin are both aspects of his creatureliness, of his dependence upon and freedom before God. Man has no inalienable claim to life; it is a gift of the Creator. He cannot possess his freedom apart from knowledge of and obedience to God. So sin, disobedience, leads to death. Sin and death constitute the universal lostness of man. Christ is the saviòr who saves men from both sin and death. "If in this life we who are in Christ have only hope," writes Paul, "we are of all men most to be pitied." (I Cor. 15:19). To have found life of infinite and eternal meaning, and then to lose it through the natural mortality of man, would be worse than never to have known it. It would mean the ultimate and radical separation of fact and value, and give evidence of the fundamental irrationality of existence. Christian faith denied this irrationality and held that Christ had "brought life and immortality [incorruptibility] to light through the gospel" (II Tim. 1:10). It was the power of this faith that created the Church and introduced into the ancient world not only the assurance of a redeemed life for the individual and the sacred community after death, but also a profound sense of confidence in the world as rational and dependable because it is the creation of God.[1]

Christian faith inherited the Jewish idea of resurrection. Not all Jews held this belief; Sadducees rejected it, Pharisees accepted it. It was a matter of dispute in the Jewish household. Paul reasoned with the Jewish king Agrippa, "Why is it thought incredible by any of you that God raises the dead?" (Acts 26:8). Jesus took the side of the Pharisees, with the assertion that the God of Abraham, Isaac, and Jacob "is not God of the dead but of the living" (Matt. 22:31, 32). In the Old Testament which assumes everywhere the mortality of man death can be set aside

[1] Cf. Cochran, op. cit. pp. 483-8.

by the act and power of God. A good man can be "translated"
to heaven as were Enoch and Elisha. This, however, was a very
special and exceptional thing. But the idea of resurrection, insofar
as it was held in Judaism, involved the general destiny of man.
Resurrection meant the reuniting of body and soul. This idea is
based on the assumption that death is the separation of the soul
from the body, a universal primitive notion. But resurrection had
a moral significance with the Jews in that it brought the whole
man before God for judgment; as he had done his good and evil
in the unity of body and soul, so he would be judged in the
wholeness of soul and body. The pattern of this final or general
resurrection persisted in the Christian community. It is the form
of the judgment as Jesus makes use of it in the twenty-fifth chapter of Matthew. Elsewhere in the New Testament it is found.
But there is a focusing of faith upon what has now happened
in the resurrection of Christ. This is God's act in the present, and
in the instance of one known and believed in as the Lord and
Savior. The power of God is not set at some far distant future,
and seen in a mass dealing with the race. It is seen and known
now and with direct reference to one man. This man was put to
death and "God raised him from the dead" not in some future
judgment, but almost immediately, "on the third day." God deals
now with the dead; he deals with the individual, and the company
of those who are united with Christ in faith. God is not far away
either in time or in space; his act of creation, his judgment, and
his "salvation" are present realities. Men are dealing immediately
with God in Christ, who while he lived in the flesh was Immanuel,
God with us. Conclusive evidence of God in Christ was the resurrection, which proved to the faith of the disciples that when God
is with and in man even death is not able to destroy him. Christ
really died, but "God raised him from the dead." In Christ, God
casts his lot with man. In Christ man becomes one with God.
This is the real and fulfilled nature of human life. As one with
nature man comes to his end in death; but as one with God death
is not final, but a radical form of judgment and adjustment. For
the essential power of life is not in nature the creation, but in God
the Creator. Resurrection, then, in the Christian faith, is not just
a continuance of the Jewish idea of a final event involving judg-

ment at the end of the world, nor a reunion of the soul with a restored body. It is a present act of the creator God. It is not the reunion of a separated soul and body, but the radical reconstitution of the man who, alive or dead, has never ceased to be for God.

Thus Christian faith "accepts" death. Man is mortal; only God has immortality, or deathlessness. We must set this faith against the idea of the natural immortality of the soul. Platonism, Hinduism, and idealism generally hold to that idea. The body dies, but the soul is immortal; it is the deathless part of man. So we speak not of the immortality of man, but of the soul. But this is not the Christian doctrine of man and his destiny. Man, the whole man, is a creature, a mortal. There is no part of him that is by nature immortal, or deathless. There is in him no soul or spirit that survives death by its nature and power. The whole man dies; so with Christ. It was not just his body that died; Christ died. So with every man. The risen Christ is the same man, but he is now a new being, first evidence of the new creation which like the old creation that passes away is the work of the one creator God. The essential distinction is not that between the "natural" and the "spiritual," but the more radical distinction between the old creation and the new creation of God. It is the *man* who is risen, not the soul, the man in his wholeness and precisely as the whole or spirit than man is. It is the resurrection of the body *(soma)*, not the flesh *(sarx)*, despite the wording of the creed. The body, however, is not the old body, but the new creation of God. It is the *spiritual person*, man in his fullness and wholeness who, as such, always has participation in the life of God which gives promise of "resurrection."

Death is essentially a mystery, part of the mystery of life. Yet we can know some things about death as we know many things about life. I once heard a biologist describe what might be called the chemistry of death. The two things about death that are of most direct concern to man as man are (1) separation and (2) dissolution. These two represent, respectively, the moral and the physical aspects of death. Moral life is life in relation with other persons. The personal community is maintained by love, it is destroyed by hate. Morally, hate is murder; spiritually, hate is sin,

for it is the rejection of God and disobedience to him. It destroys
the life of the spirit which is fellowship and communion, the
sharing of a common world with other persons, men and God.
And this separation is death; the phrase "dead in sin" is literally
correct. Existence in hate is death; existence apart from God is
spiritual death.

Death also is dissolution. Man is an organism of vast complexity and a unity of many delicately adjusted chemical, biological, psychological, and mental processes. Death means the
disorganization, the dissolution, the "corruption" of this amazing
creature. The co-ordination of activity ends abruptly at death and
the dissolution of parts and substances follows in the course of
nature. The man ceases to be. The active person in society, the
unit of the historic process, is withdrawn. His voice is no longer
heard, humanity closes ranks; another may take his place, but no
other can be he. He is effectually and finally separated from the
world of men; he is not there. It is not just that the body has
died, so also have the psyche and the mind; the person is dead.

Christian faith acknowledges death in both the meanings set
forth above. It confesses that man is universally subject to both
alienation from God and corruption; it finds in Christ a savior
from both sin and death. This "scheme," for so it is for Paul, is
described in Romans 5 and I Corinthians 15:21,22. In Christ men
are reconciled to God; in Christ men share in the resurrection of
the dead. The "salvation" of men from sin and death is an act
of grace on the part of God. This is seen directly in man's deliverance from sin as forgiveness and reconciliation. Forgiveness
is an act of grace; reconciliation is life restored in God. The sinner is restored by an act of God. This is a spiritual re-creation. If
any man is in Christ he is a new creature (II Cor. 5:17).

The same is true of the new life called resurrection which is a
creative act and gift of God. Apart from the creative power of
God, resurrection is blank miracle and meaningless. As the manifestation of that creative power by which the world exists and
man is brought into being as a son of God, resurrection is both
possible and meaningful. It is no more a miracle than is the first
creation; it is mystery but not miracle. Rather, it is miracle and
mystery, "miracle" being simply something beyond human power

as mystery is that which is beyond human comprehension. God the Creator continues his creative act when death destroys the human person who is part of the created world and so essentially mortal. But this is not the simple resurrection of Jewish expectation, namely the reuniting of a soul with the body from which it has been separated by death. For death is the disintegration of both soul and body. The whole man has died; there is no "soul" somewhere to be brought back to a reassembled body. The disintegration has been thorough and final. That person is dead.

But that person, as we have said many times, is the whole: body, soul, mind, spirit. This person, part of nature and of history, dies, that is, disintegrates. The living, complex individual is no more. But in its wholeness as spirit there is the identity and reality which is preserved or restored through resurrection. We make a sharp distinction here between traditional meanings and the one I shall give to "spirit," especially in this connection. Traditionally, the "spirit of man" has been conceived as capable of surviving death because it was either (1) a part of deity, (2) a simple psychic atom, hence indestructible, or (3) a pure "form," such as Aristotle's entelechy. The essence of each one of these conceptions lies in the fact that the spirit, by its own power or nature, is transcendent or immune to the dissolution of death. All these ideas have been rejected for one reason or another. The first is pantheistic; the second loses its force in a time when even material atoms have turned out to be highly complex in structure and therefore not indestructible; the last is an element of rationalism and for those not rationalists an empty concept. In each case there is a metaphysical entity which seems a more acceptable and rational basis for the idea of a future life as immortality than the miracle of resurrection. It is metaphysics versus miracle. By and large the Christian faith has held to the miracle, although on occasion each of the other ideas has been introduced into the apologetic for it. If the rational demonstration of, or argument for, immortality fails, there is still theological strength in miracle in that it is an act of God, and reason cannot prescribe limits to God's power or claim to explain his acts either of creation or resurrection.

But while the act of God is mystery in the proper sense of the word, it is still possible to think intelligibly about the life after death which is the gift and the creation of God. Our starting point, or basic assumptions, are those of Christian faith: (1) the free and unconditioned creative power of God, (2) the fact that man the spiritual person is a creature of God, (3) the essential nature of man as existing in relation to God and to other men, and (4) the fact that God loves each and every man with an infinite redemptive and creative love. There is nothing novel in any of these statements; what we do here is to take all of them with complete seriousness. Neither metaphysics nor sheer miracle is the basis of our hope of eternal life, but the creative power and the love of God. Man lives after death not because he never wholly died, nor because some part of him is immortal, but because he always exists for God, in life or in death. Death can and does separate man from his fellow man and from this world, but not from God. The perspective of God is a broader perspective than that of man. The continuity between this life and the life after death is in the act of God, not something in man as man. For our knowledge of existence there is no conceivable structure or essence remaining or persisting through the radical dissolution of death. But the spiritual person exists for God, by God's own act of creative love. Death is a complete darkness, and formlessness and emptiness so far as human thought or imagination is concerned. In death we are wholly and unconditionally "in the hands of God" as we were before we ever existed in this world. But out of this darkness and formlessness and emptiness God creates anew the one who has died.

The life eternal is thus not the life of a wraith, but of a full and complete personal existence. God gives it a body as it pleases him. We can think or speak of this life and "body" only by analogies, as did Paul in I Corinthians 15, and by contrasts. But the reality asserted in these analogies and contrasts is a reality of fullness and fellowship. It is the reality of full personal existence in which the self-centeredness of the individual is overcome in the fellowship. The value and integrity and freedom of the individual exist precisely in the fellowship of love. Love is at once the free act of the person and the bond with other persons. In this life the particularity of existence makes full and true community impossible. The legitimate demands of both nature and history set a man against his neighbor in some degree, even though he loves his neighbor. Many hardly know at all the meaning of love; and those who love are constantly called to repent their denial of it, or their limitation upon it which is really denial. This is the universal sin of man, from which he needs redemption. Christ became a part of this world of sin, "became sin," Paul says (II Cor. 5:21). But he conquered the sin by a complete love, an incorruptible faithfulness to God and man. He likewise "became death," that is, he died. He shared in that darkness, and formlessness and emptiness which are death. As a living man in this world he "let go" as do all men. No structured existence, no metaphysical being remained; only the love which bound him to men, all men, in the world he was leaving in pain and failure, and to God whose love is the power of creation and resurrection. So God raised him from the dead, the "first fruits of them that sleep."

The redeemed life, the life of resurrection is essentially a life in fellowship, the fellowship historically created by Christ. To be "in Christ" is to be in this fellowship. This is the opposite of individual immortality. The risen life, before or after death is participation in the body of Christ, the fellowship of love, the life of the Spirit. The fellowship is true community, not a collectivity. The real "world" of those who are raised from the dead is the world of personal being. We have known personal existence in this life in a physical universe. For science the physical universe is "nature"; for faith it is "creation." It is, in any case, the locus of our personal being and life. When death comes this world "passes away," we are permanently separated from it as a physical universe, or created world. But "in Christ" we are one with God through his grace. We cannot but think that some other "locus" or medium for our personal existence will be provided by the creative power of God. A full personal life means a body. Paul faces this natural question in I Corinthians 15 with some speculation. But it all comes down to the assertion that "God gives (it) a body as he has chosen." The future life, just as this life, is wholly dependent upon the creative act of God, and that is an affirmation of faith and not of reason. The first Christians were not troubled by metaphysical problems because they took seriously the common Jewish belief in God as Creator. No development of human thought or knowledge reaches to that basic faith either to prove it or to supplant it. It is the faith of the Christian then and now.

Eternal life is the gift of God, and is the full and final manifestation of his power as Creator. The whole life of man finds its ultimate reference and meaning in God and in the aspects or "stages" of his creative action. Thus man in "this life" is known fundamentally not as a natural species, or as individual and society in the historic process, but as the creature of God. His high distinction is not just that he is a rational mind, but that he is made in the image of God. As spiritual person his essential nature is found in the self-transcendence (which is self-fulfillment) of his relation to other persons and to God. He finds his completion in others, as mankind finds its completion in God.

The three manifestations of God's creative action are (1) the creation of the world, and of man as both member and master of it, (2) the re-creation (regeneration) of men through the grace of forgiveness and redemption, and (3) the final creation of man through "resurrection" in the "new heaven and earth." Creation, redemption, resurrection are all the creative work of God. They represent the course God takes to bring man the spiritual person into being, and to awaken in him that free response and give him that spiritual maturity that will enable him to share in the life of the eternal kingdom. There are questions of procedure, of the "how" of this action of God that cannot be answered. One is the question of the "body" with which Paul deals, and answers only speculatively and by analogy. Another is the question of those who die without ever having known the re-creation of redemption. If we do not think in terms of a literal hell and heaven, nor of a double predestination, that is, to salvation or to damnation—and indeed neither term applies to the Christian—then what shall we think about those who die unrepentant and unreconciled to God? This is naturally a vastly important question because it concerns the great majority of mankind, those who lived and died before Christ and those who have lived and died after Christ but who either never heard his word of grace and salvation or hearing it, ignored or rejected it.

I think the answer to this question is evident from our knowledge of God in the Christian faith. All men, in every time and
place, in life and in death, are creatures of God and included in
his love and in his purpose of redemption. This life is an opportunity for men to know God and to serve him in repentance and
faith, as it is an opportunity for man to love his fellow man. But
these opportunities are obscured or lost in actual historic conditions. Even those who have heard of Christ and the Christian
gospel largely only half understand, or almost wholly misunder-
stand it. It is literally true, as Jesus said, that the way that leads to
destruction is broad and easy and many go that way, but that the
way that leads to life is narrow and few find it. So it is in this
world as we know it. But those who have either failed to hear
the word in this life or have refused to follow it, still in death
are in the presence of the same God, and are objects of his purpose that all men should be saved. The reconciliation to God
which is redemption and which gives one part in the eternal kingdom calls for repentance. This is always, indeed, an uncoerced
response. But the "Hound of Heaven" will pursue every man
until a free response is won. It is not a question of reincarnation
in this world, nor of going on from world to world in a series
of existences. It is a question of the personal response to God.
Nels Ferre has put this vividly:

There are no incorrigible sinners; God has no permanent problem
children. Heaven, to those who truly love all, can be heaven only when
it has emptied hell. . . . The *mercy* of God, says the Bible, is *everlasting;*
and love *never* fails.[2]

For the destiny of man is not a "heaven" but God. God the
Creator created this world; he may, at his pleasure, create other
worlds. It is quite possible that there are many "worlds," not
duplicates of this physical universe somewhere outside it. There is
no "outside" to this physical universe or world. But the existence
of other creations with their own space and time systems, and
perhaps wholly different specific structures of existence, is not
only possible but thinkable. It is pure but unprofitable speculation
to think about them, however, and wholly irrelevant to the ques-

[2] Nels F. S. Ferre, *The Christian Understanding of God*, New York, 1951,
p. 229.

tion of the destiny of man. For the real "world" and universe of man is God himself. Both Old and New Testaments, while they use the imagery of the "new heaven and new earth," rise above the usual level of cosmic speculation and affirm that God himself is our home. "God is our refuge and strength." "The eternal God is your dwelling place, and underneath are the everlasting arms" (Exodus 33:27). "In him we live and move and have our being" (Acts 17:28). The first Christians thought of Christ as this divine home with a known character and quality. Paul was ready to depart from the body and to be with Christ. The Fourth Gospel reports Jesus as saying, "I am the vine, you are the branches; ... abide in me and I in you" (John 15:1ff.). It is not "heaven" but the kingdom of heaven that is the destination. Heaven is a myth-ological place; the kingdom of God is the non-mythological but spiritual home of the human spirit; it is the life of God himself. "Worlds" are the creations of God; he creates such worlds as fit his purpose. But God himself is the ground of our existence; life eternal is life in God. And it is not the denatured and devitalized existence of a spiritual essence or abstract, but the full, personal life in which "all things are yours, and you are Christ's and Christ is God's."

CHAPTER XIII

THE TRUTH OF THE CHRISTIAN FAITH

CHRISTIAN FAITH and Christian theology cannot be equated although they can never be completely separated. Christian faith is the personal response of man as spirit, that is, in his wholeness, to God revealed in Christ. The response is faith, obedience, love. Christian theology is the interpretation of Christian faith by man as mind, that is, as thinker. Faith is a matter of life, conduct, relationship; theology is systematized belief in the form of ideas; it is "doctrine," which means primarily "teaching." It is therefore both the form of thought about the faith, and the terms of communication of the faith. It is both a matter of personal understanding, and the common language of the believing community. In the faith the primary Actor is God; in theology the actor is man. The deep relatedness of faith and theology or belief is disclosed by the fact that, although the "otherness" of God is basic to the faith, God still must be heard, seen, and known by the human person. That hearing, seeing, and knowing is faith. The absoluteness of the God who reveals himself cannot be attributed to the faith of man because actual faith involves a form of belief, and believing is a human act. The truth of the Christian faith lies in God. But God is present to each and every believer as Holy Spirit. There is always this inward reality to "teach" and enlighten, as well as to give life and comfort to the Christian believer. "Faith" is a gift of the present God. Both in the individual and in the community of faith God is present. Belief or theology that constantly rises out of faith is thus subject to the corrective and creative action of the Holy Spirit.

This might seem to point to a theology that is directly the creation of God, and therefore infallible. And such a claim has been made for "doctrine." The Church of Rome holds that it is preserved from error in its official dogma. It has, as it were, domesticated the Holy Spirit and claims his full authority for dogma. The theoretical basis of this claim is the authority of tradition as the product of the Holy Spirit in the whole Church and through its concrete life in history. This is more fundamental than the strictly scriptural basis of scholastic Protestantism. The Reformers were more aware of the inner testimony of the Holy Spirit than were their scholastic successors. Had the whole Reformation movement been as vividly alive to the immediate guiding and enlightening presence of the Holy Spirit as the Reformers themselves, both the Church and its theology would have been greatly benefited. It would have meant not an infallible theology but a constantly developing theology and the refusal to make any formula or creed permanent and final. Both Roman Catholicism and Protestantism however sought to fix the theology of the Church in dogma as that which "is believed always, everywhere and by everyone."

The error of this strategy for the "preservation of the faith" lies in the fact that theology is a system of ideas. And ideas are the finite forms of human thinking. All ideas are the product of human thought, are forms of human thought, are acts of the human mind. Ideas, imaginal or conceptual, are formed through the process of time by the environment of man and his conscious or unconscious effort to understand and act in that environment. The reason itself which is the mind engaged in systematic dealing with ideas is formed by the world in which man lives. The initiative of the human subject and even his mental creativity are real and essential, but that initiative and creativity work within and upon a "given" world. The world includes persons as well as things; it is spirit as well as nature. The ideas formed in the total experience of the thinking creature represent within his conscious life the simplest and most factual objects, and also the most complex, pervasive and mysterious realities. But the ideas can never be identified simply with that to which they refer. They are never flawless or final; they are constantly subject to revision. In short no human idea has the absoluteness of truth possessed by the reality to which it refers. This is true of the world of nature; it is even more true of the world of spirit, of God.

For ideas are always ideas of "something." Thinking is constructive and even creative, but it always refers to "reality" of some kind. This is the irreducibly metaphysical aspect of knowing, and poses the permanent problem of knowledge or epistemology; how can the mind know the thing itself that its idea is about? There are three stages to the development of this problem: (1) rationalism, (2) idealism, and (3) skepticism. Rationalism itself has two forms: first, it says with Parmenides, "Thought and being are one." Then, after the introduction of empirical science, it says with Spinoza, "The order and connection of ideas is the same as the order and connection of things." [1] The postulate of Paul Tillich is akin to the first of these two; the structure of reason is identical with the structure of Being.[2] Subject and object being essentially one, or identical, knowing is possible.

Idealism, what I have called subjective rationalism above,[3] holds that only minds and their ideas are ultimately real; personal idealism fills out the picture by making not just the knowing mind, but the whole personality real, and the personality is conceived as the full unity of consciousness: thought, feeling, and will. The "knowledge" of God and of his dealings with man, theology in short, arises from a speculative construction in which the content and process of consciousness itself are primary materials. This content and process of consciousness is knowable because it is the consciousness itself. Consciousness, therefore, by immediate knowledge of itself, and by speculative elaboration arrives at a religious philosophy, or a philosophical theology. The existence and nature of God and the destiny of man are known by this method. The God known is not present except in idea; he does not reveal himself as an Other present and acting upon the world and making

---

[1] *Ethics*, Prop. VII.
[2] Cf. Paul Tillich, *Systematic Theology*, vol. I, p. 77. "Subjective reason is the rational structure of the mind, while objective reason is the rational structure of reality which the mind can grasp and according to which it can shape reality."
[3] Page 198f.

demands upon man. But he is known through the development of
ideas and the religious consciousness. The Christian tradition and
the person and teaching of Jesus Christ are accepted and interpreted in the idealistic system. They constitute revelation in the
sense of the disclosure of true ideas of God and man and human
destiny.

Skepticism rejects rationalism in both kinds, and also idealism.
It denies all claims to knowledge of "something," that is metaphysics. It holds that the mind and its ideas cannot be brought
into direct and dependable relation to a world or a God essentially independent and "other." Thus skepticism produces various
forms of thought; existentialism, logical analysis, and ideologies
representing the special interests of individuals or groups. Man is
turned in upon himself, either as a thinker, or as a member of
society, or as an "individual." There is no God whose will and
nature furnish a basis and a directive for human life. The nature
known by science is reduced to a system of forces that can be
used by man through technology. This is the outcome of the
development of thought that step by step gave up the enterprise
of knowing "something," that is what it is, and the Someone
whose will and purpose determine what man should be.

Christianity and Christian theology have felt the impact of
this long and diverse development. Rationalism has held that it
provided terms for true theology; idealism has tended to identify
itself simply with Christian belief. And there are various kinds of
existentialists who profess to set forth the true and original Christian faith, as well as existentialists who make no profession of
Christian faith or of any religious faith at all. But the skepticism
which produced the "age of ideology" is the consequence of the
philosophical subjectivism which resolves man into a mind whose
essential act is knowing, or a will that acts on its own, or a feeling complex that is an end in itself. Insofar as Christian theology
has gone along with this subjectivism it has suffered the fate of
the general philosophical failure.

But Christian faith is not an idealism, or a rationalism, or an
arbitrarily chosen existentialism. It is faith in the living God, the
Creator, the Judge and Redeemer of men. Its ideas are not *concepts* of being, or formulas for the process of nature; they are

conceptions formed out of the daily living interaction with the world and one another, and formed by the worship and service of God. Not alone the fortunes of individual existence but the struggles, achievements, and disasters of a people under God provide dramatic and imaginative forms for the representation in thought of God and his dealings with men. This is the concreteness and reality of the God of Israel. It is here that the personal-spiritual nature of God emerges. It is remarkable that the knowledge of God derived from this religious-historical experience exhibits the paradox of a God who is transcendent, invisible, inconceivable, and yet is immediately at hand, wholly involved in the life of his people and upholding all things by the word of his power. The presence and action of God are unlimited precisely because no place, or thing, or thought can hold him. His Word is the medium of his creative power, and of his communication with the people through the prophets.

The Word became flesh in Jesus Christ. The early Christian Church had conceptions of God derived from the prophets which they saw fulfilled in Christ. Fulfilled, corrected, and overflown. Christ came "in the fulness of time." Without historic preparation the idea of God as Spirit who is also Person (the living God who acts) would have had no meaning or content. By "Spirit" was and is meant the transcendent but also the present One who creates the world but is not to be confused with it. It means the freedom which manifests itself in the creative act and in the act of love. Creativity without love is wild, blind, and meaningless; love without the power of creativity is a vain sentiment. Faith in the God known in Christ is faith in One in whom love and power are united in a supra-moral, supra-rational creative and redemptive work. This is the ultimate meaning of the Spirit-Person; God deals with man as person in Christ. Herein is disclosed the true and ultimate nature of God. He is not an individual among individuals. He is not a unity of consciousness. He is Subject, acting in freedom. The man he has created in his own image is a subject who is also spirit-person in that he has real freedom both to create and to love. Because his freedom is not wholly united with love he is a sinner needing redemption. He can and does disobey God, and can seek to be himself lord of his life and of as much of the world as he knows and feels can be made subject to himself. But he can also by confrontation with the holiness of God know himself as a sinner, and by confrontation with the suffering love of God he can be moved to repentance. This personal reality of God and his human creature is the ultimate power and reality. All the rational and creative activities of man in history and in his dealings with nature are secondary to this personal relation with God. The *truth* of Christian faith is found in this basic conception of the ultimate personal nature of God and man himself, and the corresponding character of personal acts, relations, and fellowship as constituting ultimate reality. God, not the idea of God, nor the divine, nor the absolute, nor truth or love taken as general qualities, is the Alpha and Omega. The exposition in this volume of the Spiritual Person, as over against both simple abstractions like Being, or complex concreteness such as personality as the unity of consciousness, derives from the conception of God which arose in Israel especially with the prophets, and which came to full expression and incarnation in Jesus Christ.

This is a truth about "something"; or *Someone*. The Someone is God, the ultimate term for Christian faith and theology. There is no principle or reality prior to God. God acts in creation and in redemption; he reveals himself in both forms of action and in the immediate presence and help he gives to the man of faith, the "pure in heart." Thought about God, and knowledge of God, is theology. God is not *substance*, or *being*. Substance is a physical category, and being is a mental category. The original meaning of metaphysics is that system of principles upon which all knowledge of nature is based, the "first principles of knowledge." Metaphysics is then strictly speaking the knowledge of nature (*phusis*) in most general terms. Knowledge of God is not therefore metaphysics, unless one's idea of God is basically naturalistic and "God" is simply the most general idea of the world itself. This is the charge made against metaphysics with complete validity by Ritschl. He declared that any idea of God derived from our knowledge of the world is simply the idea of the world. Knowledge of God is therefore not metaphysics but theology.

Knowledge of God is not *ontology*. Ontology is a category of the mind, of reason. But reason is a function of the mind, of the cognitive consciousness. And God is not a mental function. God is the transcendent *Subject* of all his acts and relations. This is the basic meaning of Spirit. God is Spirit. We may not venture to analyze the "structure" of God, even upon the analogy of the human spirit. This was the fallacy of Personal Idealism. Man is a creature of God "in his image." Man also is spirit or spiritual person. But the human *person* is not a substantial soul, or a unity of consciousness, or a psychosomatic individual. This human spiritual person is the transcendent *subject* of all the functions of the individual—mental, psychic, or somatic. The *person* is the *spirit*, the center and circumference, the essence and the whole-ness of complete personal existence. But the creature is an indi-vidual who is both nature and spirit. His temporal origin is in nature but his eternal origin and destiny is God. He is a creature of both necessity (nature) and freedom (spirit). But the freedom is not merely, or only, freedom of the will. Indeed, it is not the will but the whole person (spirit) that is free. And this freedom is not only moral, it is also creative. Above all it is the basis of truly personal relations and fellowship. Because man is spirit, and free, he can live in faith and obedience with God and in love with his fellow man.

Thus the ultimate terms of Christian faith and theology are God and man, the two parties: God, the Party of the First Part, the absolutely first, who is *the* (not *a*) Spiritual Person. There is no metaphysical knowledge of God, because God is not the ultimate abstraction from nature. There is no ontology of God because God is not the ultimate category of reason. But there is a theology, a knowledge of God in terms of his personal acts toward men and his primary act of free creation of the world. The God of metaphysics does not create the world; he *is* the structure of the world. The God of ontology does not create the world; he is the essence of the world. But the God of Christian faith creates the world; he is with it in all its life and joy and agony; he is the Father of spirits; he is the dwelling place and destiny of man. This is the truth of the Christian faith, faultily and inadequately "known" in Christian theology. The ideas of theology are derived from human life in history, and with God in worship and communion. They are not formal *concepts* which

are pure mental forms wholly defined by other such forms and
related by logic. They are *conceptions,* ideas in which there is
structure indeed, perhaps various structures, but ideas clothed in
meanings derived from the most varied and inclusive experiences
of man as a spiritual person in relations with God, with nature,
and with other men. These ideas refer directly to the human and
divine realities of man and God. They are ideas of *Someone* and
someones, of the real world of persons in history and in eternity.
They are no more subjective than are the ideas of science or
history. The *Other* and the *others* are real and the fullness of
man's life in relation thereto is due to the infinite variety and
creativity of this world of the spirit.

The primary act of human consciousness in the knowledge of
God is faith, as the primary act of the mind in the knowledge of
nature is perception. Both faith and perception carry a conviction
of objective reality as well as some specific complex of quality
and character. Perception may be analyzed into pure sensation
and interpretation, but it is not pure sensation first and then interpretation. Some elementary idea or interpretation gives at least
vague structure to the perception. The advance of knowledge
consists in a revision of earlier forms of perception. Perception
without its minimal element of rational structure is mere feeling.
But that is not yet perception. Faith likewise can be analyzed into
the pure sense of presence, and intelligible thought. The naming
of a deity, the relating of a god to a place, or an object; the association of gods with a tribe or a nation; these are the common
rational elements in the elementary idea of God. The question is
never, Is there a God? That would be nonsense for the human
race for the greater part of its history. The question may be,
Where is God? Or, What does God do? Or, What does God say?
These questions are practical; they arise from man's sense of the
mysterious power and presence, akin to but greater than himself,
and upon whom his security and well-being depend.

Nature is largely unknown, but knowable; it is the element
in man's total experience that can be indefinitely structured or
made intelligible; there is no mystery in it. God, or to use a more
general term, Spirit, is first known as mystery, and as knowledge
grows the mystery deepens. Mystery is not just the unknown,

it is the incomprehensible in the known. Primitive man knew his
gods much more completely than does civilized man; they were
more nearly like his finite self and the simple forms of nature as
he knew it. As man knows more of nature it becomes more complex; as man knows more of God he becomes a greater mystery.
In both cases the knowing starts from a primary act, in knowledge
of nature from perception, in knowledge of God (Spirit) from
faith. Both these forms of knowledge have a reflex effect of giving man more knowledge of himself. For man is also nature and he
is spirit. He can know nature because he is in immediate contact
with nature and is "nature" himself. He can know spirit—God
and human persons—because he is "spirit" himself and the divine
and human spirits are immediately present to him. In this sense
subject and object are not separate but together and essentially
akin. The epistemological problem of getting a subject which is
a knowing mind directly related to an object which is a "something" outside it arises from the assumption of an essential difference and distance between them. But in fact the knower is a
personal being who is himself part of nature. He is essentially a
part of the total "object," the nature to be known. There may be
a finite distance between his body and any other body or natural
object; but direct contact is still possible. Man even has direct
contact with the stars through the light which fills the space
between and, despite light years of distance, makes the stars immediately present. Yet man is not the stars; both man and the stars
are parts and positions in nature. Thus real and "objective"
knowledge is possible.

Perception of nature is possible because the knower "touches"
nature immediately; there is no distance between man and nature.
The knowing organ is his body which through his senses perceives the qualitative variety of natural objects, and by his action
as an individual body in nature perceives the general character
of its motions. Faith in God (Spirit) is possible because man is
immediately in the presence of Spirit. There is no distance between God and man. Man himself is spirit. He "knows" his fellow men as men because they are spirit. He knows them not by
perception but by faith. He does not "know" that his human
companion is also a person by inference from his actions which

reveal a "mind" that is "inside" him and invisible. He knows immediately that "other" not by perception but by faith. Indeed, that is the way he knows himself as a peculiar creature, identical and responsible, with his rights and his duties and his mysterious likeness to God and other persons. The knowing organ is his own spirit, which is the man in his wholeness and freedom. He learns slowly the nature of the gods, and finally, God, by the faith which is his response to the immediate presence of God. Man is daily, momentarily dealing with God, and either learning God's ways or departing further from them. In his own response and active relation to God he comes to know more clearly and more adequately both God and himself.

The advance in knowledge of God precedes advance in knowledge of man himself as spirit. Man does not create God in his own image; he gets the clue to a truer knowledge of himself from his prior knowledge of God. Man's present preoccupation with himself, his inquiry into his body, his psyche, and even his spirit, is a modern concern. It is the age-long preoccupation of prophets and men of faith *with God* that has brought man to a knowledge of himself as a true person with the powers of spirit. The history of revelation is first of all the story of God's self-revelation; but the direct consequence of this self-revelation is the awakening in man of a true knowledge of himself. "Because I am holy you shall be holy." Because God is righteous, man must be righteous. Because God is love, man must love. This is the history and also the logic of faith and the knowledge of God by faith. By knowledge of nature man knows himself as a species; by knowledge of spirit man knows himself as a community of persons. This knowledge is generally unclear and uncertain. The Christian faith finds it clarified and made essentially complete in the person of Christ. "We all, with unveiled face, beholding the glory of the Lord, are being changed into his likeness from one degree of glory to another: for this comes from the Lord who is the Spirit" (II Cor. 3:18). This historical person Jesus was not God, but he was a man who in his wholeness as spirit was completely one with God. God found no obstacle in Jesus, but was present, and acted in his true character.

The revelation of God in Jesus Christ was also, however, the revelation of man. The Christian sees in him the true nature and act of God, and also the true nature and act of man. He is the true man. This is the primary content of the Christian faith. It is not merely that Jesus is "like" God, who presumably is somewhere up in heaven. He is completely one with God because God is immediately and actively present. It is this immediate "real" presence of God that seems to be rejected in many theories of the incarnation. But for God to be "present" is the basic presupposition of all religious faith. The problem in human life generally is not that God is not present but that he is not acknowledged, that his acts are resisted, that he cannot reveal himself as he is but that he is obscured and denied.

The faith of Christians in Jesus Christ is the form of their faith in God. It is not just the affirmation that God has made himself known in Christ, but a recognition in Christ of the God men always and everywhere know as the mystery and the power upon which their lives depend for both security and meaning. *This* is he! This is not just what God is like; this is the true God. This is also the true man who as the image of God can and does communicate the living presence and the true nature and act of God. An individual human person mediates the presence and power and truth of the divine Person. Body, soul, and mind of a man become the organ in history of the human spirit brought to its completion in God. Christ is the Word of God, the full and true and living medium of God's self-communication to man. "The Word became flesh." It is because the man Jesus is spirit that he can be one with God who is Spirit. It is because Jesus is "flesh" that he is one with mankind. His oneness with God is his free act of obedience; his oneness with man is his free act of *agape*. The oneness with God is not symbolic or figurative; it is real and actual. His oneness with man lies not merely in being one of the species; it is full spiritual unity in love, which made him subject to the whole range of human existence, good and evil, life and death.

Jesus Christ is the truth of the Christian faith. Christian theology becomes true insofar as it formulates belief in terms that faithfully express this truth of faith. But every theology, including this one, is a structure of human thought and is neither infallible nor complete. We can but humbly and critically labor to recreate our thoughts in the presence of Christ and with our eyes and hearts fixed on him. We need instant illumination and guidance of the Holy Spirit. But our ideas as formed first by the heritage of Israel and then by the Christ known in the Gospels and the faith of the first Christians must be given priority over speculative rationalistic or naturalistic conceptions. It was the great accomplishment of the Greek mind to forge intellectual methods and techniques for the knowledge of nature; chief among these are the formal concept, the rules of logic, and the *ratio* of mathematics. It was the great achievement of the Hebrew mind, under God, to give form and force to the categories of spiritual personality, to discover in God as Spirit the power of creation, the personal origin and Lord of human life, the Judge of history, and the Redeemer. Impersonal nature disclosed her truth essentially to the Greek mind; the personal God revealed himself essentially to the Hebrew mind and heart. Thought is clarified and organized in Greece; the will is disciplined and ordered in Israel.

Both these traditions are heritages for the Christian faith. Both are required for a full theological exposition of the meaning of life in history under God. The personal and the impersonal poles of reality and truth are involved both as method and as content in Christian theology. But God, the Person, is the absolute First. Nature is the form of the world he creates. Faith, therefore, is directly concerned with and responsive to God. It must speak in the terms of spiritual freedom and personal relation. These are the ideas, the conceptions forged in the believing community and derived from men's dealings with God. They are more like names and descriptions than definition; they indicate and identify the God who speaks and acts, and the men who have heard his word and done his will. They are freighted with personal meanings and insights, with promise and hope and the sense of divine mystery. They are ideas that defy precise formulation, logical analysis, and finality of definition. Their truth lies not in their precision, a purely technical value, but in their fullness of meaning and their inexhaustible power to vitalize and empower the human spirit. This faith must live today, and this truth of the spirit must make men free, in an age almost overwhelmed with a knowledge of nature couched in ideas derived from the work of the Greek mind.

Conflict between these two forms of "truth" can well be disastrous. There is no need of conflict; one of the great tasks of the present and the immediate future is the creative harmonization of the two traditions. If the effort to achieve such harmony denies the *ratio*, the concept, the "clear and distinct idea" of the knowledge of nature in hopes of preserving a living faith in God, the end will be obscurantism and superstition. If the spiritual and personal reality of the *conception*, the living Word of God, is denied and with it the creative and redemptive action of God himself, then a bleak future lies before mankind, a way devoid of spiritual guidance and moral wisdom; *power* impersonal and destructive of the human spirit will have its day. The truth of the Christian faith embraces both traditions; it is concerned with God, and with nature as his creation, and with man, made in his image. It should be the endeavor of Christian theology to exhibit the meaning of the faith in true understanding of nature, man, and God.

A legitimate and indeed inescapable question arises when the claim to truth is made for the Christian faith; does that mean that all other religious faith is false, or untrue? This has traditionally been the claim of Christian theologians. Followers of other religions were held to be victims of false teachings and even of demonic deception. Such claims are not made, at least so bluntly, today. But the question arises still about the truth or non-truth of the non-Christian religions. And it is a serious question not to be set aside by the bland assertion that there is much truth and goodness in all religions, an assertion which is so true as to be platitudinous. Nor can any informed person affirm that all religions teach essentially the same thing. More often than not the chief element of faith in one religion is the chief error for another; for example, the death of Christ on the cross for the Christian faith is key to the whole doctrine and for the Moslem faith is declared to be a deception perpetrated by the disciples of Jesus. Back of this specific contradiction between the two great faiths lie fundamental differences in conceptions of God and his dealings with man—theological differences. This is merely an illustration of real differences that extend to the point of mutual contradiction.

Neither can the question of the truth of religions be set aside
by the assertion that religion is not a realm of "truth." This is
more often an unspoken assumption than an open assertion. It is
closely related to the idea that there is much truth in all religions.
"Truth" becomes a minor and relative matter; it means that certain
insights into the spiritual life of man are valid, or that certain
practices are helpful. Or, more seriously, it can and often does
mean that religion is fundamentally a part of the total cultural
complex of human life and shares in the relativity of culture. It is
undoubtedly true that religion and culture constitute a unity. In
primitive religion the unity is simple and unchallenged.

But there comes a "crisis" in which this simple unity is brought
in question. It met the challenge of the rational mind in Greece,
and in Israel the challenge of the divine demand. Reason, as the
critical study of nature which it was in Greece, tends to relegate
religious belief to the realm of mythology. Gods and spirits are
objects of a superstitious popular fancy; the enlightened mind
does not concern itself with them. But the rational mind itself
tends to be absolutized, and rational systems of cosmology are
correlated with the conscious and moral life of man, furnishing
a sort of secular religion such as Stoicism. The rejection of dogmatic Christianity during the Enlightenment produced a comparable system known as deism. In the Orient, reason did not
become a critical, mathematical, and empirical instrument for the
knowledge of nature as it did in Greece. Accordingly it was free
to elaborate almost without limit cosmic-religious conceptions of
the world of the spirit, of God or the gods. No historic or natural
factuality put any curb on this speculative exercise of reason. All
beliefs were admitted and no criterion of "truth" in an exclusive
sense disturbed the free development of beliefs. The Orient assimilated not only religion but also reason to culture. Religion
and culture remain an uncriticized unity in great ethnic religions.
Even Buddhism which began as a critical and empirical study of
the human consciousness, soon fell into the general practice of
unlimited cosmic speculation. All of it was rational; none of it
false, none of it true.

In Israel the challenge was not primarily rational but moral.
The critical judgment fell not on mythologies but upon the moral

life of the people. This was a judgment first upon the nature religion of Canaan, the *baalim*. The consequences for moral conduct of deifying the productive process which is always an evil of nature religions stirred the wrath of the prophets who in the name of Jahveh, and by his authority, denounced these immoralities and the worship of the *baalim* with which they were associated. It was primarily not a theoretical rejection of polytheism, nor a rational denial of the existence of the *baalim*, but a moral judgment against the fertility cult and its sexual evils, and a religious repudiation of apotheosized impulses and forces of nature. This was the negative side of the development of a conception of God as moral, and as requiring moral righteousness of men. But the same moral judgment of the righteous God was directed against the lax morals of Israel and Judah themselves, especially injustice and oppression of the weak and poor. A true *humanity* emerges as the demand of Jahveh. The prophets were not rational moralists, or sociologists; they were passionate spokesmen for God who spoke to them and sent them out to make his judgments known.

In short, the "crisis" for Israel was the judgment of a righteous God upon historical existence. It was directed to the moral conduct of men. It was a very this-worldly kind of religion not concerned with an analysis of the human consciousness in order to achieve individual deliverance from the evils of existence, nor with cosmic speculation. It was a direct impact of the eternal God upon the history of man in which purity of personal conduct and justice in social and civil life were demanded. There were two implicit "truths" in this prophetic disclosure of divine judgment.

(1) As mentioned above, it made God known as righteous will. This is the usual way of stating the matter but this use of the term "will" can easily be misleading. What the prophets really did was to make God known as a truly personal deity. "Will" is one aspect of the total act of the Person. The special relevance of the term is that it means that God *acts*. He acts in righteous judgment; he demands righteous conduct of man. But he also creates the world, and rules it. He loves his human creatures and labors with them through a troubled history seeking to make them

like himself. In short God is the Spiritual Person, Creator and Lord of men; the God of love who seeks their redemption.

(2) Another truth disclosed in the prophetic movement is that God requires that men serve him faithfully in the secular life. The prophets did not teach "religion"; indeed they denounced the common practice of religion. Not only the idolatry and polytheism of Canaanite religion, but the elaborate sacrificial system of the children of Israel also. The passionate words of Micah are too well known to repeat. What the prophet told the people was that God's first demand is for justice and kindness and humanity. But this is all in the "secular" life; it has to do with the everyday (temporal) conduct of men, the morality, the social order, the civil law and its administration.

This prophetic beginning was consummated in Jesus Christ. Jesus was not a religious teacher in the ordinary sense of the word. He did not "found" a religion. Like the prophets, most of his direct comment on prevailing religion was critical even to the point of denunciation. But neither was he, as many have assumed, a teacher of ethics or morality. He did not teach a moral system any more than he taught a religion. What Jesus did was to transcend both religion and morality and teach men to know God and to do his will. Jesus spoke for God, not for "religion," or even "morality." He brought men personally face to face with God in his teaching and in his life, and said, "Serve God," and what he meant by serving God was so simple the wayfaring man, though a fool, could understand; it was to live with men in love and forgiveness, and to minister to their needs, bodily and spiritual. Jesus was always supremely interested in the two parties, God and man. He called men to serve God and love their fellow man. This was almost completely devoid of theological or moral theory. It includes no instruction in what we call "religion." The only direct instruction in religion that Jesus gave was a brief formula for prayer. He summed up the whole meaning of religion and morality in the two commandments, to love God and man. The teachings of Jesus were certainly in the realm of moral conduct, but they were direct comments on and descriptions (as in the beatitudes) of the good and the evil in human life. This is done in parable, precept, and direct command. He did not, for example, state a doctrine of vicarious suffering; he did say that unless a grain of wheat falls into the ground and dies it does not bear fruit. He said the same thing more cryptically: "He who finds his life will lose it, and he who loses his life for my sake will find it" (Matt. 10:39). And all of this he witnessed to by dying on the cross. He had said, "If any man would come after me, let him deny himself and take up his cross and follow me" (Matt. 16:24). There is no ethical system of instruction here. What, then, is there?

There is in Jesus Christ, and his teaching, a direct confrontation of man the human person with God the divine Person. The whole substance of religion and morality is derived from this prior reality of the God-man and the man-man relation. The nature of the Person as creative, as responsible, as existing in communion and community, and the "law" of personal relations which is *agape*, the way of reconciliation through vicarious suffering—repentance on the part of the wrongdoer, and free forgiveness on the part of the wronged—this is the "truth," this is the revelation of God, this is the "gospel" of salvation for man. This is the "truth" about God and man. Out of this "theological" truth, for it is theological and not either metaphysical or ontological, still less scientific, a "Christian" morality and a "Christian" religion can be formed. The history of Christianity is the history of the varied developments in the realms of morality and religion. But more basic than either, a permanent point of origin for both, is the "event" of Jesus Christ which provides the "truth" and the reality that all moral and religious action must seek to articulate in the life of believers.

Both morality and religion are the works of man. There is no revealed morality and no revealed religion. What God reveals is himself, his holiness, and his love. The structure and concrete content of both morality and religion are the works of man. It is men not gods that are religious; in religious life are expressed the apprehensions and responses of the human spirit to God. These apprehensions and responses never have the absoluteness of the revelation, nor the infallibility that pertains only to God's judgments. But morality is the service of God among men, and religion is response to the self-manifestation of God. Both morality and religion, therefore, are profoundly and creatively affected by the Christian revelation.

The religious development consciously centered on the Christian fact and revelation represents the making of a religion, the Christian religion. It might be more accurate to say that a number of religious forms, or religions, came into being. "Christianity" from quite early in its history was really a family of religions. Some members of the family, such as the Ebionites, dropped out quite early. Some, such as the Gnostics, the Marcionites, and the Manichees, were ejected from the family circle and repudiated. A certain general division between East and West eventuated in the two great rival branches—the Orthodox and the Roman Catholic. But there were also Nestorians, Arians, and others. And in the sixteenth century Protestantism, itself varied in form from the beginning, broke off from the Roman world. It is possible to speak of the Christian religion because all these religious movements claim Jesus Christ as the head and supreme authority for their beliefs, rites, and morality. The unity does not inhere in the religious fact which is a human and historical product, but in the revelation of God in Christ. But none of the varieties of religion called Christian can lay valid and exclusive claim to the reality and authenticity of Christ. Much of the actual structure, ritual, and ecclesiastical form of the various Christian religions, and vast areas of their doctrine, have only remote connection with his person or work. They are "non-theological" factors.

The truth of the Christian faith, therefore, does not inhere in any of the historic forms or branches of the Christian religion. The faith of the Christian is not faith in the Christian religion; it is faith in God as revealed in Christ. More generally, the really religious man is not interested primarily in religion but in God. Religion is man's way of expressing and cultivating that faith. The Christian religion, in any of its forms, is the way in which men who believe in Christ seek to express and cultivate that faith. But it is man who is religious not God; religion is something that man does and in its finest and truest expression it still carries with it the finiteness and imperfection of all human doing. Religion, actually, can easily become an obstacle between man and God. It was this that stirred the indignation of Jesus. It was not that the practices of religion are bad; prayer, sacrificial offerings, ritual observances as sincere expressions of faith and as ways of communion with God are good. But if they become ends in themselves or are used to coerce, they present barriers between man and God and defenses behind which man, under the form of serving God, seeks the absolutizing of his own will. Religion at its best needs constant renewal and reform. Martin Luther tried to get back of religion to direct relation with God. Such is the meaning of his doctrine of salvation, *sola fidei, sola gratia*. Protestantism soon fell into a basic error; namely, the idea that a bad form should be replaced by a good form, and then that good form identified as the faith. The Anglican Church reforms the Roman Catholic religion and then established a fixed Anglican form which could not contain the Wesleys. The Disciples of Christ "restored" the New Testament Church, and then put an end to all further "restoration." Such is the history of the Christian religion.

The form of religion tends to interpose itself between the Christian and Christ. In any actual religion, therefore, there is a form which can be and easily does become a substitute for God. Present-day interest in religion and the sense of the importance of religion does not by any means prove that men are becoming more Christian. Often it means that men are insulating themselves from Christ and the direct relation to God that he makes possible, for the sake of furthering their own security, importance, and peace of mind.

All this is relevant to the question about the truth of the non-Christian religions. The Christian does not find ultimate "truth" in his religion; he finds it in Christ, and as he finds it he is at once engaged in the effort to make his religion more true, that is more expressive of the spirit and will of Christ. The radical revelation of God in Christ, however, is always the ultimate point of reference. In the non-Christian religions this revelation of God is not even present. Let us, at once, say that in all religion and in all religions there is a revelation of God; or, more accurately, all religion is response to the revelation of God. But the response tends powerfully to misinterpret and obscure the meaning of the revelation. We have just been pointing out this tendency of religion in Christianity. The saving thing in Christianity is not the perfection of the religious act of man, but the constant fact of the revelation in Christ and the Holy Spirit as present interpreter of that fact. This "saving thing" is often ineffective for Christ is stereotyped and the Holy Spirit ignored. Among the non-Christian faiths at their best there are high attainments in morality, in spiritual culture, and in theological insights. These all represent the moral, psychological, and intellectual possibilities of man. There is much truth and much good in all these best fruits of the world's religions. The forms of morality are largely dictated by the actualities and demands of social existence. Spiritual culture reflects the common psychological structure of man. Theology likewise is cast in the common form of human thought. The basic sense of the divine presence in all times and all religions has been a stimulus to sensitive spirits in their religious quest. The accomplishment of man in his religious quest is vast and impressive. God has never left himself without a witness, and men have always and everywhere been in some way stirred by that witness.

But the greater part of this religious development has turned in upon itself; it has lacked the direct criticism of the prophet and the creative power of the incarnation of God which the world knows in Christ. Not only the historic fact of Christ, but also the theological preparation of the prophets, is lacking. This is the main line of God's self-revelation. The development of the critical reason in Greece finally led to the true way to know nature. Today all the world is embracing that way. Science is not *a* way to be set alongside the works of the witch doctor or even the empirical medicine of China. It is *the* way. Likewise the prophetic-Christian revelation of the personal nature of God and man and the way God deals with man, the demands he makes and the redemption that he offers, this too is a disclosure of Truth. We cannot claim that the Christian religion is the true and only religion. But it is the claim of the Christian faith that it is essentially a faith in God as he truly is, and a knowledge of man as what he really is. The personal-spiritual truth of man and God revealed in Christ provides the ultimate criterion for all religion and all morality. There is no ontological or metaphysical reality beyond the Creator God and the human creation that bears his likeness. The "law" of this order of reality, faith, love, communion, fellowship, this is the ultimate order of reality. It is not to be set alongside other ways, such as the Atman-Brahman, the Tao, or Nirvana. The truth of Christian faith is the truth of God. It is never adequately understood and expressed in the Christian religion. What it will do to any religion theologically, morally, psychologically we cannot tell. But this faith is the gift of God to man, not just to Christians; it is Truth that should be made known to all.

INDEX